Prisons of Poverty

Contradictions

Series Editor: Craig Calhoun, Social Science Research Council

For more books in this series, see page vi.

Prisons of Poverty

Loïc Wacquant

Expanded Edition

Contradictions Series, Volume 23

University of Minnesota Press
Minneapolis
London

Originally published in French as *Les Prisons de la misère* (Paris: Raisons d'agir Editions, 1999). Copyright 1999 Raisons d'agir Editions, Paris.

Copyright 2009 by Loïc Wacquant and the Regents of the University of Minnesota

Published by the University of Minnesota Press
111 Third Avenue South, Suite 290
Minneapolis, MN 55401-2520
http://www.upress.umn.edu

Library of Congress Cataloging-in-Publication Data

Wacquant, Loïc
  [Prisons de la misère. English.]
  Prisons of poverty / Loïc Wacquant. — Expanded ed.
    p.   cm. — (Contradictions ; 23)
  Includes bibliographical references and index.
  ISBN 978-0-8166-3900-7 (hc : alk. paper) — ISBN 978-0-8166-3901-4
(pb : alk. paper)
    1. Poverty policy—United States. 2. Poverty policy—Western
Europe. 3. Think tanks—United States and Western Europe.
4. Neoliberalism. I. Title.
  HV9950.W3213 2009
  365'.973—dc22
                                                    2009006972

Printed in the United States of America on acid-free paper

The University of Minnesota is an equal-opportunity educator and employer.

20 19 18 17 16 15 14   10 9 8 7 6 5 4 3

For Ashante and Abdérazak
and their brothers in injustice
on both sides of the Atlantic

Contents

Introduction

The Return of the Prison

Virulent denunciations of "urban violence," intensified surveillance of so-called problem neighborhoods, increased anxiety over and repression of youth delinquency, harassment of the homeless and immigrants in public space, night curfews and "zero tolerance," the relentless growth of custodial populations, the deterioration and privatization of correctional services, the disciplinary monitoring of recipients of public assistance: throughout the European Union, governments are surrendering to the temptation to rely on the police, the courts, and the prison to stem the disorders generated by mass unemployment, the generalization of precarious wage labor, and the shrinking of social protection. *Prisons of Poverty* retraces how this new punitive common sense was forged in America by a network of Reagan-era conservative think tanks as a weapon in their crusade to dismantle the welfare state before being exported to Western Europe and the rest of the world, alongside the neoliberal economic ideology that it translates and applies in the realm of "justice." And it shows how the transition from the social state to the penal state, spearheaded by the U.S. turn to hyperincarceration as queer antipoverty policy, portends the advent of a *new government of social insecurity* wedding the "invisible hand" of the deregulated labor market to the "iron fist" of an intrusive and omnipresent punitive apparatus.

The demonstration unfolds in three steps. The first part of this book, "How America Exports Its Penal Common Sense," tracks the processes and pathways whereby the *neoliberal punitive doxa* composed of notions and measures aiming to criminalize poverty—and thereby normalize insecure work at the bottom of the class structure—was incubated in the United States and is being internationalized, indeed globalized. Three stages are distinguished in the transatlantic diffusion of this new way of thinking and tackling the question of "security" in the city: (1) the gestation, showcasing, and dissemination, by American think tanks and their allies in the bureaucratic and journalistic fields, of terms, theses, and measures ("zero tolerance policing," the "broken windows theory," "prison works," and so on) that converge to penalize social marginality and its correlates; (2) their selective importation, through a labor of translation and adaptation to the national cultural idiom and institutional framework, by the public officials and political leaders of the different receiving countries; (3) the "academicization" of the categories of neoliberal penality by pseudoscholarly research tailor-made to ratify the abdication of the social and economic state and to legitimize the bolstering of the penal state.

I pay particular attention to the pivotal role played by the Manhattan Institute in formulating and packaging the aggressive policy of "quality of life" implemented by mayor Rudolph Giuliani and his police commissioner William Bratton in New York City, made into the Mecca of crime fighting by a shrewd propaganda campaign. I find that the transatlantic spread of American-style "law and order" was facilitated by the close ties established between U.S. pro-market think tanks and the kindred policy institutes that have mushroomed across Europe during the past decade, especially in England. As in matters of employment and social welfare, London has served as the Trojan horse and acclimation chamber for neoliberal penality with a view toward its propagation across the European continent. A major player here is the Institute for Economic Affairs, which brought to the United Kingdom, first, Charles Murray to advocate cutting welfare to stem the growth of a destructive "underclass," then Lawrence Mead to urge the adoption of paternalist "workfare," and finally William Bratton to proselytize "zero tolerance" policing. But if the export of the new American crime-fighting products proved so successful, at the level of public rhetoric and policy framing if not implementation, it is because it suited the outlook and served the political needs of the party leaders and state managers of the importing countries, as they converted to the religion of the "free market" and to the imperative of "small government"—in social and economic affairs, that is. This applies with particular irony to Lionel Jospin and the French socialists after they returned to power in 1997 in the wake of the mammoth antineoliberal demonstrations of December 1995 that toppled the conservative majority: like their British, German, and Italian counterparts, the French socialists joyfully joined the coalescing "Washington consensus" on punishment in an effort to shore up their political legitimacy by offering increased criminal security as diversion to, and Band-Aid for, the increased social insecurity generated by their economic policy.

The second part of the book examines the transition "From Social State to Penal State" in the United States, where it has been engaged with vigor for a quarter-century, and in the European Union, where it is now being offered as a no-nonsense cure for the noxious combination of joblessness, immigration, and criminality. It starts with a compact analytic and empirical characterization of the ascent of America's carceral state along five dimensions: (1) vertical expansion through the runaway rise of inmate populations at all levels of the custodial system; (2) horizontal expansion via enlarged probation, punitive parole, and the growth of electronic and genetic databases allowing for intensified surveillance at a distance; (3) the disproportionate increase of correctional budgets and personnel among public administrations, just as education and social assistance outlays are dwindling; (4) the resurgence and frenetic development of a private industry of imprisonment lavishly supported by Wall Street; (5) a policy of "carceral affirmative action" resulting in the demographic predominance of African Americans and deepening racial disparity and hostility among confined populations. I argue that the "upsizing" of the penal sector of the American state is causally and functionally related to the "downsizing" of its welfare sector in the post-Keynesian age. Both partake of the making of a regime of *liberal paternalism* that gives the hypertrophic penal system a central place in the emerging apparatus for the management of poverty, at the crossroads of the deregulated low-wage labor market, welfare programs revamped to buttress casual employment, and the collapsing black ghetto as device for ethnoracial control. In sum, the ramping up of the prison in post-Fordist America pertains to the re-drawing of the perimeter and mission of Leviathan (this punctures in passing the activist myth of the "prison-industrial complex" and its hallucinatory vision of incarceration for capitalist profit and inmate labor exploitation).

Having mapped the contours of the U.S. penal state, I document several trends that converge to constitute, as it were, a "European road" to the penal treatment of poverty and inequality, character-ized by the *conjoint* intensification of *both social-welfare and penal interventions* (rather than the replacement of one by the other, as in America): the steady rise of incarceration rates among most members of the European Union since the stagflation decade of the 1970s; the massive overrepresentation, among their inmates, of the most pre-carious segments of the working class, including the unemployed, non-European immigrants, and drug addicts; the hardening of pun-ishment, more openly turned toward incapacitation as against re-habilitation; and the persistent overcrowding of jails and prisons, ef-fectively reducing confinement to its function of warehousing of the undesirable. The castigatory shift of public discourses on urban dis-order, especially pronounced among socialist and social-democratic officials, betrays a similar drift toward a police-and-prison response to diffusing urban poverty and related social dislocations that, para-doxically, stem from having amputated state capacities for social and economic action. One is thus founded to predict that a "downward" convergence of Europe on the labor and welfare front would result in an "upward" convergence on the penal front, translating into an-other upsurge in the carceral population. Indeed, the making of *penal Europe is already well under way,* as police, justice, and penitentiary unification succeeds monetary unification as the next major platform for European integration, while "social Europe" languishes at the stage of vague vision and rhetorical project.

The third part of *Prisons of Poverty,* special to this edition, re-turns to the United States to dig deeper into the origins of the puni-tive turn in public policy toward the poor and identify some of the political protagonists and strategies that have fostered the penaliza-tion of urban marginality. It offers a summary account of the "Great Penal Leap Backward," whereby the United States turned from leader in progressive criminal justice, poised to show the world the path toward "a nation without prisons" in the mid-1970s, to world champion in incarceration and ardent advocate of all-out penal expansion on the international stage. I show that the rolling out of the carceral state was caused not by rising crime rates but by the changing political mood and policy response toward brewing street delinquency and its main source in the public mind, deepening dereliction concentrated in the racialized core of the dualizing metropolis. The incarceration boom in America after the breakup of the Fordist–Keynesian social compact emerges at the confluence of three independent causal series: (1) the de-autonomization of the penal sector inside the state as a result of the crisscrossing conservative and libertarian critiques of criminal justice; (2) the rabid politicization and mediatization of crime spawning a new cultural industry of the fear and loathing of (lower-class and dark-skinned) offenders; (3) the deployment of the prison as device for the containment of a supernumerary population, deemed deviant and devious, let loose by the implosion of the African-American ghetto.

Tracing the diffusion of the neoliberal *doxa* and the differential arc of the penalization of poverty on the two sides of the Atlantic in the closing decades of the twentieth century reveals much about the transformation of the state and class domination in the age of hegemonic neoliberalism. It also discloses that the unforeseen return of the prison to the institutional forefront of advanced society is not driven by trends in crime or by the increased efficiency of police and justice bureaucracies now guided by scientific theory (as the semischolarly tale of "broken windows" would have it), but rather is the result of political choices informed by cultural values and made to matter by asymmetries of power. That carceral expansion is not a destiny but a policy means that it can be questioned, slowed down, and eventually reversed by other policies. It is my hope that the present book will contribute empirical materials, conceptual tools, and political pointers to that effect.

Acknowledgments

Prisons of Poverty is a revised and expanded edition of the French book *Les Prisons de la misère*, published in 1999 and initially intended for a mixed readership of academics and activists (which accounts for its dynamic style and tone). The original work benefited from the munificent material support of a MacArthur Foundation

Fellowship, the matchless intellectual stimulation of Pierre Bourdieu (at whose insistence it was published in the Raisons d'Agir series), and the professional generosity of colleagues in criminology and penology at research institutions on three continents who guided and goaded me in my irreverent forays on their terrain. I thank Tarik Wareh for the excellent draft translation of the French version he produced and Zach Levenson for timely help with the index. I am also grateful for an Alfonse Fletcher Fellowship, which facilitated the revisions of the book and preparation of the afterword to this edition.

One

How America Exports
Its Penal Common Sense

For the past decade, a moral panic has been welling up across Europe that is capable, by its scope and virulence, of profoundly redirecting state policies and durably remaking the visage of the societies it affects. Its *apparent object* (too apparent, indeed, since it tends to consume public debate) is "youth" delinquency and "urban violence," that is, the disorders of which "sensitive areas" or "problem neighborhoods" are taken to be the crucible and the brewing "incivilities" of which their residents are said to be the primary victims as well as the foremost perpetrators. So many terms that one is well advised to keep in quotation marks, since their meaning is as vague as the phenomena they are alleged to designate—phenomena of which nothing proves that they are specific to "youths," that they pertain only to certain "neighborhoods," and still less that they are distinctively "urban." Yet one finds them characterized thus everywhere, and because of this very fact they appear to be self-evident. They swell the speeches of politicians, saturate the daily papers, invade and inebriate television, and there is no shortage of media-savvy politologists and magazine sociologists adept at surfing the wave of "current issues" to deliver on the spot those minute-made books that, under cover of "debunking received ideas," grant them the dignity of societal facts or even categories of analysis.

These notions did not spring spontaneously, ready-made, out of reality. They partake of a vast discursive constellation of terms and theses that come from the United States on crime, violence, justice, inequality, and responsibility—of the individual, the "community," the national collectivity—that have gradually insinuated themselves into European public debate to the point of serving as its framework and that owe most of their power of persuasion to their sheer omnipresence and to the newly recovered prestige of their originators.[1] The banalization of these topoi conceals a *stake* that has little to do with the problems to which they ostensibly refer: the redefinition of the missions of the state, which is everywhere withdrawing from the economic arena and asserting the necessity to reduce its social role and to enlarge, as well as harden, its penal intervention. Like a father who for too long has been overly tender and lax, the European welfare state would henceforth be duty-bound to become "lean and mean," to "downsize," and then deal severely with its unruly flock, elevating "security," narrowly defined in strict physical terms and not in terms of life risks (occupational, social, medical, educational, etc.), to the rank of paramount priority of public action.

Withering away of the economic state, diminution and denigration of the social state, expansion and glorification of the penal state: civic "courage," political "modernity," even progressive boldness (under the marketing name of "the Third Way" or "social liberalism"), would now demand that one embrace the most repressive clichés and measures. "Defenders of the Republic, let us not be afraid!" is the gallant exhortation of the French advocates of a new repression that bills itself as "of the left" in government—among them figure two former ministers and an adviser of François Mitterrand, an editorialist for the center-left cultural weekly *Le Nouvel Observateur,* and two directors of the Catholic-left magazine *Esprit*—in an opinion piece published with fanfare by *Le Monde* in September 1998 that openly expresses the new official thought on the subject: in the name of the people, in their interest (as duly defined by us), let us reestablish law and order, so that we may snatch victory in "the race that has now been entered into between reactionary restoration and republican refoundation."[2]

One would here need to reconstitute, link by link, the long chain of institutions, agents, and discursive supports (advisers' memorandums, commission reports, official missions, parliamentary exchanges, expert panels, scholarly books and popular pamphlets, press conferences, newspaper articles and television stories, etc.) by which *the new penal common sense aiming to criminalize poverty*—and thereby to normalize precarious wage labor—*incubated in America is being internationalized,* under forms more or less modified and misrecognizable (including sometimes by those who propagate them), in the manner of the economic and social ideology founded on individualism and commodification of which it is the translation and complement in the realm of "justice." We shall limit ourselves here to selective indications bearing on the most visible channels and routes, which nonetheless suffice to give an idea of the transcontinental scale and impact of this worldwide operation in ideological marketing. We shall also focus on the relations between the United States and Western Europe, while acknowledging that Washington's influence, on both the economic and penal planes, is making itself felt even more strongly in Latin America and—by a supreme irony of history—in many fledging countries born of the breakup of the former Soviet empire.[3]

One shall likewise have to be content, for space reasons, to retrace the impact of only one "think tank" or policy institute each in the United States and in England, whereas, to give full force to the analysis that follows, it would be necessary to reconstitute the complete network of multiplex relations that tie these organizations to one another, on the one hand, and to a varied gamut of agents and institutions that hold positions of power within the political, economic, journalistic, and academic fields, on the other. For the success of this or that protagonist (person or organization) in the vast transcontinental traffic in ideas and public policies within which the internationalization of the penalization of poverty takes place is due not to the "influence" that it enjoys in its individual capacity—to suppose so would amount to taking the effect for the cause—but, rather, to the position it occupies within the structure of relations of competition and collusion, of subordination and dependency, that tie it to the whole set of the other participants, and which is at the basis of the effects it is capable of wielding.[4]

This much to recall, against the charismatic conception of the intellectual as lone knight mounted on his writings and armed solely with his ideas, and its collective complement, conspiracy theory (which attributes to the conscious aims and coordinated strategies of a ruling group, or in this case country, what is the product of multiple institutional gear-meshings and linkages, which are controlled by no one, however powerful), that the authors and organizations whose proposals and activities are analyzed below are nothing else, from the angle that interests us here, than the personal and institutional materialization of systems of material and symbolic forces that run through them and beyond them.[5] Their writings and interventions are so many local and limited manifestations, in a given national space, of the constitution of a *new transnational regime* of relations among the political-bureaucratic field, the economic field, the journalistic field, and the intellectual field, of which partake, inter alia, the global integration of the major media and publishing groups, the unprecedented expansion of the international market for corporate law dominated by Anglo-American firms, the transatlantic exportation of U.S. electoral marketing techniques, and the recent proliferation across European countries of foundations and policy "think tanks" with a half-academic and half-political vocation or façade, as well as novel derivative "professions" (such as "pollster," "image consultant," and "expert in urban policing")—and a regime that forcefully pushes toward the worldwide alignment of public policies onto that particular historical incarnation of neoliberal utopia that is fin de siècle America.[6]

Manhattan, Crucible of the New Penal Reason

This wide-ranging network of diffusion originates in Washington and New York City, crosses the Atlantic to lash itself down in London, and from there stretches its channels and capillaries throughout the Continent and beyond. It is anchored in the complex formed by the organs of the American state officially entrusted with implementing and showcasing "penal rigor," which has held sway uncontested in the United States for two decades, resulting in a quadrupling of the carceral population unprecedented in the annals of democratic societies, during a period when the crime rate was flat and then sharply declining.[7] Among these organs figure the U.S. Department of Justice (which periodically leads veritable *dis*information campaigns on crime and imprisonment) and the State Department (which, through the agency of its embassies, actively proselytizes, in each host country, in favor of ultra-repressive criminal justice policies, particularly regarding drugs), the semipublic and professional associations tied to the administration of police and corrections (Fraternal Order of Police, American Correctional Association, American Jail Association, etc.), as well as the media and the commercial enterprises that participate in the business of incarceration (private firms in the areas of imprisonment, correctional health care, construction, identification and surveillance technologies, insurance, financing, etc.).[8]

But, in this domain as in a good many others since the denunciation of the Keynesian social compact, the private sector makes a decisive contribution to the conception and implementation of "public policy." In point of fact, the preeminent role that falls to neoconservative "think tanks" in the constitution and subsequent internationalization of the new punitive *doxa* spotlights the organic bonds, as much ideological as practical, between the decline of the social-welfare sector of the state and the deployment of its penal arm. It turns out that the policy foundations and institutes that paved the way for the advent of "real (neo)liberalism" under Ronald Reagan and Margaret Thatcher by painstakingly undermining Keynesian notions and policies on the economic and social front between 1975 and 1985 have also operated, a decade later, as a pipeline feeding the political and media elites with concepts, principles, and measures designed to both justify and speed up the establishment of a penal apparatus at once prolix and protean.[9] The same parties, politicians, pundits, and professors who yesterday mobilized, with remarkable success, in support of "*less* government" as concerns the prerogatives of capital and the deployment of labor are now demanding, with every bit as much fervor, "*more* government" to mask and contain the deleterious social consequences, in the lower regions of social space, of the deregulation of wage work and the deterioration of social protection.

On the American side, more so than the American Enterprise Institute, the Cato Institute, or the Heritage Foundation, it is the Manhattan Institute that has popularized the categories and policies aimed at suppressing the "disorders" fostered by those whom Alexis de Tocqueville, already, called "the lowest rabble of our big cities." In 1984, this organization, founded by Anthony Fischer (Margaret Thatcher's mentor) and William Casey (who had been CIA director during Reagan's first term as president) to apply market principles to social problems, launched *Losing Ground*, the book by Charles

Murray that would serve as the "bible" for Reagan's crusade against the social-welfare state.[10] This book massages and misinterprets data to "demonstrate" that the rise in poverty in the United States after the 1960s was caused by the excessive generosity of policies intended to support the poor: such support, we are warned, rewards sloth and causes the moral degeneracy of the lower classes, and especially the "illegitimacy" that is alleged to breed all the ills of modern societies— among them "urban violence."

Charles Murray was an unemployed political scientist of mediocre repute. The Manhattan Institute put up 30,000 dollars for him to write Losing Ground: American Social Policy, 1950–1980, *and organized unprecedented hype around the book together with its allies in the media and bureaucratic fields. A public-relations specialist was hired specifically to promote it; some thousand complimentary copies were sent out to a select list of journalists, elected representatives, and scholars. Murray was "placed" on the circuit of television talk shows and university conferences, and meetings were organized with newspaper and magazine editors and columnists to discuss his thesis. The Manhattan Institute even held a splashy symposium on* Losing Ground, *for which the participants (journalists, public policy experts, and social scientists) received "honoraria" of up to $1,500 in addition to free lodging in a luxury hotel in the heart of New York.[11] Because it appeared at the acme of Reagan's popularity and sailed along with the prevailing political wind—(much) less (social) government—this work riddled with logical fallacies and empirical errors became an instant "classic" in the debate on welfare in the United States.[12] It is true that it followed closely on the heels of George Gilder's ode to capitalism—and the capitalists, those epic heroes of the battle for the creation of wealth—*Wealth and Poverty, *which the* Economist *had welcomed with this salute: "Blessed Are the Money-Makers." Already for Gilder, the source of poverty in America was to be found in "the family anarchy among the inner city's concentrated poor" supported by welfare, whose effect is to corrupt the desire to work, to undermine the patriarchal household, and to erode* *religious fervor, which have always been the three mainsprings of prosperity.*[13]

After a book of tabloid philosophy fancying itself a defense of libertarianism, In Pursuit of Happiness and Good Government, *which depicts the state as the fundamentally harmful force responsible for all the world's ills and calls for a return to a mythologized Jeffersonian America,*[14] *and which such fashionable highbrow publications as the* New York Review of Books *nonetheless felt obligated to cover on account of its author's rising political clout, Murray was again the object of intense media attention for that authentic treatise in scholarly racism, written in collaboration with Harvard psychologist Richard Herrnstein,* The Bell Curve: Intelligence and Class Structure in American Life, *which maintains that racial and class inequalities in America reflect individual differences in "cognitive ability."*

According to The Bell Curve, *IQ determines not only who attends college and who succeeds on campus but also who becomes an unemployed drifter or an enterprising millionaire, who lives within the sacraments of marriage rather than in unwed cohabitation ("illegitimacy—one of the central social problems of the times—is strongly related to intelligence"), whether a mother raises her children properly or neglects them, and who fulfills their civic duties conscientiously ("brighter children of all socioeconomic classes, including the poorest, learn more rapidly about politics and how government works, and are more likely than duller children to read about, discuss, or participate in political activities"). As one might have guessed, IQ likewise governs the propensity to crime and the likelihood of imprisonment: one becomes a criminal and lands behind bars because one suffers, not from being materially "deprived" in a deeply inegalitarian society, but from being "depraved" mentally and morally. Writes Murray: "Many people tend to think of criminals as coming from the wrong side of the tracks. They are correct insofar as that is where people of low cognitive ability disproportionately live." In sum, all the "social pathologies" that afflict American society turn out to be "remarkably concentrated at the bottom of the IQ distribution."*

It follows logically that the state must refrain from interven-
ing in social life to try and reduce inequalities that are grounded
in nature, lest it perpetuate "the perversions of the egalitarian
ideal that began with the French Revolution." For "egalitarian
tyrannies, whether of the Jacobite [sic] *or Leninist variety, are*
worse than inhumane. They are inhuman."[15]

Consecrated as the premier "idea factory" of the New American
Right federated around the trinity of the free market, individual responsibility, and patriarchal values, and armed with an annual budget in excess of five million dollars, in the early 1990s the Manhattan
Institute organized a conference on "the quality of life" that led to
a special issue of its journal *City*. (This magazine has as its goal to
"civilize the city" and it invests heavily in this project: during that
period, ten thousand copies of every issue were distributed free of
charge to politicians, senior public officials, businessmen, and influential journalists along the northeastern seabord, so that it quickly
became one of the main common references of state decision makers
in the region.) The key idea of the conference was that the "sanctity
of public space" is indispensable to urban life and, *a contrario,* that
the "disorder" in which the poorer classes revel is the natural breed-
ing ground for crime. Among the participants in this "debate" was
the city's star federal prosecutor, Rudolph Giuliani, who had just lost
the mayoral election to the black Democrat David Dinkins, and who
would draw from it the themes of his victorious campaign of 1993.[16]
In particular, Giuliani took from this debate the guiding principles
of the police and justice policy that would turn New York into the
world showcase for the doctrine of "zero tolerance" giving the law-
enforcement authorities carte blanche to hunt out petty crime and to
drive the homeless and the derelict back into the shadows of dispossessed neighborhoods.

It is the Manhattan Institute, yet again, that popularized the
"broken windows theory" formulated in 1982 by George Kelling and
James Q. Wilson (the leading light of conservative criminology in the
United States) in an article published by the *Atlantic Monthly* magazine. A derivation of the popular wisdom captured by the French saying "he who steals an egg, steals an ox," this so-called theory (practi-

cal musings about policing based largely on experiments conducted by a Stanford psychologist on people's propensity to engage in pilfering an abandoned car whose windows had been smashed) maintains that it is by fighting inch by inch the small visible disorders of every day that one will vanquish the major pathologies of urban crime. The Institute's Center for Civic Initiative, whose objective is "to research and promulgate creative, free-market solutions to urban problems," and which counts among its fellows Richard Schwartz, the architect of the Giuliani administration's "workfare" programs and CEO of Opportunity America, Inc. (a private job-placement firm for welfare recipients), financed and promoted the book by George Kelling and Catherine Coles, *Fixing Broken Windows: Restoring Order and Reducing Crime in Our Communities.*[17]

This theory, which has never been validated empirically,[18] served as a pseudo-criminological alibi for the reorganization of police work spurred by William Bratton, the head of security for the New York subway promoted chief of the city's police in March 1994. The primary objective of this reorganization was to soothe the fear of the middle and upper classes—those that vote—by means of the continual pestering of the disreputable poor in public spaces (streets, parks, transit stations, buses and subways, etc.). Three means were deployed to achieve this goal: large increases in the staff and equipment of the police squads, the "reengineering" of bureaucracy via the devolution of operational responsibilities to precinct captains with mandatory quantified target goals, and a computerized monitoring system (along with its centralized database of criminal and cartographic information that officers can consult via portable computers on board their patrol car) that makes possible the ongoing redeployment and rapid intervention of forces, resulting in an inflexible enforcement of the law, particularly against such minor nuisances as drunkenness, public urination, disturbing the peace, panhandling, solicitation, and "other antisocial behaviors associated with the homeless," according to Kelling's own terminology.

"In New York, we know who the enemy is," declared William Bratton, the city's chief of police, in a conference delivered in 1996 at the Heritage Foundation, one of the New Right think tanks closely allied to the Manhattan Institute in its campaign to take apart the welfare state. To wit: the "squeegee men," those destitute street entrepreneurs who accost drivers at traffic stoplights to offer to clean windshields for petty change (Giuliani turned them into the reviled symbol of the social and moral decline of the metropolis during his victorious mayoral campaign of 1993, and the popular press openly likened them to social vermin or "squeegee pests"), petty drug retailers, prostitutes, beggars, the homeless, drifters, and perpetrators of graffiti and other urban depredations.[19] In short, the enemy is the subproletariat that mars the scenery and menaces or annoys the consumers of urban space. It is this group, castigated under the catchall pseudo-scholarly category of "underclass," that has been the priority target of the policy of "zero tolerance," whose avowed objective is to restore the "quality of life" for those New Yorkers who know how to behave in public, that is, the predominantly white middle and upper classes, the ones who are gradually reclaiming the central city and still vote in municipal contests.

As its name indicates, this policy consists of a rigid and intransigent enforcement of the law aimed at repressing minor infractions committed on the streets so as to restore the sentiment of order and to force the members of the lower classes to "moralize" their public behaviors. To fight without mercy, one by one, the petty daily disorders that the latter cause in public space—street peddling, aggressive panhandling, urination, drinking, littering, and loitering—the New York police use a computerized statistical system (CompStat, a scientific-sounding acronym that stands plainly for "computerized statistics") that enables every precinct captain and each patrol to deploy their resources and activities based on continually updated and detailed, geographically coded information on incidents and complaints in their sector. Each week, the heads of the various police districts meet at the headquarters of the NYPD for a ritual session of collective evaluation of the results for each precinct, and to shame those commanders who do not deliver the expected drop in the official crime figures.[20]

But the genuine innovation of William Bratton did not rest on the specific policing strategy he implemented, which targets entire categories rather than isolated offenders, multiplies specialized measures and means of suppression, and relies on the systematic use of "just-in-time" computerized crime data, by opposition to "community policing" and to "problem-solving policing."[21] It resides, first, in having jostled and overturned the sclerotic and cowardly bureaucracy that he had inherited by subjecting it to the latest wave of management theories on business "reengineering" (associated with the names of Michael Hammer and James Champy) and "target management" à la Peter Drucker. From the outset, Bratton flattened the organizational chart of the police department, reassigned personnel, and ordered the mass firing of high-ranking officers: three-fourths of precinct captains were dismissed, so that their average age dropped from over sixty to about forty years. He transformed neighborhood police stations into "profit centers," the "profit" to be generated being the statistical reduction of recorded crime. And he merged all criteria of evaluation of police services as a function of this sole indicator. In short, he directed the city's law-enforcement bureaucracy as a corporate head would a firm deemed to be underperforming by its stock owners: "I would pit my command staff against any Fortune 500 company," proudly declared the new "CEO of the NYPD," who pored over the evolution of criminal statistics daily with religious zeal: "Can you imagine running a bank if you couldn't look at your bottom line every day?"[22]

The second asset enjoyed by Bratton in his remaking of the city's police, which would also be very hard to replicate in the European context, is the extraordinary expansion of the human and financial resources allocated by New York for the enforcement of public order. In only five years, the city increased the budget of its police department by 40 percent to $2.6 billion, equal to four times the appropriation given to its public hospitals. And it hired or absorbed a veritable armada of 12,000 officers for a total payroll of more than 47,000 in 1999, including 38,600 uniformed staff (see Table 1). This stupendous growth has given New York the highest ratio of police per capita of any U.S. metropolis, with 66 officers per 10,000 residents in 1996,

Table 1. Growth of the New York Police Department, 1985–99

	1985	*1990*	*1995*	*1999*
Civilian personnel	6,255	9,563	9,352	8,638
Uniformed personnel	26,073	26,844	37,450	38,621
Total	32,328	36,407	46,802	47,259

Source: Annual reports of the New York Police Department, 1985–99.

nearly twice the rate sported fifteen years earlier. By comparison, in the same period, the city's social services absorbed a budget cut of one-third and lost 8,000 positions to find themselves with only 13,400 employees.[23]

By embracing the doctrine of "zero tolerance," Bratton turned his back on the "community policing" strategy to which he owed his previous success as police chief in Boston. The conversion is hardly conclusive, if one compares the performance of New York City with that of San Diego, a metropolis that applied community policing during the same period:[24] from 1993 to 1996, the Southern California city posted a drop in crime *identical* to that recorded by New York City, but at the cost of only a modest increase in police staffing of 6 percent. The number of arrests effected by the forces of order diminished steadily by 15 percent during those three years in San Diego, whereas it increased by 24 percent in New York City to reach the phenomenal figure of 314,292 arrestees in 1996 (the number of persons stopped for minor drug-related offenses alone doubled to surpass 54,000, that is, more than a thousand arrests per week). Finally, the volume of complaints against the police sagged by 10 percent on the shores of the Pacific while they ballooned by 60 percent in Giuliani's city.

It is this new policy that city leaders, but also the national and international media (followed by certain European researchers whose main source of data on the U.S. city is their dutiful daily reading, from Paris, London, or Stockholm, of the *International Herald Tribune*), were quick to credit for the decline in the crime rate posted by New York City in recent years—conveniently ignoring the facts that this decline *preceded* by several years the introduction of these police tactics and that crime also dropped in American cities that did not apply them (such as Boston, Chicago, San Francisco, or San Diego).[25] Among the "lecturers" invited in 1998 by the Manhattan Institute to its prestigious "Luncheon Forum" to enlighten the upper crust of politics, journalism, and philanthropic and research foundations on the northeastern corridor: William Bratton, promoted "international consultant" in urban policing, who cashed in on the glory of having "reversed the crime epidemic" in New York (and on the agony of having been fired by Giuliani for being more popular than the mayor) with a pseudo-autobiography in which he preaches the new credo of "zero tolerance" to the four corners of the globe—beginning with England, the land of welcome and acclimation chamber for these policies on their way to the conquest of Europe.[26]

> But I think that what the reduction in crime [in New York] has really accomplished is that the philosophy that the Manhattan Institute and that the Heritage Foundation have been discussing for years is being applied in cities across the country with great success.
>
> —Rudolph Giuliani, keynote address to the Livable Cities Conference, sponsored by the Heritage Foundation, the Manhattan Institute for Policy Research, and the State Policy Network, April 1999.[27]

The Globalization of "Zero Tolerance"

From New York, the doctrine of "zero tolerance" as instrument of legitimation of the penal management of troublesome poverty, that is, visible poverty that causes disruptions and annoyance in public space and thus fosters a diffuse sentiment of insecurity, or even simply a nagging sense of unease and incongruity, has propagated itself across the globe with lightning speed.[28] And with it has spread the military rhetoric of waging "war" on crime and "recapturing" public space, a rhetoric that assimilates (real or imaginary) criminals, the homeless, vagrants and panhandlers, and other urban derelicts to *foreign invaders*—facilitating the conflation with immigration, which always pays off at the ballot box in countries swept by powerful xenophobic currents—in other words, with allochthonous elements that must imperatively be expurgated from the social body.

Basking in the aura of New York's "success" (the Big Apple is routinely and misleadingly portrayed as the metropolis with the highest crime rate in the nation, suddenly gone to leading the pack of America's "safe cities," whereas it was never either one or the other statistically),[29] this theme gives local politicians the opportunity to jump on the bandwagon of American "modernity" and, thence, to effect a paradoxical rhetorical pirouette allowing them simultaneously to reaffirm on the cheap the state's determination to "get tough" on "disorder" and to discharge the same state of its responsibilities in the *social and economic* genesis of insecurity in order to appeal to the *individual* responsibility of the residents of "uncivil" areas, upon whom it is now incumbent to exercise proximate social control, as expressed by this statement—one of a hundred others like it—by Henry McLeish, the Scottish (and New Labor) home affairs minister, published under the bellicose title "Zero Tolerance Will Clean Up Our Streets":

> I am asking Scots to walk tall. This is a war and there are many battles to be fought. People need to reclaim the streets. We can be far too complacent about second-rate services and standards in our communities. Mindless vandalism, graffiti and litter despoil our housing estates. The message is that this kind of behaviour will not be tolerated. People have a right to a decent home and decent community. But too many people are not exercising their responsibilities.[30]

The Giuliani experiment has produced eager emulators on every continent. In August 1998, the president of Mexico launched a "National Crusade against Crime" by means of a plank of measures presented (as is the norm nearly everywhere) as "the most ambitious in the history of the country." Its openly flaunted objective: "to imitate programs like 'zero tolerance' in New York City." In September 1998, it was the turn of the minister of justice and security of Buenos Aires, León Arslanian, to indicate that this province of Argentina would join in applying "the doctrine elaborated by Giuliani." Arslanian also revealed that a cluster of abandoned industrial warehouses on the edge of town would be converted into *galpones penitenciarios* (detention centers) so as to generate the needed extra prison space. In January 1999, following the visit of two high-ranking officials of the New York Police Department, the new governor of the state of Brasília, Joaquim Roriz, announced the implementation of *"tolerância zero,"* thanks to the immediate hiring of an additional 800 civil and military police in response to a wave of violent crime of the kind that chronically roils the Brazilian capital. To the critics of this policy who pointed out that it would translate into a sudden 30 percent increase in the carceral population at a time when the state's correctional system was already on the verge of explosion, the governor retorted that the state would simply have to build new penitentiaries.

On the other side of the Atlantic, at the beginning of December 1998, while the Jospin government was readying itself to come out in the open with the repressive turn of policy it had been preparing for months, the Americanologist Sophie Body-Gendrot, an accredited commentator on questions of "urban violence" (she is the coauthor of an official report on the topic presented a few months before to the minister of the interior that borrows and amplifies all the current journalistic clichés on the question), was smoothing the way by recommending on the national station France-Inter, during a broadcast of the popular radio program *The Phone Is Ringing,* the implementation of a *"tolérance zéro à la française"*—though no one could say for sure what such "Frenchness" might consist of. The following month, on the other bank of the Rhine, the Christian Democratic Union (CDU) was waging a brisk campaign on the theme of *"Null Toleranz"* in the Frankfurt region, while simultaneously gathering signatures for a petition against dual citizenship, so as not to risk being outflanked by future Chancellor Gerhard Schröder and his overtly xenophobic statements on crime and immigration.[31] Since William Bratton's triumphant tour the previous fall—the former police chief was received as a messiah by the city's highest dignitaries—the New York City doctrine had been vaunted as the painless and plain panacea for all the ills of society: crime, vagrancy, and "social parasitism," not to forget the claim of (mainly Turkish and Yugoslav) resident foreigners to German citizenship, hastily assimilated to the undesirable presence of illegal aliens *("Null Toleranz für straffällige Ausländer").*

In Italy, the Giuliani-brand *"moda repressiva"*—as observers from across the Alps call it—was the rage as early as 1997. The police treatment of street poverty fascinates a wide gamut of elected officeholders, on the Right as well as on the Left, either in its original form, imported straight from the United States, or in the watered-down, "Europeanized" retranslation of it offered by Tony Blair and Jack Straw in England. Thus, when, at the beginning of 1999, a series of murders in the center of Milan spiked up yet another media panic over "immigrant crime," the mayor of the Lombard capital and his chief deputy dramatically flew off to New York City while the government of Massimo D'Alema adopted a plank of repressive measures inspired by the recent British crime legislation (criminalization of certain misdemeanors, increased powers for the police, dismissal of the director of the prison administration, known for his progressive positions favoring inmates' rights and programs geared toward rehabilitation). As for the mayor of Naples, Antonio Bassolino, he took *zero tolleranza* to heart, applying it not only to minor and middling delinquency, but also to driving infractions, as in New York, where, since the winter of 1998, drunk driving is punished by the immediate and automatic confiscation of the car at the point of arrest by the police.[32]

In February 1999, the city of Cape Town launched a large-scale "zero tolerance" operation aimed at checking a wave of violence of a prototerrorist nature allegedly perpetrated by radical Islamic groups opposed to governmental corruption. (In August 1996, William Bratton had flown to Johannesburg for a "consultation" with the local police chief, George Fivaz, during a visit copiously covered by the South African and U.S. media, but which had not borne any fruit.) The South African copy makes the New York original pale by comparison: police roadblocks and checkpoints between neighborhoods, night sweeps by shock commandos armed to the teeth aimed at poor areas (such as the township of Cape Flats), and ubiquitous officers in full combat regalia on the streets around Water Front, the rich touristic enclave of the city center. In March, at the other end of the globe, the minister of police of New Zealand was returning from a mission to New York to proudly proclaim to his fellow citizens that, all things considered, their national police had nothing to envy when compared to that of the Big Apple, since "New Zealand has never had a corrupt police force," and it "has enforced zero tolerance from the beginning." His proposal to import from the United States the "devolution of responsibilities" and the setting of quantitative targets for precinct captains, as well as the redeployment of police forces in high-crime zones, instantly garnered the approval of the country's main political leaders.

Meanwhile, the chief of police of Cleveland County in England, a pioneer of "zero tolerance" in the United Kingdom, was intervening in Austria before the Polizeiführungsakademie (national police academy) to sing the praises of this American import on behalf of British Interior Minister Jack Straw. The following week, a national symposium was held on this same policy in Canberra under the aegis of the Australian Criminological Institute. In June 1999, after William Bratton had come in person to sermonize the Ontario Crime Commission, it was the turn of Toronto's mayor Mel Lastman to announce with considerable fanfare the imminent launch of "the greatest crackdown on crime that the city has ever known," on grounds that the criminal trajectory of the Canadian metropolis followed that of New York, albeit with a lag of two decades, and that, in any case, the efficient policing of any large city follows the same simple principles in all places and at all times, those taught by the self-proclaimed "international crime consultants" issued from the ranks of the New York police who now crisscross the planet or pontificate in training seminars offered to their American and foreign colleagues in Manhattan. It is these selfsame principles that William Bratton invoked on a second trip to Buenos Aires in January 2000, at the invitation of the candidate for mayor of the local right-wing party, during which he toured the *villas miseria* (shantytowns) of Pompeya and Barraca, where unemployment, desperation, and delinquency concentrate, to expound with assurance: "The cause of crime is the bad behavior of individuals, it is not the consequence of social conditions." The following spring, all the major political parties of both Right and Left contending in the regional and municipal elections vied to advertise themselves as the most determined advocates of *"tolerancia cero"* and *"mano dura."*[33] One could multiply ad infinitum examples from countries and cities where the recipes of the Bratton–Giuliani duo are in the process of being evaluated, programmed, or applied (generally in adulterated forms).

From the realm of street policing and punishment, the U.S. notion of "zero tolerance" later spread as if through a metastatic process to designate in turn, and pell-mell, the strict application of parental discipline within the family, the automatic expulsion of students who bring weapons inside their school, the swift suspension of professional athletes who commit violent acts outside of stadia, the punctilious control of drugs within prisons, but also the staunch refusal of racist stereotypes, the severe repression of discourteous behavior among airline passengers, and intransigence toward double-parking along commercial boulevards, litter in public parks, and children who do not wear their seatbelts in the backseat of cars. It has even been extended to international relations: thus, in the spring of 1999, Ehud Barak demanded of Yasir Arafat that he demonstrate "zero tolerance" toward terrorism, while the British troops intervening as part of the United Nations peacekeeping force in Kosovo professed to apply "zero tolerance" for any disorder on the streets of Pristina.

Irony has it that this tactic of legalized police harassment is spreading from one end of the planet to the other at the very moment when it is being seriously called into question in New York itself, in the wake of the gruesome murder in January 1999 of Amadou Diallo, a twenty-two-year-old Guinean immigrant killed in a hail of gun-fire (he was hit by nineteen of the forty-one bullets fired at him) by four police officers from the "Street Crimes Unit" in pursuit of an alleged rapist while he was standing peaceably in the doorway of his apartment building. Coming on the heels of the Abner Louima scandal, in which a Haitian immigrant had been sexually tortured in a Manhattan police precinct the year before, this police killing triggered the largest civil disobedience campaign that the United States has witnessed in years. For two full months, daily picketing and demonstrations took place in front of the police headquarters, during which more than 1,200 peaceful protesters—including some hundred local and national African-American elected officials, among them former mayor David Dinkins, the president of the NAACP, and many retired black police officers—were arrested, handcuffed, and charged with "disorderly conduct."

In the wake of these events, the aggressive tactics of this special unit of 380 men (nearly all of them white) that was the spearhead of the policy of "zero tolerance" have become the object of several administrative investigations and two judicial inquiries led by federal prosecutors, on suspicion that these officers carry out arrests based on "racial profiling" and systematically flout the constitutional rights of their targets.[34] According to data obtained by the National Urban League, in two years, this squad, which operated in plainclothes and patrols in unmarked cars, stopped and searched 45,000 persons on mere suspicion based on dress, appearance, behavior, and—above all other indicators—skin color. More than 37,000 of these stops proved groundless, and the charges against half of the remaining 8,000 were dismissed by the courts, leaving a residue of barely 4,000 justified arrests: fewer than one in eleven. A 1999 poll conducted by the *New York Daily News* found that about 80 percent of black and Latino young men in the city had been stopped and searched at least once by the police during the previous year.[35]

In point of fact, incidents with the police have multiplied since the implementation of the city's "quality-of-life" initiative: the number of complaints filed before the Civilian Complaint Review Board spiked by 60 percent between 1992 and 1994 to reach an all-time high in 1996. The vast majority of these complaints concerned "routine patrol incidents"—as distinct from encounters in the course of judicial inquiries—whose victims were black and Latino residents in three-fourths of the cases. Blacks accounted for 53 percent of the complaints filed, whereas they are only 20 percent of the municipal population. And 80 percent of complaints against police brutality were recorded in only 21 of the 76 districts making up the city, all of them ranking among the poorest.[36] A painstaking statistical study of the use of the "stop-and-frisk" policy commissioned by the New York State Department of Justice as part of its judicial review found that African Americans made up one-half of the 175,000 individuals controlled during 1998, and fully two-thirds of those checked by the elite Street Crimes Unit. This "racial disproportionality" was particularly pronounced in white neighborhoods, where 30 percent of police stops targeted blacks. Not surprisingly, African-American and Latino areas are the privileged terrain for deployment of this technique: only one of the ten city districts where the practice of "stop and frisk" was most intense is majority white. Additionally, four arrests in ten turned out to be devoid of any legal basis. Worse yet, the Street Crimes Unit, whose unofficial motto is "We Own the Street," arrested an average of 16.3 blacks for every one charged with an offense, compared to 9.6 for white arrestees. These disparities cannot be fully explained by crime-rate differentials between neighborhoods and groups: they stem in good measure from the discriminatory application of the policy itself. And such bias, the New York State attorney general stresses, "undermines the credibility of the police and, in the final analysis, undermines the mission of law enforcement itself."[37]

Even the main New York police union has come to distance itself from the "quality-of-life" campaign that its officers are charged to lead, following the murder indictment of the members of the squad responsible for Amadou Diallo's death. After the Patrolmen's Benevolent Association unanimously, and for the first time in its 105-year existence, passed a "no-confidence" vote publicly demanding the suspension of Police Commissioner Howard Safir in April 1999, the president of the union urged its 27,000 members to exercise the maximum degree of restraint before making arrests on such puny grounds as jaywalking, taking one's dog out without a leash, or riding a bicycle without a bell, as required by the city's policy: "Now that crime is way down, an adjustment in strategy is required. If we don't strike a balance between aggressive enforcement and common sense, it becomes a blueprint for a police state and tyranny."[38] The police officers of New York themselves, then, turn out to be far less enthusiastic about "zero tolerance" than its overseas zealots.

This is because one of the major consequences of "zero tolerance" as it is practiced day to day—rather than theorized by the "thinkers" of the policy institutes and their epigones in the academic and political fields—has been to dig an abyss of distrust (and, for young people, of outright defiance) between the African-American population and the forces of order, reminiscent of the relations they entertained in the segregationist era. A poll conducted in March 1999 revealed that *the overwhelming majority of blacks in New York City consider the police to be a hostile and violent force* that poses a threat to them: 72 percent judged that officers make use of excessive force, and 62 percent that their acts of brutality against persons of color are common and habitual (versus only 33 percent and 24 percent of whites, respectively). Two-thirds thought that Giuliani's policy had aggravated police brutality, and only one-third said that they felt safer in the city today, even though they resided in the neighborhoods where the drop in violent crime has been the most pronounced statistically. As for white New Yorkers, 58 percent and 87 percent of them declared exactly the opposite: they praised the mayor for his intolerance toward crime and they felt unanimously less threatened in their city.[39] "Zero tolerance" thus presents two diametrically opposite faces, depending on whether one is the (black) target or the (white) beneficiary, that is, depending on which side one finds oneself of the caste barrier that the rise of the American penal state has the effect—if not the function—of shoring up.

Another consequence of the "quality-of-life" policy pursued by the New York police, which has also been scarcely discussed by the advocates of that policy, is the unprecedented clogging of the courts it has caused. Although the municipal crime rate has been falling steadily since 1992, the number of persons arrested and tried in the city has increased continuously. Between 1993 and 1997, the volume of arrests shot up 41 percent to reach the astronomical figure of 384,600, which is *more than the total number of crimes recorded* by the police (355,900) after the latter had dropped by 59 percent.[40] In 1998, the seventy-seven judges of New York's criminal courts who exercise jurisdiction over misdemeanors (i.e., offenses punishable by less than one year of confinement) were in charge of 275,379 cases, or 3,500 cases *each*, twice the caseload they handled in 1993 with approximately the same resources. For defendants who wish to go to trial, the average wait has reached 284 days (as against 208 in 1991), even for minor cases such as simple shoplifting or a bounced check. It is quite common for a judge to hold hearings on up to a thousand cases *per day* without any of them being resolved, whether because their examination is postponed as no judge is available to set a trial date, or because the public defender is not able to free herself (each handles over one hundred cases at any given moment), or because the defendants, weary with waiting, resign themselves to pleading guilty and ask for a plea bargain that exempts them from trial in exchange for a reduced sentence. Some defendants adopt the opposite strategy: they skillfully play on the endless delays and repeated postponements to secure the dismissal of the charges against them. Thus, even though the number of trials in New York's criminal court has fallen from 967 in 1993 to 758 in 1998 (amounting to one trial for every 364 cases), the volume of cases closed by dismissal of charges on grounds of excessive delays has doubled in that period from 6,700 to 12,000. Even Rudolph Giuliani's spokesperson for penal policy was forced to acknowledge that, every year, thousands of offenders escape all punishment owing to the shortage of judges, so that the "the impact of the Police Department's work in driving down crime can potentially be lost."[41]

For precarious members of the lower class, relegated to the margins of the labor market and forsaken by America's "semi-welfare" state, who are the main target of the policy of "zero tolerance," the gross imbalance between the activism of the police and the profusion of means devoted to it, on the one hand, and the overcrowding of the courts and grievous shortage of resources that paralyzes them, on the other, has every appearance of an *organized denial of justice*.[42]

London, Trading Post and Acclimation Chamber

On the British side, the Adam Smith Institute, the Center for Policy Studies, and the Institute of Economic Affairs (IEA) have worked in tandem to disseminate neoliberal ideas on social and economic matters,[43] but also the punitive theses elaborated in the United States and introduced under John Major before they were carried forth and amplified by Anthony Blair. For example, in late 1989, the IEA (founded, like the Manhattan Institute, by Anthony Fischer, under the illustrious intellectual patronage of Friedrich von Hayek) orchestrated, at Rupert Murdoch's initiative and with considerable pomp, a series of meetings and publications around the "thought" of Charles Murray. Murray used this platform to beseech the British to hasten to severely shrink their welfare state—absent the possibility of eliminating it—so as to thwart the emergence, in the United Kingdom, of a so-called underclass of alienated, dissolute, and dangerous poor, cousin to the hordes said to be "devastating" the inner cities of America in the wake of the permissive social measures taken as part of the "War on Poverty" of the 1960s.[44]

This intervention, trumpeted by the *Sunday Times* and followed by a veritable blizzard of unusually effusive articles in the British press (the *Times,* the *Financial Times,* but also the *Guardian,* the *Independent,* etc.), led to the publication of a collective book. In this volume, one can read, alongside Murray's ruminations on the need to bring the weight of the "civilizing force of marriage" to bear on lower-class "young males [who] are essentially barbarians" and on their partners so prone to get pregnant since, for them, "sex is fun and [having] babies endearing,"[45] a chapter in which Frank Field, then in charge of welfare within the Labor Party and Blair's future minister of welfare reform, advocates punitive measures designed to prevent single mothers from having children and to force "absentee fathers" to assume financial responsibility for their illegitimate offspring as well as an "availability-to-work" test to push people into whatever jobs happen to be on hand.[46] This book testifies to a solid consensus taking shape, between the most reactionary segment of the American Right and the self-proclaimed avant-garde of the European "New Left," around the idea that the "undeserving poor" ought to be put back firmly under control by the (iron) hand of the state, and their errant behaviors corrected by public reprobation and by tightening the noose of administrative constraints and penal sanctions.

"Scrapping the Welfare State to Save Society" from the "New Rabble"

The best part of a thousand people turned up to a forum sponsored by the Sunday Times *and the Institute of Economic Affairs in London last week to hear him. He has been able to tap into a deep fear of unmarried mothers and the rising costs of the welfare state. Murray's polemic—which first appeared in the British press in 1989—prepared the ground for the outbursts against unmarried mothers which have become a feature of Toryism. We have Rupert Murdoch to thank. It was he who invited him to speak at one of the annual gatherings of his news editors in Aspen, Colorado. Murray was spotted by Irwin Stelzer, a Murdoch adviser, who pressed him to visit Britain and try to apply his theories here. The result has been the wholesale import of classic American libertarianism. What Milton Friedman was to early Thatcher economic policy, Murray is to Major's Back to Basics. ("Get the Poor off Our Over-Taxed Backs," The* Guardian, *September 17, 1994)*

In an article bluntly titled "Get the Poor off Our Over-Taxed Backs," Madeleine Bunting, a reporter for the left-of-center Guardian, *draws an ironic but ultimately flattering portrait of Charles Murray, "the American guru who inspired the 'Back to Basics' program" of John Major in the closing years of the Tory government, for whom "the welfare state must be scrapped to save society from the underclass" that is already sowing social ruin and moral desolation in England's cities after having ravaged the segregated neighborhoods of the American metropolis.*[47]

Murray "articulates the unspeakable with the assurance of a man who believes his time has come." And with good reason: the neoconservative revolution whose "theorist" he has been proclaimed by the think tanks and fashionable journalists (U.S. News and World Report *listed him among the "32 men and women who dominate American politics" in 1993, and the* Times of London *referred to him reverentially as "Dr. Charles Murray," as if he were some great scientist, in the article reporting the release by the Institute of Economic Affairs of its booklet on the silent but ominous threat that the "underclass" poses to British society; and, with no fear of ridicule, the IEA's director places Murray in the august lineage of Adam Smith and Friedrich von Hayek)*[48] *is triumphing without even having to give battle in the United States and the United Kingdom, where the parties supposed to represent the forces of progress, the Democratic Party and New Labor, are tripping over themselves to adopt the dogmas and administer the antistate elixirs promoted with guns blazing by the Manhattan*

Institute's very own Bradley Fellow. Isn't President Clinton himself "on record as saying that Murray's analysis," *according to which illegitimate unions and single-parent families are the cause of poverty and crime,* "is essentially correct," *even if he does not wholeheartedly endorse the solution advocated by Murray—namely, abolishing overnight all forms of assistance to single mothers and using the monies thus saved to put their children up for adoption or into large state orphanages?"* [49] *Murray likewise calls for the wholesome restoration of the acid stigma that yesteryear attached to women who conceived children outside the sacrament of marriage, because* "the welfare of society requires that women actively avoid getting pregnant if they have no husband": "It is all horribly sexist, I know. It also happens to be true."* [50]

Murray readily concedes that he hardly knows British society, aside from quick visits of "sociological voyeurism" *in the company of officials to some of the country's* "problem neighborhoods." *No matter: his* "analyses" *pertain less to social diagnosis (which would require a minimum of scientific work) than to prognosis of an imminent disaster that only draconian cuts in the nation's social budgets would be susceptible to averting—just as in France some argue that only bringing formerly working-class neighborhoods back under firm police control will make it possible to check a* "drift of the middle classes" *toward the extreme Right. Murray explains:*

> The debate on social policy [in the UK] is lagging behind America by about seven to ten years. I get into the arguments here that I was getting into in 1986 in the US. The feeling of déjà vu is very powerful. But in terms of the things I'm worried about, Britain is now far ahead of the US. . . . The potential for really explosive upheaval is very, very high. You have single parenthood rapidly rising; as benefit budgets rise, they cause hostility amongst those paying the taxes. . . . The middle classes will get real angry. [51]

By the time Murray returned to the attack in 1994, on the occasion of a sojourn in London sponsored by the *Sunday Times* during which he again received wide and complacent press coverage, the notion of "underclass" was well established in the language of UK policy as well as in the social sciences—under the impetus of research bureaucracies anxious to demonstrate their usefulness by sticking to the political-journalistic themes of the day. So he had no difficulty convincing his audience that his dismal predictions of 1989 had all been realized: "illegitimacy," "dependency," and crime, the three leading indicators of the growth of the loathsome "underclass," had increased in unison among Albion's new poor and, together, threatened the sudden death of Western civilization.[52] (A few days after Murray launched his warning in the press, the budget minister of the Tory government, Kenneth Clarke, echoed him by asserting in a major public speech that the reduction in social expenditures made by the Major government aimed "to prevent the emergence of an underclass excluded from the possibility of working and dependent on welfare.") And so, in 1995, it was the turn of his ideological comrade in arms, Lawrence Mead, the neoconservative political scientist from New York University, to come and explain to the British at yet another IAE colloquium that, if the state must imperatively refrain from helping the poor materially, it nonetheless behooves it to support them *morally* by imposing on them the requirement of (substandard, low-paying) work. This is the theme, since then canonized by Anthony Blair, of the "obligations of citizenship," used to justify the mutation of *welfare* into *workfare,* and the institution of forced wage work under conditions excepting from social and labor law persons "dependent" on aid from the state—in 1996 in the United States and three years later in the United Kingdom.[53]

A major American inspirer of the British policy of welfare reform, Lawrence Mead is the author of the book *Beyond Entitlement: The Social Obligations of Citizenship,* published in 1986, whose central thesis is that the U.S. welfare state of the 1970s and 1980s failed to reduce poverty, not because its assistance programs were too generous (as Charles Murray maintains) but because they were "permissive" and did not impose strict behavioral mandates upon beneficiaries. For nowadays, as opposed to yesteryear, "unemployment has more to do with functioning problems of the jobless than with economic conditions," so that "work, at least 'dirty,' low-wage jobs, can no longer be left solely to the initiative of those who labor": it must be made mandatory, "just as a draft has sometimes been necessary to staff the military." The state therefore does not have to make the desired behavior more attractive—for example, by increasing the minimum wage (which has been in free fall since 1967 in real value) or by improving social insurance and health coverage—but to staunchly punish those who do not submit to it: "Non-work is a political act" that demonstrates "the need for authority."[54]

In plain terms, employment in insecure jobs paid at subpoverty wages must be raised to the rank of a civic duty (in particular by curtailing the possibility of subsisting on public aid outside of the deskilled labor market), or else it will find no takers (or employers might have to raise wages). This diagnosis is fundamentally correct. Mead has the merit of seeing and making us see that the generalization of precarious work, which some present as an "economic necessity," admittedly regrettable in certain aspects but ideologically neutral and in any case materially ineluctable, rests in reality on the direct use of *political constraint*. It partakes of a class project that requires, not the destruction of the state as such in order to substitute for it a stateless liberal Eden of the universal market, but the *replacement of a "maternalistic" welfare state with a "paternalistic" punitive state,* which alone is capable of imposing desocialized wage labor as societal norm and foundation for the new polarized class order.

In *The New Politics of Poverty: The Nonworking Poor in America,* published six years later, Mead argues that the social question that looms over advanced societies—both in America and in Europe, though with a lag there—is no longer "economic equality," an obsolete notion, but the "dependency of the poor" incapable of working by reason of social incompetence or moral ineptitude: "We need a new political language in which competence is the subject instead of the assumption. We need to know how and why the poor are deserving, or not, and what suasions might influence them." It follows that a "new politics of individual behavior," stripped of the remnants of the "sociologism" that had hitherto vitiated every approach to the problem by abusively claiming that poverty has social causes, supersedes "social reform."[55]

Whence, finally, the need for a strong state, an inflexible moral guardian, which is alone capable of overcoming the "passivity" of the poor by the discipline of work and the authoritarian remodeling of their dysfunctional and dissolute "lifestyle," which Mead "theorizes" in a collective work with the revealing title *The New Paternalism:*

"Traditional antipoverty policy is compensatory. It attempts to fill in the deficits of income and skills that the poor suffer because of disadvantaged backgrounds. . . . By contrast, paternalistic programs emphasize obligations. The idea is that the poor need support, but they also require structure. And behavioral rules are to be enforced through government. The law enforcement side of social policy serves the freedom of others, but it also claims to serve the poor themselves."[56] To put it differently, although they might not want to have any part in it, the dispossessed fractions of the working class are the expected "beneficiaries" of the historic transition from welfare state to punitive state.

The paternalistic programs that will furnish the poor with the "directing framework" supposed to enable them (at long last) to "live in a constructive manner," and thus to reduce the burden they impose on the rest of society, have as their target—this is neither a surprise nor a coincidence—two populations that partly intersect and largely complement one another: recipients of public assistance to the destitute and the clients of the criminal justice system, that is to say, the women and children of the (sub)proletariat as concerns welfare and their husbands, fathers, brothers, and sons as for the penal apparatus.[57] Lawrence Mead thus advocates "more government" on both the social *and* the penal fronts, but on the express condition that this "social" function as penal in disguise, as an instrument of surveillance and discipline of recipients primed to dispatch them to its crime-control counterpart should they fail to meet mandated work standards. Mead concedes at last that "the implications" of state paternalism "are particularly momentous for racial minorities, who are over-represented among the poor" (he forgets to mention that they are even more overrepresented in the penal sector of the state). In their case, its deployment might at first sight "seem like a reversal, and for blacks even a return to slavery or Jim Crow" (the regime of legalized segregation and astringent ostracism prevalent in the Southern states from Emancipation until the civil rights revolution of the 1960s). But he is swift to assure us that "paternalism is really a postracial social policy" since it emerges at the moment "when racial theories of poverty are less plausible than they have ever been" and because in any case "today's poor and those who serve them are integrated, drawing elements from all racial groups" *[sic]*.[58]

The fact that a high-ranking dignitary of the New Labor government, Frank Field, would come in person to comment on Lawrence Mead's theses, after having previously served as Charles Murray's discussant in the same setting, speaks volumes about the degree of mental colonization of the British policy makers by the United States (the cover of the conference book's new printing in 1997, after New Labor's electoral victory, trumpets in big block letters, "Frank Field, MP, Minister for Welfare Reform").[59] Such submission does not fail to both amaze and delight the New York University political scientist: "I am honoured by the attention British social policy experts have given my work. It is thrilling to discover that my reasoning, developed from afar, has contributed something to what Americans would call 'the mother of all welfare states.'"[60]

"The Best Answer to Poverty Is to Direct the Lives of the Poor"

The following excerpt from a text by Lawrence Mead titled "The Debate on Poverty and Human Nature" has the merit of providing a pseudophilosophical catalog of the new commonplaces that guide American (and hence British) social policy in the "post-welfare" era[61]—as commentators like to say, with one of those pithy formulas that expresses in a crude manner the objective pursued all along by the supporters of welfare "reform": its abolition. In this catalog, we find the regression toward an atomistic vision of society as a simple serial collection of individuals guided in turns by their rational interest and (whenever their behavior seems to defy the calculus of utility or to go against conservative common sense) by a "culture" from which their strategies and life chances magically spring forth; the individualistic explanation of a social fact, in flagrant violation of the first precept of the sociological method (according to which one always explains a social fact by another social fact), decreed null and void in the new "meritocratic society" that has finally come into being; and the erasure of the antagonistic division between social classes, advantageously replaced by the technical and moral opposition between the "competent" and the "incom-

petent," the "responsible" and the "irresponsible," with social inequalities being no more than a reflection of these differences in "personality"—as with Murray and Herrnstein's differences in "cognitive capacity"—and on which therefore no public policy can hope to gain traction.

This ultraliberal vision coexists, curiously, with the authoritarian conception of a paternalist state that must at once enforce elementary "civilities" and impose deskilled and underpaid wage labor onto those who do not want it. Social work and police work thus obey the selfsame logic of control and straightening of the behaviors of the faltering or inept members of the working class. It is not indifferent that this text was published in an anthology offering "Christian perspectives on a policy in crisis," insofar as the religious impulse plays a noteworthy role in the return of neo-Victorian moralism among the dominant classes of the Anglo-American zone: sociodicy and theodicy join the better to legitimate in concert the new liberal-paternalistic order.

Social policy has gradually given up reforming society and instead focuses on managing the lives of the poor. One cause, no doubt, is conservative political trends in the nation, but the more fundamental reason is that structural explanations of poverty have become implausible. If poverty is due mainly to behavior rather than social barriers, then behavior, rather than society, must be changed. Above all, unwed childbearing must be discouraged and work levels raised. . . .

That is why social policy has turned toward enforcing work. Since 1967, and especially since 1988, AFDC [Aid to Families with Dependent Children] has required rising proportions of welfare mothers to participate in work programs as a condition of eligibility for aid. States are using child support laws to require more absent fathers to work to help support their families. In addition, schools have enforced standards more firmly, homeless shelters police the conduct of their residents, and law enforcement has become tougher. The evidence is that such paternalist policies, which combine support for the poor with demands for functioning, offer more hope to ameliorate poverty than just doing more for the poor—or doing less. The best answer to poverty is not to subsidize people, or to abandon them. It is to direct lives. . . .

My own view is that government should directly enforce the civilities most essential to public order. It must repress lawbreaking, draft soldiers, and so on. With slightly less urgency, it should enforce the obligations that

Americans must discharge to be regarded as equals in the public realm. To achieve equal citizenship is America's innermost purpose. Political participation is part of equal citizenship, but few feel that voting should be mandatory. The case is otherwise with employment. People regard working as essential to their social standing, so to assure employment by those not working is the major domestic imperative American government faces. . . .

In a meritocratic, postreform society, these identities of competent and incompetent have become the chief stratification, eclipsing older class differences. Experts and commentators type some people as "privileged" and others as "disadvantaged" on the basis of personal style, without any knowledge of their economic circumstances. People are termed "rich" if they have an upstanding, reliable manner, and "poor" if they do not. No structural reform of the society could alter these identities. For in our current politics, personality, not income or class, is the defining quality about a person. The great divide in society lies not between the rich and less rich, but between those who can and those who cannot assume responsibility for themselves.

—Lawrence Mead, "The Debate on Poverty and Human Nature" (1996)

The paternalist state wished and called for by Lawrence Mead must also be a punitive state: in 1997, the IEA brought back Charles Murray yet again in order, this time, to promote before an audience of policy makers and hand-picked journalists the notions, much in vogue in American neoconservative and neodemocratic circles, that "prison works," and that escalating correctional expenditures, far from constituting an unbearable financial burden, are a wise and profitable investment for society.[62] (This thesis, which is supported by America's highest judicial authorities, such as the attorney generals for the United States, California, Florida, and Texas, is so glaringly untenable as soon as one ventures outside the borders of that country, given that there exists *no correlation between crime rates and incarceration rates* on the international level, that the IEA had to resign itself to formulating it in the interrogative.) Murray relies on a discredited statistical study by the U.S. Department of Justice which concludes that, by the mere virtue of its "neutralizing" effect, the tripling of the incarcerated population of the United States between 1975 and 1989 prevented 390,000 homicides, rapes, and robberies in 1989 alone, to profess that "short of the death penalty," prison is "by far the most effective" means of "restrain[ing] known, convicted criminals from murdering, raping, assaulting, burglarizing, and thieving."[63] And he articulates in these muscular terms the penal policy that should go hand in hand with the retrenchment of the social state: "A lawful system has only a minor interest in the reasons why someone commits the crime. The criminal justice system is there to punish the guilty, exonerate the innocent, and serve the interests of the law-abiding."[64] In sum, the state need not concern itself with the causes of crime among the poorer classes, other than their "moral poverty" (the new explanatory "concept" in fashion), only with its consequences, which it should suppress with zeal and efficacy.

A few months after Murray's visit, the IEA invited the former police chief of New York City, William Bratton, for purposes of advertising "zero tolerance" at a press conference dressed up as a scholarly colloquium, in which the police chiefs of Hartlepool, Strathclyde, and Thames Valley participated (the first two having taken the initiative of introducing "proactive policing" in their districts). This was only logical, since "zero tolerance" is the indispensable police complement to the rising incarceration spawned by the criminalization of poverty in Great Britain as in the United States. At this meeting, which was again covered with much ballyhoo by docile media, one learned that "the forces of law and order in England and the United States agree more and more that criminal and subcriminal *[sic]* behaviours such as litter, insults, graffiti, and vandalism should be firmly checked to prevent more serious criminal behaviours from developing," and that there is an urgent need to "restore the morale of police officers who for years have been undermined by sociologists and criminologists who insist that crime is caused by factors, such as poverty, over which the police have no control."[65]

This pseudosymposium was prolonged, as is customary, by the publication of a collective book, *Zero Tolerance: Policing a Free Society*, whose title summarizes well the political philosophy to be implemented: "free," that is, (neo)liberal and noninterventionist at the top, in matters of taxation and employment; intrusive and intolerant at the bottom, for everything to do with the public behaviors of the members of the lower class caught in a pincer movement by the generalization of underemployment and precarious wage labor, on the one side, and the retrenchment of social protection and the profligacy of public services, on the other. Widely diffused among the experts and members of Blair's government, these notions directly informed the

Law on Crime and Disorder voted by New Labor in 1998, recognized
as the most repressive penal legislation passed in the United Kingdom
since World War II.[66] And to avoid any ambiguity as to the target of
these measures, the British prime minister justified support for "zero
tolerance" in terms that could hardly be more clear: "It is important
that you say we don't tolerate the small crimes. The basic principle
here is to say, yes it is right to be intolerant of homeless people on
the streets."[67] One measures the banalization of these theses in Great
Britain by the fact that the *Times Literary Supplement* judged the
booklet of the Institute for Economic Affairs, *Zero Tolerance,* worthy of review and indeed of exaltation: in an article forthrightly titled
"Towards Zero Tolerance," the inspector in chief of the British prisons invites us "to welcome warmly and to encourage [this] admirable
little book" on the grounds that it shows us how the police can be
"not agents of law-enforcement but partners in a concerted effort
with communities that aims to reestablish the conditions in which a
free society can blossom."[68]

From the United Kingdom, where they constitute the yardstick
by which all authorities are henceforth enjoined to measure their police and judicial practices, the notions and measures promoted by the
neoconservative "think tanks" of the United States and their British
trading posts have spread throughout Western Europe—in Sweden,
Holland, Belgium, Spain, Portugal, Italy, Germany, and France. So
much so that it is difficult nowadays for an official of a European
government to express herself on "security" without some "Made in
USA" slogan coming out of her mouth, be it dressed up, as French
national honor demands, with the adjective *républicain* or qualified
by "à la" (Spanish, Italian, German, etc.): "zero tolerance," curfews,
vitriolic denunciations of "youth violence" (that is, of so-called immigrant youth from neighborhoods left fallow by capitalist restructuring), proactive repression of vagrancy and minor public disorders, the
diligent targeting of petty drug traffickers and consumers, the erosion
or lowering of the juridical boundary between minors and adults, incarceration of repeat-offender youths, privatization of criminal justice
services, and so on. All these *mots d'ordres*—in the double sense of
motto and incitements to "law and order"—have crossed the Atlantic
and the Channel before finding a more and more hospitable reception on the Continent, where, in what is the crown of the hypocrisy or

ignorance on the part of politicians, their proponents present them as national innovations necessitated by the unprecedented evolution of "urban violence" and crime in their localities.

Importers and Collaborators

Indeed, it is plain that the export of these law-and-order themes and theses hatched in America for the purpose of reaffirming society's moral ascendancy over its "undeserving poor" and bending the (sub) proletariat to the discipline of the new labor market is thriving only because it is meeting with *the interest and approval of the authorities of the different importing countries.* This approval assumes a variety of forms, ranging from the jingoistic enthusiasm of Anthony Blair to the shameful and awkwardly denegated acceptance of Lionel Jospin, with a whole gamut of positions in between, as testified by Gerhard Schröder's oscillations between these two poles over time.

This implies that one must include among the agents of this transnational enterprise of symbolic conversion, aimed at making the new *punitive ethos,* necessary to justify the rise of the penal state, accepted as self-evident by universalizing it (within the narrow circle of the capitalist countries that think of themselves as the universe, that is), the leaders and officials of the European states who, one after the other, have converted to the imperative of the "restoration" of (republican) order after having convinced themselves of the benefits of the ("free") market and the necessity of a smaller (social) state. In those urban areas where the state has given up on bringing firms and jobs, it will put up in their stead police stations and patrols, perhaps in anticipation of building prisons later.[69] The expansion of the penal apparatus can even make a significant contribution to the creation of jobs in the surveillance of those cast off from the world of work: the 20,000 "adjunct security officers" and 15,000 "local mediation agents," who were to be massed in "sensitive neighborhoods" before the end of 1999, represent a good tenth of the "youth jobs" promised by the French government as part of their campaign to fight unemployment. The "Action Bulletin No. 71" guiding the implementation of "Local Security Contracts" between French cities and the state under the aegis of the interior ministry likewise advocates "creating a ladder of 'private security occupations' in the field of youth occupational and social integration" and "making a special effort toward the recruitment of security deputies so that these represent, at least partially *[sic]*, the sociology of urban neighborhoods."[70]

But the countries that import the American instruments for a resolutely offensive penality, fit for the enlarged missions incumbent upon the police and penitentiary in advanced neoliberal society—to reaffirm the moral authority of the state at the moment when it strikes itself with economic impotence, to bend the new proletariat to desocialized wage labor, to warehouse the useless and undesirable of the social order *in statu nascendi*—do not content themselves with passively receiving these tools. They often borrow them on their own initiative and always adapt them to their needs as well as to their national traditions, political and intellectual. Such is the purpose of those "study missions" that have multiplied in recent years across the Atlantic.

Following in the footsteps of Gustave de Beaumont and Alexis de Tocqueville, who set out, in the spring of 1831, on a carceral excursion across the "classical soil of the penitentiary system," parliamentarians, penologists, and high-ranking civil servants of the European Union's member countries regularly make the pilgrimage to New York, Los Angeles, and Houston, with the aim of "penetrating the mysteries of American discipline" and the hope of better activating the "hidden springs" of its inner workings back in their own homeland.[71] Thus, it was in the aftermath of such a mission, graciously financed by Corrections Corporation of America, the leading private incarceration firm in the United States and the world—as measured by sales (over $400 million in 1997), inmate beds (almost 50,000), and the yield of its stock on the NASDAQ market (its value multiplied fortyfold in its first ten years of existence)—that Sir Edward Gardiner, head of the commission on interior affairs in the House of Lords, was able to discover the virtues of prison privatization and to steer the United Kingdom onto the road of for-profit incarceration. Gardiner later demonstrated the sincerity of his personal endorsement of privatization by taking up a position on the board of directors of one of the main firms that compete for the booming and lucrative punishment market: the number of inmates locked up in British private establishments exploded from 200 in 1993 to nearly 4,000 six years later.

Another medium for the diffusion of the new penal common sense in Europe is official reports, those *pre-thought* writings by means of which politicians cloak the decisions they intend to make for political (and often narrowly electoral) reasons[72] in the garb of the pseudo-science that those researchers most attuned to the media and state problematic of the moment are particularly adept at producing on order. These reports are based on the deceitful quid pro quo that follows: in return for a fleeting media notoriety—which she will endeavor to cash into academic prebends and privileges in the most heteronomous sectors of the university field—the hired researcher agrees to abjure her intellectual autonomy, that is, her capacity to pose the question at hand in properly scientific terms, which requires her *ex definitione* to break with the official definition of the "social problem" assigned and in particular to analyze its political, administrative, and journalistic preconstruction. To take but one instance, this would mean retracing the invention and political uses of the recently proliferating category of *"violences urbaines,"* which is a pure *bureaucratic artifact* devoid of statistical coherence and sociological consistency, rather than docilely descanting on its presumed causes and possible remedies in the very terms dictated by the state administration that created it for its own internal ends.[73]

These studies typically rely on the support provided by reports produced under similar circumstances and according to analogous canons in the societies taken as "models" or singled out for a "comparison" that generally boils down to fantasized projection, such that the governmental common sense of a given country finds a warrant in the state common sense of its neighbors through a process of circular reinforcement and mutual misrecognition. One example among others: one is dumbfounded to discover as an appendix to the official report of the mission conferred by French Prime Minister Jospin upon two socialist representatives, Christine Lazerges and Jean-Pierre Balduyck, *Responses to Juvenile Delinquency*, a note by Hubert Martin, adviser for social affairs at the French embassy in the United States, which delivers a veritable panegyric on the curfews imposed upon teenagers in the American metropolis.[74] Without emitting the slightest doubt or the most timid criticism, this zealous civil servant parrots the results of a dubious survey in the form of an apology carried out and published by the United States Conference of Mayors of large cities with the express aim of defending this police gimmick, which occupies a choice place in their media "showcase" on crime and safety. According to the accounts of their promoters, which, conveniently, no serious research comes to upset or rectify (although there exist a number of such studies, and they are not so difficult to access), the institution of such curfews is alleged to be "a useful tool for public order" because it stimulates the sense of responsibility of parents and prevents acts of violence through a "wise use of the time and services of the police," thanks to "serious field preparation aimed at obtaining a local consensus."

This official of the French government thus makes himself the mouthpiece of the American mayors who "have the feeling" that curfews "have contributed to the current decline in juvenile delinquency."[75] In reality, these programs have no measurable impact on criminal activities, which they merely displace in time and space. They are very onerous in personnel and resources, as they make it necessary to arrest, process, transport, and eventually detain tens of thousands of youths every year who have not contravened any law (more than 100,000 were thus processed in 1993, twice the number of minors arrested for theft, excluding car theft). And, far from being the object of a "local consensus," as Hubert claims, they are vigorously fought over in the courts (several suits about them recently reached the U.S. Supreme Court) owing to their discriminatory enforcement and repressive purpose, which contribute to criminalizing youths of color in segregated neighborhoods.[76] One sees in passing how a police measure devoid of effects, other than criminogenic and liberticidal, and shorn of justifications other than as media ploy, manages to generalize itself, each country invoking the "success" of the others as a pretext for adopting a technique of surveillance and harassment, which, although it fails everywhere, finds itself validated by the very fact of its wide diffusion.

An American Fairy Tale for French Consumption

While it was not reviewed in any academic journal of criminology and sociology in the United States, Turnaround, *the self-celebration of "America's top cop" has been reviewed—and praised to the heavens—in France, by Julien Damon (head of the national railway's Solidarity Mission, responsible for issues related to the growing presence of homeless people in train stations), in the* Cahiers de la sécurité intérieure, *the official organ of the body officially charged with "rethinking domestic security," the Institut des Hautes Études de la Sécurité Intérieure (IHESI).*[77] *Damon praises Bratton's pamphlet as a book "to be recommended to all those who wish to be informed about the so-called 'zero tolerance' practices." In his conclusion, he even refers the reader to the promotional leaflet for zero tolerance published by the Institute of Economic Affairs,* Zero Tolerance: Policing a Free Society, *which he describes as "an English anthology [that] brings together the reflections of police officials, including William Bratton, who presents in it his theses and his methods."*[78] *This shows that the Manhattan Institute and the Institute of Economic Affairs hardly need to expend much effort to find readers, if not zealots, across the Atlantic and the Channel.*

The same issue of the Cahiers de la sécurité intérieure *contains a long article by political scientist Sébastian Roché, who has made a specialty of importing American ideologies on insecurity and disorder,*[79] *which raises the crucial question: "'Zero Tolerance': Can It Be Applied in France?" This article would delight the American colleagues who welcomed Roché to Princeton, where he effected a study "mission" as research fellow under the high authority of John DiIulio, himself a leading advocate of mass incarceration and a fashionable theorist of "moral poverty" as the root cause of crime.*[80] *In it, Roché counterposes the alleged scientific rigor and neutrality of the works of ultraconservative U.S. criminologists (such as James Q. Wilson and Richard Herrnstein—the coauthor with Charles Murray of* The Bell Curve; *the former Kansas City police chief turned Manhattan Institute Fellow, George Kelling; and David Courtwright, a neo-Darwinist historian according to whom violence in America is the product of "bachelor societies" living in a "frontier" atmosphere that gives free rein to "the biochemistry of the human species") to the amateurism of French studies, which, by contrast, "are often the product of an ideological position or professional bias." Above all, his article contains nothing that would displease William Bratton: Roché provides a remarkably superficial presentation of New York's policing strategies, citing in turn*

Wilson, Kelling, and Bratton himself, that reads every bit like a publicity flyer for the city's police department.

One example: without offering a shred data to that effect (even as he complains loudly about the lack of "systematic empirical works" in France), Roché asserts that "on security," the "opinions [of blacks] on Guiliani's [sic] policy join in level of satisfaction those of the other communities." Now, we have seen that African Americans diverge completely from white New Yorkers on this very point—and for good reason. Of course, it is not in Princeton, a little social and racial paradise cut off from everything, that one runs the risk of noticing this. And so Roché arrives at his conclusion, decreeing that "zero tolerance" is a "course" that "deserves to be explored in France," though he warns that "the repressive dimension, which is quite unavoidable, cannot be as developed *as in the United States, since violent crime is less prevalent in our country."*[81] *It thus behooves France to innovate a moderately repressive policy of police repression. This will no doubt be the object of Roché's new book, whose imminent publication is announced in a footnote:* Is There a French Broken Window?

The zeal and devotion of these transatlantic missionaries in security have not been in vain: the dogmas of the new penal religion manufactured in the United States to better "tame" the fractions of the working class bucking at the discipline of precarious and underpaid wage labor have spread across Europe, where they already enjoy the status of commonplaces among the experts now teeming around governments suddenly anxious to promote the "right to safety"—all the more fervently as they have de facto forsaken enforcement of the "right to work." These revealed truths provide the spine of the "Que sais-je?" volume Urban Violence and Insecurity *published in early 1999 under the pen of Alain Bauer and Xafier Raufer.*[82] *Raufer is the self-appointed director of studies at the University Center for Research on Contemporary Criminal Threats (a title that is an entire program unto itself) at the University of Paris-Panthéon-Sorbonne and an adjunct professor at the Paris Institute of Criminology, but also—though the book's back cover omits any mention of it—a founder of the extreme-Right group Occident Chrétien. A former student of-*

ficial at the same university and occasional guest lecturer at the Institut d'Études Politiques as well as, inevitably, at the Institut des Hautes Études de la Sécurité Intérieure, and the prolific author of countless opinion pieces regularly published in Le Monde, Le Figaro, Le Nouvel Observateur, and other mainstream media outlets, the businessman Bauer is a near-mandatory participant in official colloquia on "urban violence," where he uses his seemingly academic credentials and contacts with public officials to recruit clients for AB Associates (AB stands for Alain Bauer), the "urban security consulting group" of which he is the founder and chief executive officer.

So it shall come as no surprise that their jointly authored book offers an apologia for "zero tolerance" and private policing, and urges bringing "peri-urban France struck by crime" under firm penal control. For, according to Bauer and Raufer, the "restoration of security" in New York "made it possible to wring the necks of several pseudo-criminological 'canards,' a pestilent species of fowl that remains all too lively in our country": the origin of crime is neither demographic, economic, cultural, nor "chemico-medicinal" (that is, tied to narcotics addiction); its "remote social genesis" is an illusion or a hoax, as one prefers. "All of that is eloquently demonstrated in the stock-taking book" (i.e., the pseudo-autobiography) of William Bratton: "Over and beyond all the sociologically inspired theories, the most certain origin of crime is the criminal himself."[83] This criminological "discovery" that Bauer and Raufer generously ascribe to the former police chief of New York City is nothing other than the favorite refrain of the speeches on crime of Ronald Reagan, who himself was merely reformulating the oldest conservative social philosophy on the matter.

After crossing the Atlantic, these security fairy tales, woven out of bogus concepts, slogans disguised as "theories," and sociological falsehoods propagated by neoconservative "think tanks" in the course of their war against the welfare state, directly inform the practical implementation of European police strategies on the ground. Thus we find this faithful précis of the new neoliberal punitive doctrine in the "Bulletin No. 31" drawn up by the Institut des Hautes Études de la Sécurité Intérieure to help guide the drafting of "Local Security Contracts" in French cities:

> American research has shown that the proliferation of incivilities is merely the harbinger of a generalized rise in delinquency and crime. The first deviant behaviors, as minimal as they seem, if they become generalized, stigmatize a neighborhood, attract other deviance into it, and are the sign of the end of everyday social peace. The spiral of decline is set off, violence settles in and takes hold, and with it all the forms of delinquency: assaults, burglaries, drug dealing, etc. (cf. J. Wilson and T. [sic] Kelling, "the broken window theory").
>
> It is based on the results of this research that the police chief of New York City put in place a strategy to fight crime called "zero tolerance" aimed at those who commit incivilities, which seems to have been one of the factors in the very sharp reduction in the crime rate in that city.[84]

Much like the mercenary intellectuals of the U.S. think tanks whose ideas and slogans they borrow, the security "experts" of France's interior ministry reverse causes and effects in order to better dispose of any link between delinquency and unemployment, physical insecurity and social insecurity, the rise in public disorders and the growth of inequality. Now, it is not because "incivilities" multiply in a neighborhood (as if by spontaneous generation or through unreflective imitation) that the neighborhood *eo ipso* becomes disreputable and sinks into a flood tide of violence leading to unstoppable decline, but the exact reverse: it is economic decline and persistent segregation that feed street disorders by destabilizing the local social structure and amputating the life chances of its population.

If the black ghettos and (secondarily) the Puerto Rican and Mexican barrios of the United States concentrate within them so many "urban pathologies," it is owing to the twofold rejection on the basis of caste and class of which their residents are the object in the first place, as well as to the policies of urban abandonment and social disinvestment pursued by the American state over the past quarter-century.[85] High rates of crime are not the effect of some endogenous behavioral dynamic according to which rivulets of "minor malfeasances" would naturally converge to swell into a roaring river of "urban violence." The best available study of the "spiral of urban decay" in the United States, *Disorder and Decline* by political scientist Wesley Skogan, establishes that the most powerful determinant of social deteriorization in poor neighborhoods is the deep poverty caused by chronic unemployment and underemployment (the correlation between public disorders and the unemployment rate is +0.84), followed closely by racial segregation. Yet this study is frequently cited on both sides of the Atlantic as an empirical verification of the pseudo-theory of "broken windows."[86]

The Academic Pidgin of Neoliberal Penality

First there is the gestation and dissemination, national and then international, by U.S. think tanks and their allies in the bureaucratic and journalistic fields, of terms, theories, and measures that, knit together, concur in penalizing social insecurity and its consequences at the bottom of the class structure. Next comes their borrowing, partial or wholesale, conscious or unconscious, necessitating a more or less intricate work of adaptation to the cultural idiom and state traditions specific to the different receiving countries by the officials who then implement them, each in their domain of competence. A third operation intervenes to redouble this work and accelerate the international traffic in the categories of neoliberal understanding, which now circulate in rush-production-mode from New York to London, and then on to Paris, Brussels, Munich, Milan, and Madrid: their *academicization,* that is, dressing them up in scholarly garb.

It is through the agency of exchanges, interventions, and publications of an academic character, real or simulated, that intellectual "smugglers" *(passeurs)* reformulate these categories in a sort of *politological pidgin,* sufficiently concrete to "hook" state decision makers and journalists anxious to "stick close to reality" (as projected by the authorized vision of the social world), but sufficiently abstract to strip them of any overly flagrant idiosyncrasy that would tie them back to their originating national context. And so these notions become semantic commonplaces where convene all those who, across the boundaries of occupation, organization, nationality, and even political affiliation, spontaneously think advanced neoliberal society as it wishes to be thought.

We find a striking illustration of this process in that exemplary specimen of false research on a false object entirely *preconstructed* by the political-journalistic common sense of the day, and subsequently "verified" by data haphazardly gleaned from newsmagazine articles, opinion polls, and official publications, but duly "authenticated," in the eyes of the novice reader at least, by a few quick visits to the neighborhoods incriminated (in the literal sense of the term), with the book by Sophie Body-Gendrot, *Cities Confront Insecurity: From American Ghettos to the French Banlieues.* The title is by itself a sort of prescriptive précis of the new state *doxa* on the question: it suggests what is now de rigueur to think about the new police and penal rigor, which it proclaims to be at once inescapable, urgent, and beneficial.[87]

> The inexorable growth of phenomena of urban violences plunges all the specialists into perplexity. Must we opt for "all-out repression," concentrate our means on prevention, or seek a middle road? Must we fight the symptoms or attack the deep causes of violence and delinquency? According to a public opinion poll.

One has here, conveniently gathered, all the ingredients of the pseudo political science that the technocrats of ministerial staffs and the "Op-ed" pages of major dailies relish: as point of departure, a fact that is anything but established ("inexorable growth") but which is said to disconcert even "specialists" (it is not said which ones, and for good reason); a category of bureaucratic understanding ("urban violences") under which each can put whatever suits her interest since it corresponds to just about nothing; a public opinion poll that measures little more than the activity of the institute that produced it (and the agenda of the newspapers and magazines who commission such polls); and a series of false alternatives answering to a logic of bureaucratic intervention (repression or prevention), which the researcher sets out to resolve even though they have already been implicitly settled in the way the question is formulated. Everything that follows, a catalog of American clichés about France and French clichés about America, will allow the writer to present *in fine* as a "middle way," conforming with reason (of state), the penal drift advocated by the current socialist government if the country is to avert disaster—the back-cover text of the book hails the citizen-reader thus: "It is a matter of great urgency: by 'reinvesting' entire neighborhoods, one seeks to prevent the middle classes from sliding toward extreme political solutions" (read: the National Front).[88] An added precision: by reinvesting them with police officers, not with jobs.

The Elusive "Explosion" of "Urban Violence" Committed by Juveniles

The detailed and disaggregated examination of the production and evolution of the delinquency figures recorded by French police services between 1974 and 1997 by the best specialist of the topic, criminologist Bruno Aubusson de Cavarlay, allows one to "gain a little distance" (265)[89] *from the catastrophist statements of politicians as well as the alarmist discourses of journalists and researchers who echo them, apparently without having looked into the problem for very long.*

The gross volume of youth delinquency in France has indeed increased over the past fifteen years, but in that it has only followed the national trend for offenses, no more, no less: after fluctuating slightly, downward and then upward, the share of youths in total delinquency for 1996 is 18 percent, exactly identical *to what it was in 1980 (271). Now, it is true that, from 1994 to 1997, the number of recorded offenses decreased whereas the number of minors brought to court increased notably. But the so-called "explosion" of juvenile delinquency during this period is an* artifact *that reflects the "catching up" of the first figure by the second due to the greater diligence of the justice system in arresting and prosecuting youths during these years (270). The same goes for the increased seriousness of infractions: the shift toward violent offenses (assault and battery, threats and robbery, rape) applies to* all *offenders* and not solely *to minors, and it is in part explained by the improvement of the procedures and attitudes of the authorities, which have facilitated the filing of complaints, particularly in the case of rapes (275, 269). As for the other offenses, such as burglaries, vehicle thefts, and shoplifting, the absolute figures for minors in 1996 are even* lower *than those for 1980 (273).*

Concerning the most common so-called incivilities (insults, threats, rowdy behavior and gatherings, minor property damage, graffiti), no one can know whether youths commit more or fewer of them than in the past or than their elders, because police statistics simply do not record them! Thus it is difficult to see what would permit one to allege a "more and more important implication of youths in offenses and incivilities" as the prime minister asserts with aplomb in his letter appointing the "Mission on Responses to the Delinquency of Minors" addressed to the socialist members of parliament Lazerges and Balduyck.[90] As for "the lowering of the age of minors implicated in more and more serious and violent acts," which Lionel Jospin presents as an established fact motivating his urgent request for a parliamentary report, it is entirely based on impressions, anecdotes, guesses, and fears since, here again, "there does not exist any statistical source permitting one to measure the drop in the age of delinquents or their greater precociousness, which constantly recur in accounts from the field" (270).[91]

At the end of this rigorous exercise in statistical exegesis, Cavarlay concludes, with a firmness tempered by diplomacy, that the existing data can neither invalidate nor confirm "the hypothesis of the emergence of a new form of delinquency specific to certain minors (called 'exclusion delinquency')," any more than they authorize one to "create a new grouping of offenses labeled, without precautions, 'urban violences,' in which minors would be particularly well represented" (275). Yet it is exactly this "explosion" of "urban violences" perpetrated by youths fallen into a supposed "delinquency of exclusion" of recent make that motivates—or serves as a pretext for—the drift toward the penal treatment of poverty advocated by Prime Minister Jospin. And it is this selfsame category of "urban violences," which is statistical nonsense because it lumps together acts of a totally different nature (insults and riots, graffiti and aggravated assault, minor vandalism and armed robbery), that the minister of justice recently invoked in parliamentary debate to leave out of measures limiting the use of preventative detention those individuals who are arrested and brought to trial under emergency procedures (comparution immédiate), that is, half of all persons put behind bars on remand (40,000 every year), which are known to concern first and foremost the residents of France's neighborhoods of relegation.[92] This amounts to granting the most dispossessed a form of "carceral affirmative action" inscribed in law, and by members of parliament who are self-professed members of the Left, to boot.

All this leads one to think that, if state executives took the trouble to read the study reports that they commission (and the team in power in France in 1999 was known to be a voracious consumer of these reports), they would enable the country to avoid false and noxious debates.

They would also reduce their astonishing capacity for that kind of immobilism that thinks of itself and presents itself as a "policy of progress" but that hardly fools anyone among those very groups that suffer its consequences on a daily basis.

Who, seriously, can believe that incarcerating a few hundred more (or fewer) youths will have any impact on the problem that politicians persist in refusing to so much as name: the deepening of social inequality and the generalization of wage precariousness and social insecurity under the press of deregulation policies and the abdication of the state from the economic and urban front?

By means of a twofold, crisscrossing projection onto each other of the national prenotions of the two countries considered, this American-ologist well heeled with the French Ministry of the Interior,[93] manages at once to tack onto French neighborhoods with high concentrations of public housing the American mythology of the ghetto as territory of dereliction (rather than as instrument of *racial domination,* which is hardly the same thing)[94] and to force the ghettoized areas of New York and Chicago into the French administrative fiction of the "sensitive neighborhood" *(quartier sensible).* Hence a series of pendulum swings passing themselves off as an analysis, in which the United States is utilized, not as one term in a methodical comparison—which would immediately reveal that the alleged "inexorable rise" in "urban violence" is above all a political and media thematics designed to facilitate the redefinition of social problems in terms of security and thence stress the need for reasserting "law and order"[95]—but rather by turns as a bogeyman to be shunned and as a model to be emulated, albeit with caution. By raising, in a first moment, the specter of "convergence," the United States serves to elicit horror—the ghetto, never that in our society!—and to dramatize discourse so as better to justify taking "entire neighborhoods" into police hands. One can then take up the Tocquevillian refrain of grassroots citizen initiative, this time expanded on a global scale (since, thanks to globalization, "inhabitants of the entire planet have discovered a common identity for themselves, that of Resistance fighters for democracy"), to justify the importation into France of American techniques for the local enforcement of public order.

At the end of a meandering essay fit for poli-sci undergraduates on the hackneyed theme of "the city as social laboratory," the "stakes of the post-city," and (to put on a truly scientific air) "operational criminality in a fractal world," about which the author asserts—no joke—that its "script is borrowed from Mandelbaum's [*sic:* the correct author is Mandelbrot] mathematical theories on fractalization," Body-Gendrot puts forth this forceful conclusion, which seems to have come right out of a Manhattan Institute "luncheon forum": notwithstanding "the French regal might" that regrettably "slows the transformation of mentalities," "*governments are gradually surrendering to the evident facts:* community-based management of problems must be developed, juvenile crime police squads bolstered, the training of officers intensified, parents held criminally responsible," and "every delinquent act by a minor punished in a systematic, swift, and visible manner."[96] Evident facts that are henceforth shared in New York, London, and Paris, and which impose themselves a little more each day in the other capitals of Europe through an effect of imitation: even Sweden is now wondering whether it should inflict "zero tolerance" on itself in order to get in tune with its neighbors to the south.

In short, *Les Villes face à l'insécurité* comes at just the right moment to ratify the abdication of the social (and economic) state and to legitimize the bolstering of the penal state in formerly working-class neighborhoods sacrificed on the altar of the modernization of French capitalism. Like most of the works that have recently mushroomed on the "feeling of insecurity," "incivilities," and "urban violence," this book is part and parcel of the very phenomenon it purports to explain: far from supplying an analysis of it, it contributes to the political construction of a fortified and proactive penality entrusted with containing the disorders caused by the generalization of unemployment, underemployment, and precarious wage labor.

"Urban Violence" and Carceral Violence

During the March 1999 parliamentary debate on the bill "reinforcing the presumption of innocence and the rights of victims," Minister of Justice Elisabeth Guigou firmly opposed an amend-

*ment that would have brought the norms of provisional deten-
tion for fast-track cases resulting from live arrests* (comparutions
immédiates) *in line with those applied to cases stemming from
judicial investigations* (affaires à instruction): *"We would be depriving ourselves of an efficient tool for fighting urban violence.
Think that, with this amendment, we would not have been able
to take into remand detention the perpetrators of the acts of
vandalism committed at the beginning of this year in Grenoble"
(where despondent lower-class youths had stoned city buses).
The Socialist Party representative from a struggling working-
class district of Seine-Saint-Denis, Véronique Neiertz, went one
step further, with the support of her Communist colleague André
Guérin: "It would mean ruining the efforts deployed in the housing projects." To which the former attorney and Socialist Party
deputy Arnaud de Montebourg added: "I know emergency procedures* [comparutions immédiates] *well from having gotten my
start with them. In emergency procedures, one is confronted with
an extreme violence, with situations of horrendous poverty. But
the emergency procedure is a necessity"—and along with it, it
seems, the hasty jailing of presumed troublemakers.*

*As if the political world had suddenly started walking upside
down, it was the representative from the right-wing Union for
French Democracy (UDF), Pierre Albertini, who, for the sheer
pleasure of argumentation, put the most energy into defending
this amendment proposed by a majority-socialist commission:
"One cannot elaborate a penal policy by reckoning on the basis
of a few acts of urban delinquency, however distressing they may
be." And to recall what until recently had been a commonplace of
the Left, if not of common sense: "It would be preferable to act
on the causes of this violence."*[97] *Nothing doing—the amendment
was rejected at the government's insistence. Even* Le Monde,
*which can hardly be said to defend innovative positions on these
subjects, felt compelled to run as byline: "The 'law-and-order'
argument wins on emergency judicial procedures."*[98]

*The result is that the residents of declining public housing
projects will benefit from an additional effort at incarceration on
the part of the state, a policy of "affirmative action" in imprisonment that, if it does not approach the magnitude of the policy that
has struck ghetto blacks in the United States, is hardly different*

*in its principle and modalities. To the "horrendous poverty" of
sinking neighborhoods of relegation, the government will now
respond, not by reinforcing its social-welfare engagement, but by
hardening its penal intervention. To the faceless violence of economic marginalization, it will oppose the official violence of
carceral exclusion.*

The expression "Washington consensus" is commonly used to designate the panoply of measures of "structural adjustment" imposed
by the rulers of global finance on debtor nations as a condition for
international aid (with the disastrous results that have recently been
in glaring evidence in Russia and Asia), and, by extension, the neoliberal economic policies that have triumphed in all advanced capitalist countries over the course of the past two decades: budgetary
austerity and fiscal regression, cutbacks in public expenditures and
the bolstering of the rights of capital, the unbridled opening of financial markets and foreign trade, the privatization of state enterprises
and public services, the flexibilization of wage work and the reduction of social protection.[99] It is now apposite to extend this notion
so as to encompass within it the punitive treatment of the social
insecurity and marginality that are the socio-logical consequence of
such economic policies. And, just as France's socialist governments
played a pivotal role, in the mid-1980s, in the international legitimation of submission to the market, today the administration of Lionel
Jospin finds itself poised in a strategic position to normalize, by
lending it warrant "from the Left," the policing and carceral management of poverty in advanced society.

Two

From Social State to Penal State: American Realities, European Possibilities

If the punitive wind come from across the Atlantic is blowing so hard throughout the Old World, it is because, as in the glory days right after World War II, the political elites, business, and the "opinion makers" of present-day Europe feel an envious fascination with the United States that stems essentially from the performance of its economy.[1] The key to American prosperity and the presumed way out of mass unemployment, to believe them, would lie in a simple— not to say simplistic—formula: a smaller state. It is a fact that the United States, and alongside it the United Kingdom, New Zealand, and Australia, has curtailed its social expenditures, virtually eradicated trade unions, and vigorously pruned the rules for hiring and (especially) firing in the lower tier of the labor market so as to institute so-called flexible wage work as a norm of employment, even an obligation of citizenship through the conjoint deployment of programs of forced work ("workfare") for recipients of public assistance.[2] Proponents of neoliberal policies of dismantling the welfare state like to emphasize how eliminating labor "rigidities" has stimulated job creation and wealth production. They are much less diligent when it comes to registering the devastating social consequences of the veritable *social dumping* that these policies imply: namely, mass poverty and job precariousness, the generalization of social insecurity in the midst of regained prosperity, and the dizzying increase of inequalities fostering segregation, crime, and the dereliction of public institutions.

Aside from the fact that a number of European countries have consistently fared better than the United States on such standard economic indicators as domestic product per capita, productivity growth, real income, and even unemployment,[3] it is sometimes overlooked that the affluent America that readies itself to "cross the bridge to the twenty-first century" under the enthusiastic exhortations of William Jefferson Clinton officially counted 35 million poor people, for a *poverty rate double or triple that of Western European countries,* afflicting first and foremost children—one in five Americans under six grows up in poverty, and one in two in the black community, compared to 6 percent of children in France, Germany, and Holland, and 3 percent in Scandinavian nations. The population officially listed as "very poor," that is, surviving below 50 percent of the federal "poverty line" (a line that has sagged continually over the decades and equals only one-third of the median family income today compared to one-half twenty years ago) doubled between 1975 and 1995 to reach 14 million persons; and the economic gulf separating this population from the rest of the country keeps widening: the aggregate "poverty gap," that is, the total sum needed to bring destitute American families up to the official poverty threshold, topped $45 billion in 1995, 50 percent more than the corresponding figure for 1979 (in constant 1995 dollars).[4]

Americans residing in the nether regions of social space can hardly count on the support of the state, for social expenditures aimed at dispossessed households are the weakest of all large industrialized countries (after only Australia and South Africa) and have hit their lowest level since 1973 in relative terms. Thus the value of the main social assistance package, Aid to Families with Dependent Children (AFDC), plummeted by 47 percent in real terms between 1975 and 1995, while its coverage rate fell to less than one-half of single-parent households compared to two-thirds at the beginning of that period. In 1996, this program was replaced by a plan called TANF (Temporary Assistance to Needy Families) that sets a lifetime quota of five years of support and makes subpoverty employment the condition of assistance after two years, but does not create any jobs, while cutting aid budgets by one-fifth.[5] Forty-five million Americans (including 12 million children) are presently deprived of medical coverage although the country spends more than all of its rivals on health care as a proportion of its gross domestic product. Ten million are estimated to suffer from chronic hunger and upwards of 30 million experience food insecurity, a number rising in the wake of the 1996 "welfare reform," which caused a sharp downturn in the number of food stamps beneficiaries through a combination of budget cuts, eligibility restrictions, technical obstacles, and administrative deterrence (e.g., in Ohio the application form runs thirty pages and recipients must be recertified every three months). Seven million Americans are homeless or without adequate housing following a staggering decline in federal housing appropriations of 80 percent in inflation-adjusted terms during the 1980s. And the fastest rising category of the homeless, according to the U.S. Conference of Mayors, is families with young children.[6]

Contrary to the rose-tinted image projected by the national media and their docile relays abroad, lower-class Americans can hardly rely on the job market to improve their living conditions. Taking into account those who have given up looking for work and wage earners intermittently or grossly underemployed (it suffices to work *a single hour* in the course of the week surveyed to be counted as "employed" and thus to disappear from the statistics of the "job-seeking population"), the effective unemployment rate, by the admission of the Department of Labor itself, is closer to 8 percent than to the 4 percent ballyhooed in the news during the summer of 1999, and it continues to hover at 30 to 50 percent in the segregated neighborhoods of the big cities. Moreover, one-third of American workers earn too little to rise above the official "poverty line," set at $15,150 per annum for a family of four. The main reason for this is that the minimum wage of 1997 was 20 percent *lower* than that of 1967 in real terms and that average hourly pay *fell* by 16 percent between 1979 and 1995 for manufacturing workers and by 12 percent for service employees (in the case of men). The creation of jobs is definitely a success in terms of gross volume, but it has been achieved to the detriment of low-skill workers: wage earners holding no more than a high-school degree receive on average 44 percent *less* than their European counterparts and most lack both medical coverage (for two-thirds of them) and retirement benefits (in four cases out of five), even as they toil an average of five more weeks each year.

Indeed, the fruits of U.S. economic growth over the past two decades have been monopolized by a tiny caste of the superprivileged:

according to Harvard economist Richard Freeman, the director of the
Labor Studies Program at the National Bureau of Economic Research,
95 percent of the $1.1 trillion surplus generated between 1979 and
1996 wound up in the pockets of the richest 5 percent of Americans.[7]
Inequality of wages and incomes, like inequality of wealth, now stands
at its highest level since the Great Depression. In 1998, the chief executive officers of large American firms received $10.9 million each,
six times more than in 1990, while even with the return of sturdy economic growth the average worker's wages had increased only 28 percent during this period, barely keeping pace with inflation, to settle at
$29,267. In 1999, corporate heads took home 419 *times* the earnings
of blue-collar employees, as against "only" 42 times more a decade
earlier (for comparison, this disparity stood at 20 to 1 and 35 to 1,
respectively, in Japan and Great Britain).[8] The pay of American corporate executives has reached such dizzying heights, especially if one
takes into account stock options and deferred income, that even the
most pro-business media such as *Business Week* and the *Wall Street
Journal* have bemoaned the excessive rapacity and prosperity of the
country's CEOs.

Penal Policy as Social Policy:
Imprisoning America's Poor

But it is not enough to measure the direct social and human costs of
the system of institutionalized social insecurity offered by the United
States as a "model" for the world. One must also take into account its
socio-logical complement: the overdevelopment of the institutions that
compensate for the deficiencies of the social safety net by deploying
in the lower reaches of the class structure a police-and-prison dragnet
with an ever finer and stronger mesh. *To the deliberate atrophy of the
welfare state corresponds the dystopic hypertrophy of the penal state:*
the poverty and decay of the one have as their direct and necessary
counterpart the greatness and insolent opulence of the other. Under
this angle, five deep-seated trends characterize the penal evolution of
the United States since the onset of the social and racial backlash triggered at the outset of the 1970s by the democratic advances spawned
by the black uprising and the popular movements of protest that surged
in its wake (students, opponents of the Vietnam War, women, envi-
ronmentalists, welfare recipients) during the preceding decade and the
subsequent jettisoning of the Fordist–Keynesian social compact.[9]

Vertical Expansion, or Carceral Hyperinflation

The first of these tendencies is the meteoric growth, over the past quarter-century, of the populations confined in the three tiers of the U.S. carceral apparatus, namely, county jails (which hold persons arrested by the police and awaiting trial, or sentenced to short-term detention), state prisons, and federal penitentiaries (in which convicted felons serve sentences in excess of one year). To realize just how astounding this growth has been, in both historic and quantitative terms, one must first recall that, after a half-century of stability, the country's carceral demography was oriented *downwards* during the 1960s, so that around 1975 the number of inmates had fallen to 380,000 after a slow but regular ebbing of about 1 percent per year. The prison debate then turned on "decarceration," alternative sentences, and restricting confinement to "dangerous predators" (about 10 to 15 percent of all convicted criminals). The authorities were pondering a moratorium on penitentiary building and the gradual phasing out of juvenile confinement; criminologists were discussing whether there exist "homeostatic" mechanisms that keep imprisonment levels stable around a normal rate; some even boldly announced the twilight of the carceral institution—one book expresses well the optimistic mood prevalent among penal experts at that moment with its utopian title, *A Nation without Prisons*.[10]

Then came the "law-and-order" revolution, aimed less at fighting crime than at bolstering the economic, ethnoracial, and moral order via the punitive regulation of the behaviors of the categories deemed threatening or prone to delinquency as they became trapped at the bottom of a dualizing ethnic and class structure. And, against all expectations, the prison returned to the societal forefront to check the rising tide of dispossessed families, street derelicts, and jobless and alienated youth, as well as to soak up the desperation and violence boiling in the segregated enclaves of the metropolis as the protections afforded by the welfare state receded and desocialized wage labor generalized. America relapsed into its "monomania of the penitentiary" as a "remedy for all the ills of society," already diagnosed by Alexis de Tocqueville during his famed journey through the New World in 1831.[11] From its low point in 1973, the curve of the incarcerated population made an abrupt about-face and then took off: a dozen years later, the number of persons behind bars had doubled to 740,000 on its way to passing 1.5 million in 1995 and breaking the 2-million mark in 2000, thanks to an astounding average annual growth of nearly 8 percent through the 1990s, bringing in a net increment of 1,500 inmates every week.[12] The carceral system of the United States has now ballooned to proportions such that if it were a city it would be the country's fourth-largest metropolis.

This fivefold increase in the population under lock in just twenty-five years is a phenomenon without precedent or comparison in any democratic society, all the more so in that it occurred during a period *when the crime rate was stagnant* for most of the preceding twenty years before declining after 1993 to reach its lowest levels in three decades.[13] To realize that crime is not the driving force behind America's runaway prison buildup, it suffices to compute a simple statistic: the number of inmates per criminal offense. If this ratio stays roughly constant, it means that the rise in the carceral population has been tracking the rise in crime, as claimed by government officials, the media, and scholars who have joined in the ideological campaign for mass incarceration. The reality is the exact opposite: this measure of "punitiveness" jumped from 21 prisoners per 1,000 "index crimes" in 1980 to 49 per thousand in 1990 before zooming to 106 per thousand in 1999 (the corresponding figures for violent crimes are 227, 392, and 862 prisoners per thousand, respectively). This indicator reveals that *penal repression is five times harsher today* than it was when Ronald Reagan entered the White House.[14]

A second remarkable feature of carceral expansion in the United States is that it has been fed primarily by the *increase in admissions* to prison—they soared from 159,000 in 1980 to 461,000 in 1990 to 665,000 in 1997—and only secondarily by the lengthening of sentences: the average time served by first-time convicts in state facilities increased from 20 months in 1985 to only 25 months a decade later, owing to the growing share of petty offenders thrown behind bars. This suggests that the U.S. penal system does not merely strike harder, thanks to the adoption of determinate sentencing, truth-in-sentencing laws, mandatory minimums, and special measures targeting recidivists such as automatic life sentences for a second or third felony ("Three Strikes and You're Out"). More importantly, it casts its net much more broadly and processes a vastly enlarged number of persons who come overwhelmingly from the lower reaches of the socioracial order. A third distinctive trait of the vertical growth of the

U.S. carceral system, also consistent with the thesis of the penalization of poverty, is that carceral hyperinflation is a *national trend*, afflicting virtually every jurisdiction in the country, irrespective of the individual characteristics of states, their level of crime, and the political party in place: except for Maine and Kansas, all members of the Union posted an increase of their prison population in excess of 50 percent between 1986 and 1996.[15] During the 1990s, the United States *added* the equivalent of the entire carceral population of France and Italy put together to its stock of inmates *every single year,* even as the crime rate went tumbling down. The result is that, far from showing the world the road to the first modern "nation without prisons," it has become the biggest incarcerator on the planet, with a rate of confinement exceeding 700 inmates per 100,000 inhabitants in 2000 that stands six to twelve times higher than those of the countries of the European Union, whereas thirty years ago that gap was of the order of one to three (see Table 2). Only Russia, whose incarceration rate doubled to approach

Table 2. Incarceration in the United States and the European Union, 2000

Country	Number of inmates	Rate per 100,000
United States	2,071,686	699
Portugal	13,534	131
England and Wales	65,666	124
Spain	45,044	114
Germany	78,707	96
Italy	53,481	93
Netherlands	13,847	90
France	51,903	88
Belgium	8,671	85
Austria	6,896	83
Greece	8,038	76
Sweden	5,678	64
Denmark	3,279	62

Note: Countries are ranked by incarceration rate.
Source: For the United States, Bureau of Justice Statistics, *Prison and Jail Inmates at Mid-Year 2000* (Washington, D.C.: U.S. Government Printing Office, 2001). For the European Union, *Statistique pénale annuelle du Conseil de l'Europe, Enquête 2000* (Strasbourg: Council of Europe, 2002).

750 per 100,000 a decade after the breakup of the Soviet empire and its embrace of the market economy, has contested America's claim to the title of world champion in penal confinement before dropping to second place in 2003.

In California, which not long ago was a national bellwether in public education and public health but has since reconverted to a leader in incarceration, the number of convicts in state prisons zoomed from 17,300 in 1975 to 48,300 in 1985, before passing 160,000 thirteen years later. If one adds to them the population held in municipal jails—that of Los Angeles County alone harbors some 23,000 inmates; it is the largest detention center in the world[16]—one reaches the astronomical total of 200,000 souls in 2000 (four times the carceral figure for France, with California having under one-half of the French population). Although in the 1980s the Golden State launched "the single biggest prison construction program in history" (as its governor Pete Wilson liked to boast), inaugurating twenty-one new penitentiaries in one decade *after building only twelve during the previous* century, *its prisoners are crammed under horrendous conditions of overcrowding pushing 200 percent of capacity, after the sweeping "double-bunking" of cell blocks and the conversion of gymnasia, libraries, dayrooms, and even closets into temporary cells. Indeed, a recent report from the correctional administration compares conditions in California facilities to those that prevailed in Attica on the eve of the bloody 1972 riot that made that prison the synonym for carceral brutality around the globe.*

The stupendous growth of the inmate count in California, as in the rest of the country, is explained largely by the confinement of petty offenders and street people, particularly drug addicts, who were not sanctioned by a prison term in earlier decades and would not be put under lock in any other democratic society. Contrary to the dominant political and journalistic discourse, U.S. prisons have been filled mostly not with dangerous and hardened outlaws but with run-of-the-mill delinquents sentenced for narcotics-related infractions, burglary, theft, or for disturbing public order. Thus the share of violent offenders in the cohorts admitted to state prison declined from about one-half in 1980 to 29 percent in 1995 while the proportion of prisoners entering on a drug conviction blew up from 7 to 31 percent. That year, ten times more drug offenders and four times more burglars were thrown behind bars than murderers (104,100 and 40,000, respectively, as against 10,000). In federal penitentiaries, drug offenders outnumber violent criminals by a factor of seven to one and account for nearly one-half of all admissions. In 1998, the stock of persons held for non-violent offenses warehoused in American jails and prisons crossed the symbolic milestone of 1 million.[17]

These low-level offenders come, in their vast majority, from the most precarious fractions of the working class, and especially from subproletarian families of color living in formerly industrial cities hit by the full force of the conjoint restructuring of wage work and social protection. In county jails, the entry point of the national carceral complex, six out of ten inmates are African-American or Latino; fewer than half held a full-time job at the time of their arraignment; and two-thirds issue from households with an annual income inferior to *half* of the federal "poverty line." A mere 13 percent had some post-secondary education (compared to a national average of one-half); 60 percent had grown up without both parents, including 14 percent who lived in a foster home or orphanage; four in ten reported suffering from serious physical and mental disabilities, and one-third confessed that their parent or guardian abused alcohol or drugs or both. For many, being behind bars is sadly familiar: every other jail detainee had another member of his family incarcerated.[18]

Ethnographic interviews with a representative sample of convicts entering prison in Illinois, Nevada, and Washington state conducted by John Irwin and James Austin confirm that convicts are recruited overwhelmingly from the unskilled and un(der)employed strata of the working class. These interviews show that over half of state prisoners were put away for petty crimes involving negligible material loss or damage (in the hundreds of dollars at most) and no physical injury or threat of injury.[19] Six prisoners in ten turn out to be episodic or accidental criminals: they committed their misdeeds on impulse, because they are "corner boys" living in low-income neighborhoods where street delinquency is rife, or because they were teetering on the edge of society in extreme destitution.

Even "habitual offenders" fail to match the media picture of vicious "predators" bent on mayhem by dint of antisocial values. The majority of these (60 percent) turn out to be "disorganized petty criminals, without skill or discipline, who rarely commit acts of violence," and engage in crime by default, to compensate for their abiding inability to find a job, sustain a marriage, and lead a conventional life. Some 68 percent were convicted of either a property or a drug offense (two-thirds used narcotics at the time of their arrest). Although most had extensive criminal records, their offenses involved no victim in one-fifth of the cases and caused no injury to the victim in nine-tenths.[20] *Deprived of support by the loosening of the safety net of the social state, they find themselves in the tight embrace of the penal state, and for extended stretches typically running from ten years to life.*

The Horizontal Extension of the Penal Dragnet

But the "great confinement" of this fin de siècle does not give the full measure of the extraordinary hold that penal institutions have over the populations consigned to the nether regions of U.S. social space. First, carceral figures do not include persons sentenced to probation or released conditionally "on parole" after having served the brunt of their sentence (typically 85 percent as mandated by federal "truth-in-sentencing" standards, for a national average of twenty-nine months). Now, the number of those held in the antechambers and wings of the prison has grown apace with the population festering within its walls, owing in part to the sheer impossibility of expanding capacity fast enough to absorb the ever-mounting flow of bodies—in the 1980s, the country needed to build a new one-thousand-bed facility for new convicts every five days. It has nearly quadrupled in twenty years to approach 4.6 million in 2000, including 3.8 million on probation and 725,000 on parole. As the new century opened, some 6.5 million Americans were thus placed under correctional supervision, a figure representing over *5 percent of all males over eighteen and one black man out of every five* (we shall shortly understand why).

Over the past two decades, community supervision has reached an industrial scale for the jurisdictions that spearhead the drive to mass incarceration. Eleven states each hold in excess of 100,000 residents sentenced to probation by the courts—more than all of France with 87,000. Texas (429,000), California (287,000), Florida (237,000), and New York (174,000) supervise 1 million among them. Twelve states, led by Delaware, Washington, and Texas (with 323, 318, and 310 per thousand, respectively), sport a rate of probationers exceeding 2 percent of their adult population. During 1997, a staggering 420,000 prisoners were released on parole, including 24,000 from the gates of federal penitentiaries.

Aside from their sheer volume (equal to 34 times its counterpart of 117,000 for France), one must stress the perilous position of the 4.6 million placed under the authority of criminal justice in the community: two probationers in five (for a total of 212,000 individuals) and six parolees in ten (another 168,000) exiting supervision in 1997 were sent back behind bars within three years, either because they had committed another offense or because they had violated an administrative condition of their probation or release.

Next, in addition to new intermediate sanctions such as day reporting, "boot camps," intensive probation, and home confinement with electronic monitoring (with the help of anklets, bracelets, and other technical devices), the grasp of the penal system has widened immensely thanks to the proliferation of criminal database and the vast increase they allow in points of control at a distance.[21] In the 1970s and 1980s, at the instigation of the Law Enforcement Administration Agency, the federal agency entrusted with activating the fight against crime after it had become the fetish-theme of campaigning politicians, the police, the courts, and the correctional administrations of the fifty states established centralized and computerized data banks that have since proliferated all around. As a result of the new synergy between the "capture" and "observation" functions of the penal apparatus,[22] there now exist some 55 million criminal files (compared to 35 million a decade ago) on approximately 30 million individuals, corresponding to almost one-third of the country's adult male population.[23]

Access to these criminal databases is given not only to public bureaucracies such as the Federal Bureau of Investigation, the Immigration and Naturalization Service (which polices foreigners), and social services, but also, in many cases, to private persons and organizations. These "rap sheets" are increasingly used, for example, by employers to eliminate job applicants who are ex-convicts, and this without regard for the fact that the data they contain are often incorrect, out of date, or insignificant, sometimes even illegal. Their swirling circulation puts not only convicted criminals and those who have merely been suspected of crimes into the target sights of the police and penal apparatus, but also their families, friends, neighbors, and neighborhoods. This is all the more so in the dozen states, including Illinois, Florida, and Texas, that have made these files freely accessible via Internet sites enabling anyone to consult the criminal record of an inmate (or ex-inmate) without the slightest monitoring or justification. The diffusion of criminal records on the Internet as well as by private firms that specialize in "background checks" of employees cannot but gravely curtail the chances of rehabilitation of persons placed under correctional supervision, given the strong reticence of American employers to hire any job applicant with a criminal record.[24]

"CHECK IT OUT"

Armed with a laptop computer and $800 in seed money, Mark Moore started Tenant Information Services (TIS) in 1991. Initially, the Winston-Salem, North Carolina-based information services company provided landlords with up-to-date eviction information on prospective tenants. Today, roughly 90% of TIS' business is providing criminal background checks for some 1,000 companies, including out-of-state businesses, which resell the information to other clients.

Companies pay a $25 annual membership fee and around $7 per background check. Last year, the 12-employee firm had revenues of about $800,000. . . . [When he] started sending letters to all of his real estate clients informing them that he could offer criminal as well as eviction information, the response was overwhelming.

—Mark Richard Moss, "Making It" Section,
Black Enterprise, June 28, 1998, 48–50.

The bureaucratic enterprise of criminal filing and profiling is itself being overhauled by the mating of the latest mass-marketed computer and genetic technologies. Genetic record keeping is fast supplementing and vastly enlarging traditional data banks based on fingerprints and mug shots. Genetic databases pertaining to criminal populations have experienced exponential growth since passage of the 1994 DNA Identification Act, which allocated federal funds to systematize the assembly of such data banks and to enable their interconnection through the creation of a common source file, the CODIS (Combined Index DNA Indexing System). In October 1998, the FBI put in service this national database containing the DNA profile of hundreds of thousands of convicted felons, and into which the correctional authorities of the fifty states are now entering the saliva and blood specimens collected from their prisoners. California, for instance, is transferring the "DNA fingerprints" of its felons into the CODIS at the rate of 30,000 files a year, thanks to the recent automation of the process. In March 1999, following the proposal of the chief of police of New York, Attorney General Janet Reno convened a group of government experts, the National Commission on the Future of DNA Evidence, to study the feasibility of extending the genetic identification of convicts to all persons processed by the police, whether charged or not—amounting to about 15 million persons every year.

The penal mesh ensnaring the marginalized fractions of the working class has been further tightened by the continual reduction of early releases from prison and by the revamping of parole, from a program aimed at supporting the societal reentry of former inmates into a surveillance device designed to maximize the detection and sanction of their violations of the conditions of release. Parole and probation departments across the country have well nigh abandoned the pretense of providing jobs and have promoted drug testing to the rank of first priority, with the result that the number of "ex-cons" arrested and sent back behind bars has soared. Again, California leads the nation as the ranks of its "Parole Violators Returned to Custody" has boomed from under 3,000 in 1980 to over 75,000 in 1996, two-thirds of whom were locked up again as a consequence of an administrative revocation rather than a new criminal conviction. Nationwide, in the pivotal decade between 1985 and 1997, the percentage of parolees who successfully completed their term of parole supervision plummeted from 70 percent to 44 percent.[25]

This trend is the result of the forsaking of the ideal of rehabilitation in the wake of the converging criticisms from the Right and the Left in the 1970s and its incipient replacement by a "new penology" whose aim is no longer to prevent crime or to treat individual offenders with a view toward their reintegration into society after they have served their sentence. It is *to isolate groups perceived as dangerous and to neutralize their most disruptive members* through a standardized monitoring of behaviors and a stochastic management of risks more akin to operations research or the treatment of "social refuse" than to social work.[26]

The Onset of Carceral "Big Government"

The means for and consequence of this sudden carceral bulimia has been the spectacular swelling of the penal sector within federal, state, and local administrations. This third trend is all the more remarkable for having asserted itself during lean times for public bureaucracies, when the professed policy of elected officials, at all levels and from both ruling parties, has been to curtail the size of government. Between 1980 and 1997, the United States increased its criminal justice outlay by a full $100 billion to reach $130 billion, and corrections took the lion's share of that growth: police budgets grew fourfold to $58 billion (+$43 billion) but funds for incarceration multiplied sixfold to top $44 billion (+$37 billion), 60 percent more than the figure for the courts, when these two administrations had the same budget in 1982 (around $8 billion each). During the 1980s, state correctional expenditures increased 325 percent for operations and 612 percent for construction, three times faster than the country's military budget, even as the latter enjoyed exceptional favor under the presidencies of Ronald Reagan and George Bush the elder. As early as 1992, four states devoted more than $1 billion to the confinement of convicts: California ($3.2 billion), New York ($2.1 billion), Texas ($1.3 billion), and Florida ($1.1 billion). By 1998, ten states surpassed that figure and seventeen spent more than 6 percent of their total budget on adult imprisonment, led by Michigan with a full 15 percent.[27]

Every year since 1985, the country's budget for corrections has outstripped the sums allocated to the main welfare program, Aid to Families with Dependent Children, as well as monies allotted to food stamps. On the eve of the elimination of AFDC in 1995, the United States was spending twice as much to incarcerate ($46 billion) as to support destitute single mothers with children ($20 billion), and as much as AFDC and food stamps put together. The same divergent evolution applies to public housing: in 1980, net budget appropriations by the

Department of Housing and Urban Development amounted to three times the funds for corrections; by 1995, that ratio had been inverted, with prison and jail disbursements exceeding three times the new outlays for public housing. Considering that inmates are overwhelmingly drawn from the lowest fractions of the working class, who are for this very reason most likely to resort to welfare, food stamps, and housing support, this trend suggests that incarceration has de facto become America's largest government program for the poor.

This policy of penal expansion is by no means the exclusive province of Republicans. Between 1992 and 1997, as William Clinton was proclaiming to the four corners of the land his pride in having put an end to the era of "big government" and as the National Partnership for Reinventing Government (led by his hoped-for successor, Albert Gore) was busy cutting public programs and employment, 213 penitentiaries were built across the country—not counting for-profit establishments that proliferated with the opening of a lucrative market for private incarceration. Under Clinton's watch, the Federal Bureau of Prisons tripled its budget and nearly doubled its staff to become the third-largest prison system in the Western world with 145,000 inmates, behind only California and Texas. That incarceration was the exception to the religion of "small government" is further demonstrated by the fact that the criminal justice system of the United States *added 1 million employees to its payroll* between 1980 and 1995, including 400,000 in prisons and jails, to approach a grand total of 2 million. Put together, the federal, state, and local corrections administrations sported personnel exceeding 656,000 in 1995, which made them *the country's fourth-largest employer,* behind Wal-Mart and two agencies of temporary employment—an apt reminder of the functional relationship tying the desocialization of labor to the rise of the penal state—and just ahead of General Motors, the world's largest firm in terms of revenue.[28] No wonder that the hiring and training of prison guards have been the fastest growing of all government activities over the past two decades, according to the Census Bureau.

The sudden mutation of California's correctional administration into a megabureaucracy devouring funds and personnel after a long period of stability until 1980 is emblematic of the turn toward carceral "big government" following the demise of the

Keynesian-Fordist social compact. The annual operating budget of the state's prison system shot up from $120 million in 1970 to $408 million in 1980 before growing twelvefold to $4.8 billion in 2000. Since 1994 it has surpassed every year the budget for the entire public university system (exclusive of community colleges), long considered the jewel in the state's crown.

The number of state prison employees zoomed from under 6,000 when Reagan acceded to the presidency to 41,000 in 1998, when 3,172 parole officers and staff were supervising some 121,000 parolees assigned to 32 reentry centers and 182 CDC field offices in 81 localities. The average annual wages for guards jumped from $14,400 in 1980 to a hefty $55,000 two decades later, better than the pay of an associate professor at the University of California (and double the national average for correctional officers). Yet, even after a staggering growth of 570 percent over the past twenty years, correctional personnel has barely kept up with the inmate population, which increased sixfold since 1980. In a short decade, California swallowed $5.3 billion frantically building and renovating cells and contracted debt in excess of $10 billion in state bonds to do so. Each new prison costs an average of $200 million for 4,000 inmates and requires the hiring of an additional 1,000 staff. The result is that California now counts more correctional staff than it does social workers statewide. Meanwhile, the authorities have postponed the opening of a long-promised new university campus in the Central Valley despite the relentless rise in the number of students (which grew by 50 percent between 1980 and 1995).

In a period of budgetary penury caused by the continual lowering of effective tax rates on corporations and the upper class,[29] the increase in the funds and personnel devoted to incarceration was possible only by curtailing the monies needed for welfare, health, and education. Indeed, while the country's correctional expenditures doubled in constant dollars in the 1980s, the budget for public hospitals stagnated, that for secondary schooling shrank by 2 percent, and that going to welfare sagged by 41 percent.[30] The United States effectively made the choice to build for its poor jails and prisons rather than community clinics, day-care centers, and schools. One illustration of this trade-off:

in the space of a decade (1988–98), the state of New York increased its corrections outlay by 76 percent and cut funds for higher education by 29 percent. The gross amounts in dollars are roughly equivalent: $615 million less for the State University of New York campuses and $761 million more for the prisons—over $1 billion more if one reckons a separate line of $300 million for the emergency construction of 3,100 additional beds.[31] As in California, the curves representing the two budgets crossed paths in 1994, the year of the election of Republican Governor George Pataki, one of whose first measures, along with re-establishing the death penalty, was to increase yearly university tuitions and fees by $750, which caused a drop-off in enrollment of more than 10,000 students the following academic year.

The problem with mass incarceration as a masked antipoverty policy is that it is a financially exorbitant proposition over the medium run, due to the continual rise it generates in the population under lock, the rapid aging of that population, and the prohibitive unit price of confinement. For instance, in California each state prisoner cost $21,400 per annum in operational expenses alone in 1996, three times the maximum AFDC allowance doled out to a family of four before the abolition of that program ($7,229, inclusive of administrative costs). Defining such expenditures as a prudent "investment" in the pressing fight against crime may do to placate the electorate, but it does nothing to generate the gargantuan additional funds needed every year to pursue it further.

To contain the ever-mounting carceral bill, the authorities have implemented varying combinations of four strategies. The first is to *cut back on living standards and services* inside of jails and prisons by limiting or eliminating the amenities, programs, and "privileges" to which their occupants have access: education, sports, entertainment, and activities aimed at rehabilitation such as job development and counseling, but also legal services, visiting, and packages. However, this approach is unlikely to yield sizable benefits given that these expenses have already been compressed to the meanest share (less than 5 percent of the budget of the California Department of Corrections is devoted to academic and vocational training) with the generalization of regimes of "penal austerity."[32] Moreover, after decades of studied indifference to the treatment of inmates, the courts have taken an active role in safeguarding minimal standards of detention and they have not hesitated to put entire prison systems under judicial oversight to limit gross overcrowding or curb faulty health-care delivery.

So the second strategy is to introduce *new technologies* inside the carceral setting, from video, computers, electronic sensors, and digital devices to biometric identification, stun belts, advanced X-ray machines, and telemedicine, all in an effort to boost the productivity of carceral labor and to secure more convicts with fewer staff. But these technologies are costly and correctional facilities are a difficult milieu in which to innovate due to the premium put on safety and the vested interest of the personnel in maintaining organizational routines requiring high ratios of guards to inmates. The third strategy consists in *shifting part of the cost of confinement onto inmates and their families* and takes a variety of forms: collecting processing fees at the entrance of jails and charging detainees for room and board; instituting a "co-pay" to access the clinic outside of medical emergencies; and levying supplemental charges for various amenities such as uniforms, linens, laundry, electricity, and telephone.[33] Some counties and states have set up programs enabling them to haul their former inmates to court in an effort to recover the debt that the latter contracted willy-nilly while behind bars. But returns on these efforts have been very meager, for the simple reason that the overwhelming majority of detainees and convicts are very poor and the cost of collecting fees typically exceeds the proceeds thus generated.

As to the fourth technique for reducing the country's carceral bill, it points to the new "frontier" of the near future of corrections: *to reintroduce deskilled work en masse inside penal facilities* and to skim the wages of inmate workers to pay for their detention. Now, wage work already exists in some penitentiaries and a handful of the country's leading corporations such as Microsoft, TWA, Boeing, Best Western, Toys R Us, Victoria's Secret, and Konica occasionally resort to it on the side. But, while such private-sector use of inmate labor has been shrilly denounced by justice activists and repeatedly spotlighted by the media and inmate reporters,[34] it remains marginal for these companies and, even more so, for the carceral population as a whole. In spite of the steady growth of the Private Industry Enhancement (PIE) Program since its launching in 1989, paid work concerned only one inmate in thirteen in 1998 aside from facility support.[35] That year fewer than 2,000 state and federal convicts were on the payroll of outside companies nationwide, owing to the severe material and legal restrictions that bear on penal employment. Numerous legislative proposals have recently been put forward to eliminate these hindrances, for vocal experts consider the development of prison wage labor to be the most promising mine of correctional savings, in addition to relieving idleness, curtailing problems of discipline, fostering institutional adjustment, and increasing postrelease success.[36] It is also a matter of pressing ideological consistency: since the obligation to work is now imposed on the poor "outside" through workfare, it is only logical that it be thrust also on the poor "inside."

But there remains a yawning gap between the bold plans periodically proposed to "free prison labor" and the modest realities of work inside penal facilities: the U.S. convict workforce remains minuscule because it is unstable, unskilled, and unmotivated; setting up production behind bars is costly and complicated; and commercial carceral work comes up against virulent public resentment and potent opposition as soon as the labor market deteriorates on the outside. This leaves one final strategy for curbing the astronomical cost of the transition from social state to penal state: to extend the ideology of commodification that guides the toughening of public assistance programs for the destitute into the realm of criminal justice and to privatize incarceration.

Resurgence and Prosperity of Private Incarceration

The unprecedented expansion of the carceral wing of the U.S. state has been accompanied by the resurgence and frenetic development of an industry of private incarceration. Banned in 1925 after a series of scandals involving the murderous mistreatment of convict laborers leased to employers in the Southern states, commercial operators reemerged in the 1980s when calling on the commercial sector appeared as the best, if not the only, means to contain the ever-mounting flood of inmates and dampen the explosive growth of corrections budgets.[37] Since the founding of Corrections Corporation of America in Tennessee in 1983, this industry has captured nearly 7 percent of the inmate population, with 142,000 beds on line in 2000 (as against a mere 15,000 in 1990 and 33,000 in 1993). Analysts of the penal scene were then forecasting that its "market share" would triple in the next decade to reach 350,000 inmates (seven times the carceral population of France).[38]

Seventeen firms shared some 140 prisons scattered across twenty-odd states, based mainly in Texas, Florida, Colorado, Oklahoma, and Tennessee, but now fanning around the country. Some of these companies limit themselves to managing existing penitentiaries, to which they supply staff and services. Others specialize in medical care, food delivery, work-release programs, substance-abuse treatment, transitional services for juvenile or college-education programs. A small number offer the complete gamut of goods and activities necessary for penal custody: architectural design, financing, construction, maintenance, administration, insurance, staffing, and even the recruitment and transport of inmates coming from other jurisdictions that rent beds for their convicts. For there exists also a flourishing market in the "import–export" of convicts between states, some of which have too many prisoners and others a surplus of cells. Some counties have deliberately overbuilt their detention facilities in order to generate funds by renting out their excess beds to jurisdictions running out of room; others simply choose to export their inmates to economize on their correctional budget. In 2000, Wisconsin shipped convicts out of state even though it was under capacity simply because Corrections Corporation of America (CCA) charged $42 per day per inmate in its Mississippi or Arkansas facilities, as against $54 in a local prison.

Since Corrections Corporation of America, the Correctional Services Corporation, Securicor (based in London), and Wackenhut have gone public, the carceral industry has become one of the darlings of Wall Street. The bond market for the financing of prisons, public and private, weighs in at some $4 billion. And it appears to have a bright future ahead: in 1996 alone, construction was started on 26 federal facilities and 96 state penitentiaries. The magazine *Corrections Building News,* which chronicles the evolution of this economic sector, has a paying subscription list of some twelve thousand. Every year, the American Correctional Association, a semiprivate organization founded in 1870 that promotes the interests of this sector, brings together professionals and industrialists of incarceration for a great "corrections show" lasting five full days. Over 650 firms exhibited their products and services at the August 1997 meetings in Orlando, Florida:[39] among the wares on display were padded handcuffs and assault weapons, no-fail locks and bars, such cell furniture as fireproof bunks and block lavatories, toiletry and food supplies, restraining chairs and "extraction uniforms" (used by disciplinary squads to drag recalcitrant inmates out of their cells), electrified fences carrying a lethal charge, detoxification programs for drug addicts or "moral rearmament" plans for juvenile delinquents, cutting-edge electronic surveillance and telephone systems, advanced technologies of detection and identification, software to process and store administrative, police, and court data, anti-tuberculosis ventilation equipment, not to mention portable cells (which can be installed in one afternoon in a parking lot to absorb an unexpected influx of inmates) and turnkey prisons, and even a surgical truck for performing emergency operations in the penitentiary courtyard.

CRIME PAYS

Yearning for high returns, but leery of overpriced blue chips? One particularly attractive option is our list of America's fastest growers, an elite group of mostly smaller companies that have what it takes to keep their stocks moving: over the past year the average shareholder return for the companies on *Fortune*'s list was 75%, almost double that of the S&P 500. Go back a little further and some of the performance stats are downright dazzling: over the past three years, shares of McAfee Associates (No. 15 on our list), which makes antivirus software, zoomed 1,967%; Dell Computer (No. 47) rose 1,912%; Corrections Corp. of America (No. 67), which runs private prisons, appreciated 746%. That's a lot of lettuce.

—"Getting Rich with America's Fastest-Growing Companies,"
Fortune, September 29, 1997, 72.

The siting of penal facilities has by the same token established itself as a coveted tool for economic development and regional reconversion. Small towns in declining rural areas hit by the waning of traditional agricultural and industrial activities, in particular, have spared no effort to attract them. "Gone are the days when communities greeted the prospect of prisons with chants of 'Not in my backyard.' Prisons do not use a lot of chemicals, do not generate noise or atmospheric pollutants and do not lay off workers during recessions."[40] On the contrary, it is taken as an article of faith (by both advocates and opponents of penal expansion) that prisons bring with them stable jobs, a steady stream of business, and regular tax revenues. This is why countless local authorities, desperate to stimulate job creation in depressed counties, have vied to offer public and private prison operators alike attractive incentive packages, including government-issued debt securities, property tax abatements, investment tax credits, infrastructural modifications (water, sewer, and utility hookups, access roads, etc.), job training grants, and construction help.[41] Incarceration thus presents itself as a prosperous industry with rosy prospects, and with it all those whose interests are tied to the great lockup of the poor in America.

Carceral Affirmative Action

If carceral hyperinflation has been accompanied by a "lateral" extension of the penal system and thus a manifold increase in its capacities to monitor and neutralize, it remains that these capacities are trained first and foremost on dispossessed families and neighborhoods, and especially on the historic black enclaves of large cities. Witness the fifth key trend of U.S. carceral evolution, namely, *the rapid and continuous "blackening" of the inmate population* which explains that in 1989, for the first time in the country's history, African Americans made up the majority of new admissions to state prisons even though they comprise only 6 percent of the country's male population.

In 1995, out of some 22 million adults, blacks supplied a contingent of 767,000 inmates, 999,000 probationers, and an additional 325,000 released on parole after serving time, for an overall rate of penal supervision of 9.4 percent. Among whites, a high estimate yields a rate of 1.9 percent for 163 million adults, five times smaller.[42] As for incarceration *stricto sensu*, the gap between the two communities stands at 1 for 7.5 and it has been increasing rapidly over the past decade: 528 versus 3,544 per 100,000 adults in 1985, 919 versus 6,926 ten years later (see Table 3). In terms of cumulative probability, based on incarceration data from 1991, an African-American man has more than one chance in four of serving at least one year in prison over his lifetime and a Latino has one chance in six, as against one chance in 23 for a white male.

This "racial disproportionality," as criminologists bashfully term it, is even more pronounced among younger men, who are the primary target of the policy of penalization of poverty, since on any given day more than one of every three black men between the ages of eigh-

Table 3. Incarceration differential between blacks and whites (including Latinos), in number of inmates per 100,000 adults

	1985	1990	1995
Blacks	3,544	5,365	6,926
Whites	528	718	919
gap	3,016	4,647	6,007
ratio	6.7	7.4	7.5

Source: Bureau of Justice Statistics, Correctional Populations in the United States, 1995 (Washington, D.C.: U.S. Government Printing Office, 1997).

teen and twenty-nine are either incarcerated, under the authority of a judge or a parole officer overseeing the terms of a sentence, or waiting to appear before a criminal court. In the big cities, this proportion commonly exceeds one-half, with spikes of around 80 percent at the heart of the ghetto. One observer of the penal scene goes so far as to describe the operation of the American judicial system—using an idiom borrowed from the dark days of the Vietnam War—as a "search-and-destroy" mission against lower-class black youth.[43]

Indeed, the rapid and continuous deepening of the gap between whites and blacks does not result from a sudden divergence of their relative propensity to commit crimes and misdemeanors. It betrays first and foremost the *fundamentally discriminatory implementation of the police and judicial practices* carried out within the framework of the "law-and-order" policy of the past two decades. Proof is that African Americans represent 13 percent of consumers of drugs in the country (which corresponds to their demographic weight, according to the National Household Survey of Drug Abuse) but one-third of the persons arrested and three-fourths of those imprisoned for drug-related offenses. In ten states, black men are twenty-five times more likely than white men to be sent to prison on a narcotics charge. In Illinois, which holds the national record for black/white disparity with a ratio of 57 to 1, nonwhites are estimated to make up 28 percent of the drug-using population in the state but contribute 70 percent of drug arrestees and 86 percent of those admitted to state prison following a drug conviction.[44]

Now, the "War on Drugs" launched by Ronald Reagan with much fanfare and since expanded by his successors is, together with the repudiation of the ideal of rehabilitation and the proliferation of ultra-repressive measures (generalization of determinate sentencing and mandatory minimum sanctions, "truth-in-sentencing" statutes raising the threshold for minimum time served, automatic lifetime imprisonment for a second or third felony, increased penalties for breaches of public order), one of the major causes of the explosion in the carceral population. In 1995, six new convicts out of ten were thrown behind bars for possession or distribution of narcotics, and the overwhelming majority of those imprisoned on this charge came from poor African-American neighborhoods for the simple reason that "it is easier to make arrests in socially disorganized neighborhoods, as contrasted with urban blue-collar and urban or suburban middle-class neighborhoods."[45] The informal economy in such areas typically operates outdoors, on street corners and back alleys, in full view of neighbors, clients, and even the authorities; undercover operations and police raids are more effective because drug markets are porous and fluid, and local residents do not have ready access to legal assistance to thwart them; the police are used to behaving aggressively, if not brutally, which greatly facilitates operations designed to produce favorable statistics via mass arrests; finally, the tainted status of ghettos and their inhabitants ensures favorable media coverage and wide public approval of such police action.[46]

Penal confinement is thus a public service for which African Americans are de facto enjoying "preferential access," a trend not lacking in irony at a time when the country is turning its back on the affirmative-action programs aimed at reducing the most glaring racial inequalities in access to education, employment, and government contracts. The result is that, in numerous states, the number of black inmates easily surpasses the number of black students enrolled on the campuses of public universities: for instance, in 1998 the African-American community of the state of New York included 34,800 inmates doing time in state prison compared to only 27,900 students on the campuses of the State University of New York, while Latinos supplied 22,400 prisoners as against only 17,800 students.[47] The punitive control of ghetto blacks by means of the police and penal apparatus extends and intensifies the paternalistic tutelage that social services already press upon them. And it makes it possible to exploit—and at the same time to feed—the electorate's latent racial animus and its contempt for poor people for a maximum media and political yield.[48]

The Place of the Prison in the New Government of Poverty

More than the specifics of statistical figures and trends, it is the deep-seated logic of this swing from the social to the penal that one must grasp here. Far from contradicting the neoliberal project of deregulation and decay of the public sector, the irresistible rise of America's penal state constitutes, as it were, its negative—in the sense of obverse but also of revelator—as it manifests the implementation of a *policy of criminalization of poverty that is the indispensable complement to the imposition of precarious and underpaid wage labor* as civic obligation for those locked at the bottom of the class and ethnic structure, as well as the redeployment of social-welfare programs in a restrictive and punitive sense that is concomitant with it. At the time of its institutionalization in the United States of the mid-nineteenth century, "imprisonment was above all a method aiming at the control of deviant and dependent populations," and inmates were mainly poor people and European immigrants recently arrived in the New World.[49] Nowadays, the carceral apparatus of the United States fills an analogous role with respect to those categories rendered superfluous or incongruous by the twofold restructuring of the wage-labor relation and state charity: the declining fractions of the working class and poor blacks at the core of formerly industrial cities. In so doing, it has regained a central place in the system of the instruments for the government of poverty, at the crossroads of the deskilled labor market, the collapsing urban ghetto, and social-welfare services "reformed" with a view to buttressing the discipline of desocialized wage work.

(1) Prison and the Deskilled Labor Market

In the first place, *the penal system contributes directly to regulating the lower segments of the labor market*—and it does so in a manner more coercive and consequential than labor legislation, social insurance schemes, and other administrative rules, many of which do not cover insecure work. Its effect on this front is threefold. First, the stupendous prevalence and escalation of penal sanctions helps to discipline the reticent fractions of the working class by raising the cost of strategies of resistance to desocialized wage labor via "exit" into the informal economy. Faced with aggressive policing, severe courts, and the likelihood of brutally long prison sentences for drug offenses and recidivism, many shrink from getting or staying involved in the illegal commerce of the street and submit instead to the dictate of insecure employment. For some of those coming out of "the pen," the tight mesh of postcorrectional supervision increases pressure to opt for the "straight" life anchored in work, when available.[50] On both counts, the criminal justice system acts in concordance with workfare to push its clientele onto the peripheral segments of the job market.

Second, the carceral apparatus helps to "fluidify" the low-wage sector and artificially depresses the unemployment rate by forcibly subtracting millions of unskilled men from the labor force. It is estimated that penal confinement shaved two full percentage points off of the U.S. jobless rate during the 1990s. Indeed, according to Bruce Western and Katherine Beckett, when the differential between the incarceration level of the two areas is taken into account, the United States posted an unemployment rate *higher* than the average for the European Union during eighteen of the twenty years between 1974 and 1994, contrary to the view propagated by the adulators of neoliberalism and critics of "Eurosclerosis."[51] While it is true that not all inmates would be in the labor force if free, that two-percentage point gap does not include the Keynesian stimulus provided by booming public expenditures and employment in corrections: the number of jail and prison jobs at the local, state, and federal levels more than doubled over the past two decades, jumping from under 300,000 in 1982 to over 716,000 in 1999, when monthly payroll exceeded $2.1 billion.[52] Penal growth has also boosted employment in the private sector of carceral goods and services, a sector with a high rate of precarious jobs and turnover, and which rises together with the privatization of punishment (since the main source of the "competitiveness" of correctional firms is the exceedingly low wages and meager benefits they give their staff).

Western and Beckett argue that carceral hypertrophy is a two-pronged, delayed mechanism with contradictory effects: whereas it embellishes the employment picture in the short run by amputating labor supply at the bottom of the occupational ladder, in the longer term it can only aggravate it by making millions more or less unemployable. In their view, "incarceration has lowered the U.S. unemployment rate, but . . . sustained low unemployment in the future will depend on continuing expansion of the penal system."[53] But this overlooks a third impact of mass imprisonment on the labor market, which is to facilitate the development of subpoverty jobs and the informal economy by continually (re)generating a large volume of marginal laborers who can be superexploited at will. Former inmates can hardly lay claim to better than degraded and degrading work because of their interrupted trajectories, disrupted social ties, ignominious judicial status, and the manifold legal restrictions and civil liabilities this status carries. The half-million convicts streaming out of American prisons every year provide the vulnerable labor power suited to fuel the temporary employment sector, the fastest-growing segment of the U.S. labor market over the past two decades (it accounts for one-fifth of all new jobs created since 1984).[54] Mass incarceration thus feeds contingent employment, which is the spearhead for the flexibilization of wage labor in the lower tier of the jobs distribution. In addition, the proliferation of detention facilities across the country—their number has tripled in thirty years to surpass 4,800—contributes directly to the national growth and diffusion of illicit trafficking (drugs, prostitution, stolen goods) that are the driving engine of the booty capitalism of the street.

(11) PRISON AND THE PRESERVATION OF
        ETHNORACIAL ORDER

The massive and growing overrepresentation of African Americans at every level of the penal apparatus shines a harsh light on the second function assumed by the carceral system in the new government of poverty in America: *to complement and compensate for the collapsing ghetto as a device for the confinement* of a population considered deviant, devious, and dangerous as well as superfluous, on an economic plane (Mexican and Asian immigrants make more docile laborers) as well as on a political plane (poor blacks hardly vote and, in any case, the country's center of electoral gravity has shifted from away from declining central cities to well-off white suburbs).[55]

Under this angle, incarceration is only the paroxystic manifestation of the logic of ethnoracial exclusion of which the ghetto has been the instrument and product since its historical inception. During the half-century (1915–65) dominated by the Fordist industrial economy

to which blacks contributed an indispensable pool of unskilled labor—
that is, from World War I, which triggered the "Great Migration"
from the segregationist states of the South to the worker metropo-
lises of the North, to the civil rights revolution, which finally gave
blacks access to the ballot box a hundred years after the abolition of
slavery—the ghetto served as an "ethnoracial prison" in that it en-
sured the systematic social ostracization of African Americans while
enabling the exploitation of their labor power in the city. Since the de-
bilitating crisis of the ghetto, manifested by the great wave of urban
revolts that swept the country during the 1960s, it is the prison which
is in turn serving as surrogate "ghetto," by warehousing the fractions
of the black (sub)proletariat that have been marginalized by the transition to the dual service economy and by state policies of welfare retrenchment and urban withdrawal.[56] The two institutions have thus
become coupled and they complement each other in that each operates in its own manner to enforce the setting apart (the etymological
meaning of *segregare*) of an undesirable category perceived as threatening the metropolis with a twofold menace, inseparably physical
and moral. And this structural and functional symbiosis between
ghetto and prison finds a striking cultural expression in the lyrics and
the lifestyle flouted by "gangsta rap" musicians, as attested by the
tragic destiny of the singer-composer Tupac Shakur.[57] Born in prison
from an absentee father (his mother, Afeni Shakur, was a member of
the Black Panthers), the apostle of "thug life," hero to a multitude of
ghetto youths (and hordes of white suburban teens), died in 1996 in
Las Vegas, riddled with bullets in a car ambush set up by members of
a rival gang, after having himself been accused of shooting at police
officers and serving eight months for sexual assault.

(iii) Prison and Welfare Turned Workfare

As it was at its birth, the carceral institution is now directly connected to the gamut of organizations and programs entrusted with
"assisting" dispossessed populations, in step with the increasing organizational and ideological interpenetration between the social and
penal sectors of the post-Keynesian state. On the one side, the panoptic and punitive logic proper to the penal field tends to contaminate
and then redefine the objectives and mechanisms of delivery of public
aid.[58] Thus, in addition to replacing the right of indigent children to

state assistance with the obligation for their parents to work after two years, the "welfare reform" endorsed by Clinton in 1996 subjects public aid recipients to intrusive practices of lifelong record keeping and close supervision, and it establishes a strict monitoring of their behaviors—in matters of education, employment, drug consumption, and sexuality—liable to trigger sanctions both administrative and criminal. (One example: since October 1998, in central Michigan, welfare recipients must submit to periodic drug testing, as do convicts on parole or probation, and their testing is carried out by the state's department of corrections in offices where they mingle with parolees.) On the other side, correctional facilities must *nolens volens* face up, under conditions of permanent penury and emergency, to the social and medical hardships that their "clientele" did not manage to resolve on the outside: in the country's major cities, the biggest homeless shelter and the largest mental health facility readily accessible to subproletarians is the county jail.[59] And the same population cycles through from one pole of this institutional continuum to the other in a near-closed orbit that entrenches their socioeconomic marginality and intensifies their sense of indignity.

Finally, budgetary constraints and the political fashion for "less government" have converged to push toward the commodification of welfare no less than of incarceration. Several jurisdictions, such as Texas and Tennessee, already consign a sizable portion of their convicts to private establishments *and* subcontract the administrative handling of public aid recipients to specialized firms. This is a way of making poor people and prisoners (the vast majority of whom were poor on the outside and will be poor again when they get out) "profitable," on the ideological if not on the economic level. What we are witnessing here is the genesis, not of a "prison-industrial complex," as suggested by some criminologists following after journalists and justice activists mobilized against the growth of the penal state,[60] but of a truly novel organizational figure, a partially *commercialized, carceral-assistential contraption* which is the spearhead of the nascent liberal-paternalist state. Its mission is to surveil and subjugate, and if need be chastise and neutralize, the populations refractory to the new economic and moral order according to a gendered division of labor, with its carceral component handling mainly the men while its assistential component exercises its tutelage over (their) women and children. In keeping with the American political tradition established during the colonial era, this composite institutional ensemble *in statu nascendi* is characterized, on the one hand, by the deep interpenetration of the public and private sectors and, on the other, by the fusion of the functions of branding, moral redress, and repression of the state.

The Demonic Myth of the "Prison-Industrial Complex"

The refrain of the rise of a "prison-industrial complex" that would have succeeded (or supplemented) the "military-industrial complex" of the Cold War era, with defense industry giants retooling from supplying arms to the Pentagon to providing surveillance and punishment for the poor, the fear of the "red enemy" of the exterior being replaced by dread for the "black enemy" of the interior, and private operators acting in cahoots with corrections officials and politicians to constitute a shadowy "subgovernment" pushing for limitless carceral expansion aimed at exploiting the booming captive workforce, is a leitmotif of the oppositional discourse on prison in the United States.[61] *Anchored in a conspiratorial vision of history, this thesis suffers from four major lacunae that undercut its analytic import and ruin its practical pertinence.*

First, it reduces the twofold, conjoint and interactive, transformation of the social and penal components *of the bureaucratic field to the sole "industrialization" of incarceration. But the changing scale of confinement in America is only one element of a broader redefinition of the perimeter and modalities of state action with regard to the "problem populations" residing in the nether regions of social and urban space. It is tightly connected to, and cannot be explained in isolation from, the epochal transition from "welfare" to "workfare."*[62] *By contrast, it is very dubious whether it can be tied to the "globalization" of the overly large and vague "isms" of capitalism and racism—the two favorite culprits in this activist tale of government evil—neither of which provides the necessary and sufficient conditions for the country's unprecedented and unrivaled carceral experiment.*

Second, the imagery of the "prison-industrial complex" ac-cords the role of driving force to the pecuniary interest of firms selling correctional services and wares or allegedly tapping the vast reserves of labor held under lock. It maintains that the profit motive is crucial to the onset of mass incarceration when, in re-ality, the latter pertains first and foremost to a political logic and project, *namely, the construction of a post-Keynesian, "liberal-paternalist" state suited to instituting desocialized wage labor and propagating the renewed ethic of work and "individual re-sponsibility" that buttress it. Profiteering from corrections is not a primary cause but an incidental and* secondary consequence *of the hypertrophic development of the penal apparatus. Indeed, the fact that private concerns are reaping benefits from the ex-pansion of a government function is neither new nor specific to incarceration: the delivery of every major public good in the United States, from education and housing to safety and health care, grants a vast role to commercial or third-sector parties—relative to medical provision, for instance, punishment remains distinctively* public. *Nor is privatization necessary: banning adult imprisonment for profit did not prevent California from becom-ing a leader in the drive to mass incarceration.*

Similarly, the ritual denunciation of the superexploitation of inmates under conditions evocative of penal slavery cannot hide the fact that only a minuscule and stagnant fraction of the U.S. carceral population works for outside firms (under 1 percent by the most generous counts) and that no economic sector relies even marginally on convict laborers. As for the prisoners toiling for state or federal industries behind bars, their output is negli-gible and they are "employed" at a net loss to the government, even though their activity is massively subsidized and heavily protected.[63] *Its spectacular growth notwithstanding, it is hard to square the claim that "the prison industrial complex is becoming increasingly central to the growth of the U.S. economy"*[64] *with the raw statistics of national accounting: the $57 billion that the United States spent on corrections at the local, state, and federal levels in 2001 amounted to barely one-half of 1 percent of the gross domestic product of $10,128 billion that year. Far from being "an essential component of the U.S. economy," corrections* *remains insignificant on the production side and acts not as an overall stimulus to corporate profits but as a gross drain on the public coffers.*

Third, this activist vision is premised on a flawed parallelism between the state functions of national defense and penal administration, which overlooks this crucial difference: military policy is highly centralized and coordinated at the federal level, whereas crime control is widely decentralized and dispersed among federal authorities, one hundred state departments of justice and corrections, and thousands of county and city administrations in charge of the police, courts, and jails. The phrase "criminal justice system" hides a loosely coupled web of bureaucratic agencies endowed with wide discretion and devoid of an overarching penal philosophy or policy. Even if some farsighted ruling group had somehow concocted a nightmarish plan designed to turn the carceral system into a lucrative industry using the bodies of the dark-skinned poor as "raw materials," there is no single lever that it could have seized and used to ensure their delivery. The simplistic thesis that capitalist lucre drives carceral growth leaves unexplained the specific mechanisms that have produced the remarkable convergence of correctional trends across the different jurisdictions of the United States and only adds to the "compound mystery" of nationwide hyperincarceration in the absence of "a distinctive policy precursor."[65]

Finally, constricted by its prosecutorial approach, the woolly notion of "prison-industrial complex" overlooks the wide-ranging effects of the introduction, albeit in a limited and perverted form, of the welfarist logic within the carceral universe *itself. Correctional institutions have been profoundly transformed over the past three decades, not only by changes in the scale and composition of their clientele, but also by the prisoners' rights movement, the rationalization and professionalization of confinement, and the increasing oversight of the courts.[66] Thus judges have demanded of jail and prison authorities that they meet a battery of minimal norms in matters of individual rights and institutional services, entailing, for example, the provision of education to underage inmates and psychiatric services on a mass scale. However deficient it remains, correctional health care has improved substantially to the point where it is typically superior to the meager medical services accessible to the poorest convicts on the outside and it reaches millions yearly. So much so that public health scholars and officials have come to view the carceral system as a crucial point of intervention for detecting and treating a range of infectious disease common among low-income urban populations.*[67] *Such costly delivery of public services of first resort to destitute populations via correctional facilities is difficult to square with the castigatory notion of "prison-industrial complex" turned toward generating economic profit and social harm.*

Precarious Workers, Foreigners, Addicts: The Preferred "Clients" of European Prisons

Scrutinizing the American experience of the past three decades allows us to observe, in real-world scale and in a case that is particularly salient owing to its power of ideological attraction, the regression from the social state toward the penal state, and thus to better discern what the country's recent trajectory may owe to this regression. From the economy and politics to civic participation, popular culture, and the media, there is not a single domain of social life in the United States today that is not directly affected by the hypertrophic development of the carceral institution and its extensions. In the manner of a chemical revelator, this experience brings into bold relief the hidden face—hidden because repressed by the immense historical work of juridical, political, and cultural euphemization constitutive of the establishment of a formally democratic regime, product of two centuries of social struggles—of the *state as collective organization of violence* aimed at the enforcement of the established order and the submission of the dominated. This violence resurfaces, as it happens, sudden, massive, methodical, and targeted precisely on those who, from the standpoint of the dominant, are seen as useless or insubordinate to the new economic and ethnoracial order that is being established in the United States in the aftermath of the neoliberal revolution, and which America is offering as model to the entire world.

To understand the specificities of the American experience is not, for all that, to reduce it to the status of particularity. And one must beware of attributing the sudden ascent of the country's carceral system wholesale to that "exceptionalism" which the United States itself likes to invoke on every score, and behind which sycophants and detractors of the "American model" too often conceal the poverty of their arguments, whether apology or incrimination. Indeed, if the rise of the penal state was especially spectacular and brutal in the United States, for historically interwoven reasons that are readily identified—the narrowness of a "categorical," semiwelfare state founded on a racial divide and devoted to buttressing the discipline of the market—the temptation to rely on the judicial and penal institutions to curb the effects of the social insecurity engendered by the imposition of desocialized wage labor and by the correlative shrinking of social protection is also making itself felt throughout Europe, and particularly in France, in step with the deployment there of neoliberal ideology and the policies it inspires, in matters of labor as well as criminal justice.

Proof of this is found in the swift and continuous *increase in the incarceration rates in almost all the member nations of the European Union* over the past dozen years: between 1985 and 2000, these rose from 93 to 127 inmates per 100,000 inhabitants in Portugal, from 90 to 124 in England and Wales, from 57 to 114 in Spain, from 76 to 93 in Italy and 95 in France, from 34 to 90 in the Netherlands, from 62 to 85 in Belgium, from 36 to 76 in Greece, and from 49 to 64 in Sweden.[68] Granted, these rates remain far below that of the United States, and in most cases they have increased much less quickly than in America. Moreover, crime rose noticeably in European societies over this period, whereas it stagnated in the United States. Finally, in the majority of European countries, the ballooning of the population behind bars results from the lengthening of sentences rather than from a strong inflation in admissions, which is the opposite of the American pattern. Nonetheless, the rise in the carceral population has asserted itself over almost the entire Continent (cf. Table 4), and especially in France, where the number of inmates has nearly doubled in twenty years to nearly 60,000 in 2002, after the drop of 1997–2000 gave way to a rapid increase as the Left joined the Right in making crime fighting its policy priority. In point of fact, since 1975, the curves tracing variations in unemployment and in penitentiary demography follow a rigorously parallel evolution.

Table 4. Carceral inflation in the European Union, 1983–2000

Country	1983	1990	1997	2000	Increase %
England and Wales	43,415	50,106	61,940	65,666	51
Italy	41,413	32,588	49,477	53,481	29
France	39,086	47,449	54,442	48,835	25
Spain	14,659	32,902	42,827	45,044	207
Portugal	6,093	9,059	14,634	13,800	126
Netherlands	4,000	6,662	13,618	13,841	246
Belgium	6,524	6,525	8,342	8,671	33
Greece	3,736	4,786	5,577	8,038	115
Sweden	4,422	4,895	5,221	5,678	28
Denmark	3,120	3,243	3,299	3,279	5
Ireland	1,466	2,114	2,433	2,887	97

Note: Countries are ranked by total inmate population in 2000.
Source: Statistiques pénales annuelle du Conseil de l'Europe, Enquête 1997 (Strasbourg: Council of Europe, 2001).

As in the United States, the mid-1970s in France mark a historic break, followed by a reversal in social trends as well as a carceral evolution. To the mutation of the model of production and employment—dualization of the labor market and rise of mass joblessness followed by the extension of wage precariousness, accompanied by a proliferation of social measures aiming both to relieve the most glaring situations of distress and to flexibilize the workforce—corresponds a recomposition of the penal economy and persistent carceral inflation.

After falling by 25 percent between 1968 and 1975, France's inmate population grew continuously over two decades. Only the presidential pardons of 1981 and 1988, and the exceptional amnesties occasioned first by the arrival of Robert Badinter at the ministry of justice, then by the Bicentennial of the Revolution, momentarily checked the inexorable growth of the population behind bars: the 26,032 inmates of 1975 became 42,937 in 1985, then 51,623 in 1995 (for metropolitan France alone). The French incarceration rate thus rose from 50 inmates per 100,000 when Valéry Giscard d'Estaing entered the Élysée palace in 1974 to 71 per 100,000 when Mitterrand succeeded him seven years later, to reach 95 per 100,000 when the presidency passed to Jacques Chirac in the mid-1990s. At the same time, there was an extension of community sanctions, with some 120,000 subjected to judicial control, whether under suspended sentences with probation, on parole, or assigned to reparation by way of community service. All in all, the population under criminal justice supervision reached 176,800 as of January 1998—50 percent more than in 1989 and 2.5 times the figure for 1975. In addition, that period witnessed the extension of measures of medical and social-welfare treatment (for drug addicts) and administrative sanctions (for foreigners without papers) in cases involving neither recidivism nor associated offenses.

This strong upsurge in carceral demography is the result of a wide-ranging recomposition of the economy of penalties, characterized by the virtual elimination of the fine in favor of suspended prison sentences (with the perverse consequence of longer durations of incarceration in cases of recidivism), an upward shift of the scale of the sentence pronounced (the average quantum for unsuspended prison sentences handed down in magistrate's court jumped from 2.5 months in 1984 to 6.4 months in 1992; the average term of detention nationwide reached 7.8 years in 1996 as against 4.4 years twenty years earlier), and the withering away of early releases (parole has shrunk to the point that it was granted to only 13 percent of eligible convicts in 1996, compared to 29 percent in 1973).[69] *Meanwhile, the profile of sanctioned offenses has been redrawn, the focus of repression moving away from infractions involving a direct victim (thefts supply only one-fifth of the entering prisoners in 1997, compared to one-half two decades earlier) and toward these two "victimless" infractions that are drug offenses and immigration by undocumented foreigners, in addition to rape and other sex offenses, which are also punished more severely. In sum, the rise in the inmate population was fed by the growth in the numbers convicted between 1971 and 1987 (increase in flows), then by the lengthening of prison terms from 1983 to today.*[70]

"The new organization of penal sanctions," notes criminologist Thierry Godefroy, is arising "in connection with the control

of a growing population, that of young adults in a state of transition between school and work," while leaving available a reserve of deskilled labor with low expectations, "useful to the development of the service sector as well as to the new forms of the organization of production that rely heavily on precariousness and mobility." This redeployment of punishment raises the "penal pressure not on the 'dangerous classes' strictly speaking but on the marginalized elements of the labor market (particularly young people and foreigners), who are offered no other prospect than the acceptance of either insertion into the market of insecure jobs or carceral sanctions, especially in cases of recidivism."[71]

In contrast with the United States, then, France's penitentiary expansion has been nourished, not by all-out confinement, but by the "dualization" of penal activity and by the lengthening of custodial sentences targeted especially at immigrants and youth from the working class. Contrary to America, where public assistance dwindled to the point where it was eventually reconverted into a "springboard" toward forced wage work, in France penal growth has been accompanied by an extension of welfare-state support for the populations excluded from the labor market, through the institution of a guaranteed minimum income plan (the Revenu minimum d'insertion *or RMI), additional aid targeted at single mothers with children, state-sponsored employment schemes, public-sector youth jobs, neighborhood social development, the antiexclusion law, etc.*[72] *So that, rather than a brutal swing from the social to the penal, one observes in France, as in a number of other continental countries with a strong statist tradition, a* conjoint intensification of the social and penal treatment of the categories durably marginalized by the mutation of wage labor and the corresponding reorganization of social protection policies.

But if the mix of means utilized by the French penal state are different from those of the U.S. state, as indicated by the respective composition of their sanctions and policies, the imperative to which the redeployment of punishment responds on each side of the Atlantic is nonetheless similar: to subdue the populations refractory to precarious employment, to reaffirm the imperative

*of work as a civic norm, to warehouse supernumerary popula-
tions (over a transitional if ever longer period in the one case, for
extended periods lasting up to perpetuity in the other). In France
as in the United States, the restructuring of the penal economy
accompanies and supports the restructuring of the wage-labor
economy, with the prison serving as border and overflow catch-
ment for the deregulated market of insecure jobs.*

It is well known, since the pioneering work of Georg Rusche and
Otto Kirchheimer, which was extended and confirmed by forty-odd
empirical studies conducted in a dozen capitalist societies, that there
exists a close and positive correlation at the societal level between
the deterioration of the labor market and the rise in the population
behind bars—whereas there exists no robust statistical link between
crime rates and incarceration rates.[73] Moreover, all available studies
of judicial sanctions according to the social characteristics of those on
trial in European countries concur in indicating that unemployment
and occupational instability are severely judged by the courts on the
individual level—much as they are in the United States. What results
is, for the same crime or misdemeanor, an *"oversentencing" of individuals marginalized on the labor market to prison time.* In nearly
all advanced countries, being deprived of work not only increases the
probability of being placed on remand custody, and for a longer duration. A convict without a job is also more frequently thrown behind
bars rather than being punished with a suspended sentence or a fine,
after controlling for offense category. (In the United States, a study
found that being without a job is even more disadvantageous at the
sentencing stage than being African-American.)[74] Finally, the absence
or weakness of the inmate's integration into the world of work length-
ens the effective duration of incarceration by lowering his chances of
benefiting from a sentence adjustment or reduction, or a release on
parole.

"The fine is bourgeois or petty-bourgeois, the suspended prison
sentence is proletarian, prison time is subproletarian": the celebrated
formula of criminologist Bruno Aubusson de Cavarlay summing up
the aggregate functioning of French penal justice between 1952 and
1978 is even truer in the era of mass unemployment and deepening so-

cial inequalities.[75] Thus half of persons incarcerated in France during the course of the year 1998 had a level of education of *primary school* only (versus 3 percent who had attended a university); and one estimates that between one-third and one-half of inmates were without employ at the time of their arraignment; moreover, one in six inmates had no regular residence.[76] In England, 83 percent of inmates are issued from the working class and 43 percent left school before the age of sixteen (compared to the national average of 16 percent); over one-third were jobless and a full 13 percent were homeless at the time of their arrest.[77] Today, more than ever in the twentieth century, the "natural customers" of European jails and prisons are the precarious fractions of the working class, and most especially young people from working-class families of African ancestry.

In point of fact, throughout Europe, it is foreigners, so-called second-generation immigrants—who precisely are not immigrants—from outside Western countries, and persons of color, who figure prominently among the most vulnerable categories both on the labor market and vis-à-vis the public assistance sector of the state, owing to their lower-class distribution and to the manifold legal and social discriminations they suffer, who are massively overrepresented within the incarcerated population, and this to a degree comparable—indeed, in some places superior—to the "racial disproportionality" that afflicts blacks in the United States (Figure 1). Thus, in England, where the question of "street" crime tends to be confounded, in public perception as well as in the routine practices of the police, with the visible presence and demands of subjects of the Empire who come from the Caribbean, blacks are seven times more likely to be incarcerated than their white or Asian counterparts (and West Indian women ten times as likely). In 1993, persons of West Indian, Guyanese, and African ancestry made up 11 percent of all inmates, although they compose a mere 1.8 percent of the country's population ages 18 to 39. This overrepresentation is especially flagrant among prisoners "put away" for possession or distribution of drugs, of whom more than half are black, and among those in for burglary, where the proportion approaches two-thirds.[78]

A similar trend can be observed in Germany. In Northern Rhineland, the incarceration rates for "Gypsies" originating from Romania are more than twenty times those of native citizens; for Moroccans,

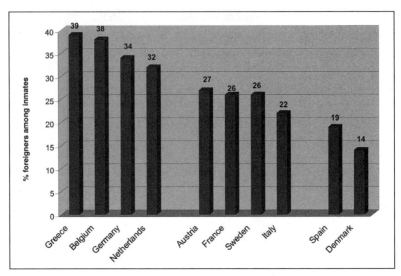

Figure 1. Overrepresentation of foreigners in the prisons and jails of the European Union, 1997. *Source:* Conseil de l'Europe, *Statistiques pénales annuelles du Conseil de l'Europe, Enquête 1997* (Strasbourg: Council of Europe, 1999).

the figure is eight times, and for Turks between three and four times. And the proportion of foreigners among those awaiting trial in custody rose from one-third in 1989 to one-half five years later. Indeed, in the Land of Hessen, the number of foreign prisoners has grown every year since 1987, whereas the number of nationals in detention fell every year. As for this swelling of the number of nonnationals behind bars, it is almost entirely due to infractions of the drug laws.[79] In the Netherlands, whose carceral population tripled in fifteen years and comprised 43 percent foreigners in 1993, the probability of being sanctioned with an unsuspended prison sentence is systematically higher even for the same first offense when the person sentenced is of Surinamese or Moroccan origin (on the other hand, the probability is higher for nationals in cases of subsequent offenses).[80] In Belgium, in 1997 the incarceration rate for foreigners was nearly six times the rate for nationals (2,840 versus 510 per 100,000); the gap between the two categories has widened rapidly since this ratio was only double in 1980. Since then, even excluding administrative detentions of undocumented immigrants, the number of foreigners entering carceral facilities has increased steadily while the flow of nationals locked up has diminished every year running to 1996. What is more, the average term of detention of foreigners deprived of liberty as a result of a criminal procedure is longer than that served by Belgians, even though they are more likely to be held on remand.[81]

In France, the share of foreigners in the inmate population went from 18 percent in 1975 to 29 percent twenty years later (whereas foreigners make up only 6 percent of the country's population), a figure that does not take into account the pronounced "carceral overconsumption" of nationals perceived and treated as foreigners by the police and judicial apparatus, such as youths born to Maghrebian immigrants or who come from the French overseas dominions and territories. This is tantamount to saying that the cells of France have grown distinctly "colored" these past years since two-thirds of the 15,000-odd foreign prisoners officially recorded in 1995 originated from North Africa (53 percent) and sub-Saharan Africa (16 percent).

The "ethnonational disproportionality" that afflicts denizens from France's former colonies stems from the fact that, *for the same offense,* the courts more readily resort to incarceration when the convicted does not possess French citizenship, suspended prison sentences and community sanctions being practically monopolized by nationals. The demographer Pierre Tournier has shown that, depending on the charges, the probability of being sentenced to serve time is 1.8 to 2.4 times higher for a foreigner than for a Frenchman (all persons tried taken together, without regard to prior records). Next, the number of foreigners implicated in illegal immigration cases has rocketed from 7,000 in 1976 to 44,000 in 1993. Now, three-fourths of those sanctioned for violating "Article 19" of the French penal code relating to unlawful entry and residence are thrown behind bars—of the sixteen misdemeanors most often tried before the courts, it is the one most frequently hit with an unsuspended prison sentence: it is in effect repressed as severely as a felony. Thus it turns out that, far from resulting from a hypothetical increase in their delinquency, as some xenophobic discourses would have it,[82] the rise in the share of foreigners in the inmate population of France is due *exclusively* to the tripling in twenty years of incarcerations for violations of immigration statutes. In point of fact, if inmates

sentenced for this administrative infringement are excluded from carceral statistics, the ratio of overimprisonment of foreigners in relation
to citizens in France drops from 6 to 3.

As in the case of blacks in the United States, aside from the fact—
a qualification that cannot be overemphasized—that African Americans have formally been *citizens* of the Union since 1868, the overrepresentation of foreigners in French prisons expresses, not only their
lower-class composition, but also the greater severity of the penal institution toward them and the "deliberate choice to repress illegal immigration by means of imprisonment."[83] We are indeed dealing here with
what is first and foremost a *confinement of differentiation* or segregation, aiming to keep an undesirable category separate and to facilitate
its subtraction from the societal body (it results more and more frequently in deportation and banishment from the national territory), as
distinct from "confinement of authority" and "confinement of safety."[84]

To the foreigners and quasi foreigners consigned to jails and prisons, often in tiers segregated according to ethnonational origin (as at
the jail of La Santé, in the heart of Paris, where inmates are distributed
into four separate and hostile wards, "white," "African," "Arab," and
"rest of the world"), one must add the thousands of migrants without
papers or awaiting deportation, especially by virtue of "double sentencing,"[85] arbitrarily held in those state-sponsored enclaves of juridical limbo, the "waiting areas" and "retention centers" that have
mushroomed over the past decade throughout the European Union.
Like the camps for "undesirable foreigners," "Spanish refugees," and
other "agitators" created by Daladier in 1938, the thirty-some centers
presently in operation on French territory—they numbered fewer than
a dozen fifteen years ago—are so many prisons that do not speak their
name, and for good reason: they are not placed under the authority of
the corrections administration, their inmates are often held in violation of Article 66 of the French Constitution (which stipulates that "no
one can be detained arbitrarily"), and conditions of confinement in
them typically infringe on both the law and basic standards of human
dignity. This is the case, inter alia, at the infamous center of Arenq
near the Marseille harbor station, where a dilapidated hangar built
in 1917 and lacking in the minimum amenities necessary for human
habitation serves to warehouse some 1,500 foreigners deported year in
and year out to North Africa.[86]

In Belgium, where the number of foreigners in the custody of the Office for Foreigners increased ninefold between 1974 and 1994, persons consigned in detention centers for foreigners *"en situation irré-gulière"* fall under the authority of the interior ministry (in charge of public order) and not of justice, and they are therefore omitted from the statistics of the penitentiary system. Five so-called closed centers, surrounded by a double row of barbed-wire fencing and placed under permanent video surveillance, serve as launching pad for the deportation of 15,000 foreigners each year: this is the official government target given as express proof of the "realistic" immigration policy carried out with the professed aim of cutting the ground out from under the far Right, which meanwhile has continued to prosper as never before.[87] In Italy, deportation orders quintupled in only four years to peak at 57,000 in 1994, even though there is every indication that illegal immigration has subsided and that the great majority of foreigners who do not have proper papers entered the country legally to fill "black market" jobs disdained by the native population[88]—as the government of Massimo D'Alema implicitly recognized when it increased by a factor of six the number of residence and work permits initially granted as part of the "regularization" program launched in early winter 1998.

More generally, it is well documented that those judicial practices that are seemingly the most neutral and the most routine, beginning with preventative (remand) detention, tend systematically to disadvantage persons of foreign origin or perceived to be such, as they are unlikely to present sufficient proofs of "community attachment" and social integration that serve to mitigate punishment. And *"la justice à quarante vitesses,"* to borrow the revealing expression of the youth of the declining housing estates of Longwy,[89] knows too well how to shift into high gear when it comes to arresting, prosecuting, and incarcerating the residents of stigmatized areas with a heavy concentration of the jobless and families issued from the labor migrations of the thirty-year boom of the postwar period who settled into those neighborhoods now designated as "sensitive" by official state jargon. Indeed, under the provisions of the Schengen and Maastricht treaties aiming to accelerate juridical integration so as to ensure the effective "free circulation" of European citizens, immigration has been redefined by the signatory countries as a continental and, by implication, national

matter of *security*, under the same heading as organized crime and terrorism, to which it has been grafted at the level of both discourse and
administrative regulation.[90] Thus, throughout Europe, police, judicial,
and penal practices converge at least inasmuch as they are applied with
special diligence and severity to lower-class persons of non-European
phenotype, who are easily spotted and made to bend to the police and
juridical arbitrary, to the point that one may speak of a genuine process of *criminalization of immigrants* that tends, by its destructuring
and criminogenic effects, to (co)produce the very phenomena that it is
supposed to combat, in accord with the well-known mechanism of the
"self-fulfilling prophecy."[91]

   This process is powerfully reinforced and amplified by the media
and by politicians of all stripes, eager to surf the xenophobic wave
that has been sweeping across Europe since the neoliberal turn of the
1980s by making an amalgam—sincerely or cynically, directly or indirectly, but with ever more banality—of immigration, illegality, and
criminality. Ceaselessly blacklisted, suspected in advance if not on
principle, driven back to the margins of society and hounded by the
authorities with unmatched zeal, the (non-European) foreigner mu-
tates into a "suitable enemy"—to use the expression of the Norwegian
criminologist Nils Christie[92]—at once symbol of and target for all
displaced social anxieties, much as poor African Americans are in
the major cities of their society. Prison and the branding it effects
thus actively participate in the fabrication of a European category
of "sub-whites"[93] tailor-made to legitimize a drift toward the penal
management of poverty which, thanks to a halo effect, tends to apply
to all working-class strata undermined by mass joblessness and flexible labor, regardless of nationality.

   From Oslo to Bilbao and from Naples to Nottingham by way of
Madrid, Marseille, and Munich, *the share of drug addicts and deal-
ers in the carceral population has undergone a spectacular rise,* which
parallels, without yet reaching the same slope, the rise observed in the
United States. Throughout Europe, antidrug policy serves as spear
and screen for "a war against persons perceived as the least useful
and potentially most dangerous parts of the population": the jobless,
the homeless, the paperless immigrants, beggars, vagrants, and other
social rejects of the city.[94] In France, the number of sentences for possession or sale of drugs exploded from 4,000 in 1984 to nearly 24,000

in 1994, and the length of sentences served for this offense doubled over this period (from 9 months to 20 months on average). As a result, the proportion of inmates "fallen" for narcotics went from 14 percent in 1988 (the first year for which it was recorded separately) to 21 percent a mere four years later, at which date it surpassed the proportion incarcerated for theft and robbery. This rate approaches or exceeds one-third in Italy, Spain, and Portugal, and it is hovers around 15 percent in Germany, the United Kingdom, and the Netherlands, where the expansion of the prison system over the last decade has served almost exclusively to absorb "junkies" (cf. Figure 2).

Even in Scandinavia, there is no country left unaffected by the sweeping penalization of narcotics consumption and the drive to confine petty users and traffickers it entails. In Norway, for example, the number of prison sentences handed down for drug infractions doubled during the 1980s to approach 30 percent of the national total today (it is perched at 20 percent in neighboring Sweden). But, over the same period, the total quantum of years of detention imposed on this count was multiplied fourfold owing to the sharp increase in the severity of the sanctions meted out. The official presentation

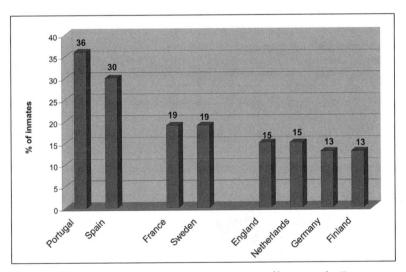

Figure 2. Share of inmates convicted for narcotics offenses in the European Union, 1997. *Source:* Conseil de l'Europe, *Statistiques pénales annuelles du Conseil de l'Europe, Enquête 1997* (Strasbourg: Council of Europe, 1999).

of correctional statistics even had to be modified in 1986 in order to record the proliferation of sentences running up to fifteen years of imprisonment, when until then the Norwegian penological norm held a three-year sentence as a ceiling not to be exceeded.[95]

The result of the extension of the penal dragnet in Europe is that, across the Continent as in the United States, *the overpopulation of prisons is weighing heavily* on the functioning of correctional services. Everywhere the carceral system loses even the pretense of pursuing rehabilitation, and incarceration gets reduced to its brute function of "warehousing" the undesirables. The members of the European Union have significantly enlarged their prison capacity over the past two decades and periodic recourse to amnesties and mass pardons (for example, in France on Bastille Day each year since 1991, and in Belgium by royal decrees about every other year), as well as waves of early releases (in Italy, Spain, Belgium, and Portugal), have become commonplace in an effort to curb the swelling of inmate stock. In spite of this, with the notable exception of the Scandinavian countries, the Netherlands, and Austria, beds are in short supply everywhere and prisons are nearly universally overflowing with inmates, with occupancy rates ranging from 110 percent in England and Belgium to some 130 percent in Italy, Greece, and the Iberian Peninsula (see Figure 3).

Yet these rates minimize actual overcrowding through various accounting artifices: for example, in the Netherlands the surplus prison population is typically transferred back to police lockups so that it does not appear in the statistics of the correctional administration; in Portugal, inmates suffering from mental health problems are not counted in the prisoner census; in Belgium, the counting of cells is less than reliable. But, above all, national averages conceal deep disparities within each country, such that an important fraction—nay, often a majority—of prisoners serve time in alarming conditions. According to the Council of Europe's most recent statistics, nearly two-thirds of all inmates in Italy and Portugal, and half of their counterparts in Belgium, are consigned to establishments plagued by "critical overpopulation" (i.e., filled to more than 120 percent of capacity).[96] In France, where the average occupancy rate of penal facilities officially stands at 109 percent, penitentiaries operate at 123 percent of their cell space, and eight of them post a population greater than double

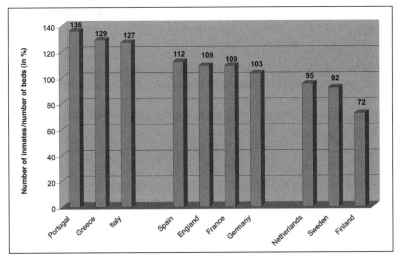

Figure 3. Overpopulation in the prisons and jails of the European Union, 1997. *Source:* Pierre Tournier, *Inflation carcérale et surpeuplement des prisons* (Strasbourg: Council of Europe, 1999).

their capacity—including two prisons at triple their capacity. In all, fully one-fourth of France's inmates are sojourning in establishments where overpopulation exceeds 150 percent.[97]

IMPRISONMENT FRENCH-STYLE, QUICK AND DIRTY

According to a study published by the ministry of justice, more than one inmate in four sits in a jail under "very difficult, indeed alarming" detention conditions. There, being confined two, three, or four men in nine square meters, up to twenty-two hours per day, is a routine reality. Thus the 330 detainees of the jail of Nîmes occupy an establishment designed for 180 persons. Two-person cells house a third inmate, who is forced to sleep on a mattress laid out directly on the floor. Cells of about twenty square meters are occupied by six inmates, who must then eat on their beds. Overpopulation is now extending to penitentiaries [where convicts serve long-term sentences]. In the Nantes correctional center, only the inmates whose sentence is longer than five years are assigned to an individual cell [whereas the French penal code stipulates that all inmates must have an individual cell]. The others are assigned two to a single man cell in which a bed, a locker, and a chair have been added. After these furnishings are put in, there remains only about two square meters available in the cell. . . .

Over one-fourth of persons placed in custody are brought to trial under fast-track emergency procedures *[comparution immédiate]*. This rate has doubled in twenty years, which reveals a penal justice that is more and more intent on speedy, nay summary, proceedings, which result in deprivation of liberty more than in any other sanction. In addition, the sentences passed by the courts get heavier and heavier. In 1997, more than 35 percent of convicts were serving prison terms exceeding five years. In magistrate's court cases, sentences of five years and more are also increasing: there were 5,245 of them on December 31, 1997, compared to 4,561 a year earlier.

Contrary to a commonly held notion, the majority of inmates (60 percent) serve the entirety of their sentences. The drying up of penalty adjustment measures [including early release and paroling] is continuing in a worrisome way, confirming the most pessimistic predictions. Given the rate at which the number of parole releases is falling, this measure will have disappeared in another five years.

—Patrick Marest, "1997, les prisons françaises," *Dedans–Dehors* (Observatoire international des prisons) 8 (July–August 1998): 12–13.

In 1993, a report by the Council of Europe's Committee for the Prevention of Torture and Inhumane or Degrading Treatment or Punishment, which is entrusted with enforcing the European convention of the same name that came into force in 1989, severely admonished France for the ignominious conditions of confinement observed at the jail of Les Baumettes in Marseille, where cells of less than ten square meters, designed for a single occupant, were housing four, in disregard of the most elementary rules of hygiene and safety. Such detention conditions are not unconnected to the one-fourth increase in the suicide rate between 1986 and 1996: one-third of suicides among France's inmates involve detainees in preventive detention in jails who take their lives within the first three months of being locked up.[98]

The same stinging condemnation was passed on "retention centers" for foreigners such as the notorious Dépôt at the Paris police headquarters, where gloomy, cockroach-infested basement cells, measuring between thirty-two and fifty square meters, each contained some dozen detainees lacking any means of distraction or outdoor exercise. Conditions in police stations and lockups, where suspects are usually held after arrest, were even worse: dilapidated, foul-smelling cells with walls sweating from the humidity, soiled bedding, faulty lighting and ventilation, etc. So much so that these conditions moved the Committee for the Prevention of Torture to break protocol and exceptionally address its observations to the French authorities immediately upon its visit. To crown it all, in a good number of countries where the committee carried out its investigations, among them Austria, Portugal, France, Belgium, and Greece, the physical mistreatment suffered by arrestees during their detention by the police is routine and well documented. Insults, kicks, punches and slaps, the withholding of food or medicine, and psychological harassment were found to bear first and foremost on the targets of choice of the European penal apparatus, namely, foreigners (real or assimilated) and young people (of working-class extraction).[99]

Discipline and Punish at the Fin de Siècle: Toward Social Panopticism

Another trend that goes in the direction of the American carceral drift: notwithstanding the great diversity of national traditions and situations,[100] on the whole *the penal policies of Western European societies have turned harsher, more encompassing,* and more overtly turned toward "social defense," to the detriment of rehabilitation, at the very moment when these societies were in the midst of reorganizing their social-welfare programs in a restrictive direction and their job markets in a permissive direction. With precious few exceptions, lawmakers everywhere have expanded the perimeter of penal sanctions and increased the custodial sentences that strike violent crimes, sex offenses, and the trade or use of drugs. The police have reinforced the resources and operations aimed at these offenses; further down the penal chain, the judicial authorities have reduced the possibilities for community sentencing and parole for a wide range of infractions. The abolition of the death penalty, in those countries that had not yet expurgated it from their criminal code, has had the paradoxical effect of lengthening the average term of confinement through the intermediary of so-called safety sentences (mandatory minimum terms of incarceration that can reach thirty years in France). And the internal functioning of carceral facilities is more and more dominated by austerity and security, with the goal of rehabilitation being more or less reduced to a bureaucratic marketing slogan.[101]

"Rehabilitation, a Residual and Utopian Mission"

For some, rehabilitation *[réinsertion]* buys a good conscience. Not people
like me, but politicians. It's the same in a jail. How many I've seen tell me,
"Don't worry, Sarge, I'm never coming back!" and wham! six months later . . .
To rehabilitate, it's not in prison that you do that. It's too late. You've got to
"habilitate" *[insérer]* people by giving them jobs, equal chances at the start,
in school. You have to do "habilitation." That we provide social assistance is
fine, but it's too late.

—A prison guard

If guards "support rehabilitation as an ideal," the whole organization of
their work belies this ideal in reality: there is no doctrine, no means or time
set aside for it (rehabilitation is included "neither in schedules, nor in terms
of staffing"), no training, no exchanges with those who are called, revealingly, "external providers" responsible for education, job training, entertainment, and social work. The ignorance in which guards are kept about
the offense committed by an inmate, the investigation, the charges, the
sentence and its length, "the suspicion of corruption that falls on [guards]
when they engage in 'social assistance,'" and the prohibition of all contact
with inmates on the outside, converge to reduce this ideal to "a word and
a cloak thrown over rags."

In the final analysis, "so long as the prison keeps its primary mission of
public security, founded upon a model emphasizing coercion, deterrence, and
repression, this will be the mission of the guards. The law-and-order expectations that currently weigh on the prison imply longer sentences, more con-
trols, and more surveillance. They appear to be incompatible with a therapeutic philosophy of rehabilitation premised upon contractual relations."

—Quotations are taken from Antoinette Chauvenet, Françoise Orlic,
and Georges Benguigui, *Le Monde des surveillants de prison*
(Paris: Presses Universitaires de France, 1994), 36–38, 43–45, 48.

A revealing case in point is the punitive evolution of the Dutch
judicial and correctional system, which for a long time was given as
a paradigm for the success of "humanitarian paternalism," from the
point of view of society as well as of the inmates. Under this regime,
deprivation of liberty was rare, prison sentences short, and time in
custody was put to active use for improving the convict's "human
capital" through education and therapeutic treatment. The erosion of
the protections offered by the welfare state in the 1990s and the pressure to align with the more repressive European norm have turned all

that upside down. Today, Dutch penal policy is governed by a "managerial instrumentalism" that gives priority to accounting concerns of cost and efficiency in an overtly retributive and security-oriented perspective.[102] The result is that the incarceration rate of the Netherlands has doubled since 1985 (it nonetheless remains near the bottom of the bracket of European variations and comes to barely one-tenth of the U.S. rate) while the population behind bars tripled between 1983 and 1996. Only a decade ago, British penologists were taking pilgrimages to the Netherlands to study the means and ends of progressive and effective penality.[103] Since 1994, it is the officials in charge of Dutch judicial policy who, anxious to rid themselves of their international image of "leniency," have borrowed from across the Channel the instruments and justifications of a resolutely punitive penal approach. A former justice minister of the Netherlands recently congratulated himself on seeing his country finally approach "the European average" on this count.

Nonetheless, the penal management of social precariousness does not always come down to imprisonment, as was noted in the American case, where the promotion of incarceration to the rank of *primum remedium* of poverty has not prevented a vigorous extension of the "external" oversight of dispossessed households and neighborhoods. In the countries of Europe with strong statist traditions, Catholic or social-democratic, where social struggles have, over the decades, established multiple avenues of recourse against the naked sanction of the labor market that function indirectly as so many safety catches against the drift toward mass confinement, the punitive regulation of the impoverished fractions of the new post-Fordist proletariat is effected mainly through the agency of ever-more refined and intrusive *panoptic mechanisms directly integrated into programs of social protection and assistance.* The laudable concern for greater efficiency in welfare support leads to putting deprived populations under a supervision that is all the more strict and punctilious as the various bureaucracies entrusted with treating social insecurity on a day-to-day basis—unemployment offices, social services, state health insurance, public hospitals, social housing, etc.—systematize their information gathering, interconnect their data banks, and coordinate their activities. They are also "modernizing" their procedures and modalities of intervention so as to minimize the "risks" posed by the populations placed in their charge and to make them compatible with the security measures that are multiplying on their borders.[104] It remains to be seen whether this social panopticism, a comparatively mild form of the punitive treatment of poverty that still predominates in Western Europe today, represents a viable and durable *alternative* to mass imprisonment, or if it simply marks a *stage* in a process of penal escalation leading in the end to a widening of the recourse to incarceration and its derivatives.

In France, the populations and neighborhoods euphemistically said to be "in difficulty" are on their way to being caught in a "computerized pincer" allowing close surveillance and thus increased control by the social services, on the one side, and the police and the courts, on the other. Several departmental councils, which since the 1983 decentralization law are responsible for welfare services (the "social integration" component of the guaranteed minimum income plan, mother-and-infant protection, social assistance to children and the elderly, etc.), have already created a single departmental data file on the individuals and households who receive aid, thanks to the ANIS (New Approach to Social Information) software package.

In the département of Ain (the administrative district northeast of Lyon), the Bureau of Welfare and Social Services has fine-tuned a supplementary computerized function that allows it to construct "typologies" of individuals and households on assistance according to such subjective appraisals reported by the social worker as "psychological difficulty," "state of dependency (expressed/recognized)," "difficulty accomplishing everyday tasks," or "difficulty at social integration." The stated goal of these typologies is to draw up social maps of the district making it possible to pinpoint zones with high concentrations of dependent and problem populations. Several civic associations, including the Ligue des droits de l'homme (Human Rights League), the Collectif informatique, fichiers et citoyenneté (Computing, Files, and Citizenship Collective), and the Collectif pour les droits des citoyens face à l'informatisation de l'action sociale (Collective for Citizens' Rights Regarding the Computerization of Social Services), have joined with several social workers' unions to call on the National Computing and Liberties Commission (Commission Nationale Informatique et Libertés, CNIL) to withdraw its authorization of the software used to make the single file and such typologies as these. The commission, which by law must approve all computerized filing systems to safeguard the constitutional right to privacy, has not seen fit to accede to their demand, even though it emphasized in its 1994 annual report its "major fear of seeing the development of a comprehensive file of underprivileged populations, and consequently a sort of cartography of exclusion premised on the definition of individual or family profiles of precariousness" liable to reinforce the territorial stigmatization and discrimination visited upon the most destitute.[105]

The interconnection of social-welfare files kept at the level of the départements is echoed by the creation of a gigantic national data bank on infractions, misdemeanors, and crimes. Authorized by the 1995 Law on Orientation and Planning on Security, the "Criminal Information Processing System" ("système de traitement de l'information criminelle" or STIC) is intended to pool the totality of computerized data collected by police agencies on violations of the law: the "central file" of the interior ministry's Department of Public Liberties, the "general file of criminal records" of the Paris police administration, local files recording law-enforcement interventions in the provinces, and finally the "criminal investigations file."[106] *Here again, under the guise of rationalizing investigative work, the authorities have created the means of accumulating detailed data on the residents of poor neighborhoods, which are most directly subjected to police combing and control, since this single database comprises not only those convicted of a criminal offense, but also the suspects, victims, and witnesses of every matter handled by the police. This is to say that it encompasses the kin, friends, and neighbors of the "clients" of the police and judicial apparatus, for a duration of five to forty years, depending on the charge filed. The Syndicat de la magistrature (the main left-leaning union of judges and prosecutors) has emphasized rightly that the STIC's exhaustive character, the extended durations over which it retains information, which de facto void the "right to forgetting," and its use of the police (and not juridical) notion of "implication"* (mise en cause) *in a procedure make it a veritable "population file," which contravenes the country's Law on Informatics and Liberties. According to a check carried out by the League for Human Rights, as of January 1, 1997, the STIC already contained 2.5 million "implicated" individuals, an equal number of victims of crimes, and a half-million indirect victims, for a total of 6.3 million offenses.*

The information dumped in this hodgepodge file includes crimes and misdemeanors, but also numerous categories of lower infractions such as "trespassing on school grounds," "willful destruction or degradation of another's property," "insult to the police," and even "soliciting" and other incivilities abusively characterized as "urban." According to several jurists and the spokesperson for the bill before the National Commission on Computing and Liberties, the (socialist) vice president of the National Assembly Raymond Forni, there is good reason to fear that such a file will be used not only for purposes of criminal investigation, but also for operations of administrative police, such as the "inquiries of morality" on persons seeking various credentials and certificates from the authorities (for a naturalization application, for example), in spite of the CNIL's explicit prohibition of such a use. It is for this reason that even the Syndicat Général de la Police (the country's main police union) disapproved of its creation. To be sure, the CNIL did not authorize the consultation of this file for "all persons whose behavior is liable to create dangers for others," as the interior ministry had requested. But it is just the same since it has granted its approval for "missions of administrative police or safety, when the nature of these missions or the particular circumstances under which they must be carried out entail the risk of disturbing public order or infringing on the security of persons"—in other words, in conditions left entirely to the judgment of the police, who in effect have the possibility of dipping into the STIC as they see fit.

The next stage in tightening the computerized surveillance of precarious populations will consist in connecting social-welfare files with police files, for example, to better implement court decisions to suspend family allowances in cases of an adolescent's repeat delinquency (this concerns several tens of thousands of

households each year), or to locate a witness or suspect by re-
tracing the pathways of social assistance and other state income
support receipt.[107] *Next, these combined files will in turn be cross-*
linked with income-tax data banks: in December 1998, the Jospin
government sneaked through the National Assembly an amend-
ment to the 1999 budget bill authorizing the treasury department
to use the NIR (Numéro d'Inscription au Répertoire national
d'identification des personnes physiques), the national Directory of
Registration Numbers for identification of physical persons (com-
monly known as the "social security number"), in order to con-
nect social-welfare files and tax files. One is reminded that, in the
1940s under the Vichy regime, the NIR included a specific code to
identify separately "Muslim natives" and "Muslim Jews," "Jewish
foreigners" and "Jewish foreign refugees."[108] *It could quite easily*
be so tailored tomorrow, under the pretext of administrative ef-
ficiency, to repertory other problem populations, such as those
residing in France's "sensitive neighborhoods."

On this front, France lags far behind the Netherlands, the in-
disputable European leader in administrative panopticism. Since
its neoliberal turn under the government of Wim Wok in the early
1990s, Holland has stressed the "obligations" of persons receiv-
ing assistance from the state and, in addition to enlarged recourse
to the prison system (its capacity was tripled between 1985 and
1995), it has developed numerous programs that place welfare
recipients, foreigners, and "at-risk" youths under permanent
supervision. Thus the files of the Dutch social-welfare offices are
directly connected to those of the tax department in order to de-
tect and punish public aid beneficiaries who would hold a job on
the side. A series of legislative measures, culminating in the File
Connection Act of 1998 (De Koppelingswet), has prompted state
agencies to put their data banks in network so as to bar the access
of illegal immigrants to the labor market as well as to the gamut
of public services, education, housing, unemployment benefits,
and health coverage. The perverse effect of these measures has
been to drive these populations further underground, obliterat-
ing basic rights (to juridical assistance, to schooling of their chil-
dren, and to emergency medical assistance, among others) that
are recognized under international conventions that Holland was

*among the first to sign, and to stimulate a vast traffic in counter-
feit papers.*[109]

    *Finally, under the guise of preventing delinquency, several
Dutch municipalities have put wide swaths of their populations
under "computer guardianship." The city of Rotterdam, for example, has created an office responsible for youth surveillance
that plans to follow stage by stage all city residents under eighteen (130,000 persons, or one inhabitant in four) with a view to
tracking from the earliest age "families with multiple problems"
and "milieus of delinquent socialization."*[110] *A research team
placed under the aegis of the municipal health services regularly
conducts questionnaire surveys of schoolchildren to measure their
material, emotional, and cognitive well-being, the properties of
their proximate social entourage, and their propensity to "risk behaviors" (consumption of alcohol and drugs, betting and games
played for money, delinquency). Teachers fill out a form providing complementary information on the family environment and
the behavior of each student (illness, absenteeism, self-esteem,
hyperactivity or excitability, deviant attitudes or behaviors). At
the end of 1998, 7,000 children ages 11 and 12 were put on file
in this way, and all Rotterdam children between 0 and 12 will be
thus monitored in a few years. Here we see very concretely how
concern for welfare (physical, moral, and social) can serve the
objective of monitoring populations placed under state tutelage,
in accordance with Foucault's classic analyses of "policing" as a
technique for governing persons.*[111]

The drift from the social to the penal in Europe is only too apparent in the *recent inflections of public discourse* on crime, so-called
urban disorders, and the "incivilities" that are multiplying as the established order gradually loses legitimacy among those condemned to
marginality by ongoing economic and political transformations. Thus
Tony Blair's New Labor has taken up as its own most of the repressive
themes traditionally dear to Tory election propaganda, under cover of
the falsely balanced slogan "Tough on crime, tough on the causes of
crime." So far the British state has proved diligent at striking only on the
crime side, that is, at low-grade street delinquency: since New Labor's

rise to power, the carceral population of England and Wales has grown at the frantic pace of a thousand persons per month—ten times faster than under Margaret Thatcher—to reach the record figure of 66,800 inmates in spring 1998. The Blair government had no sooner come into office than it increased the prison budget by £110 million while holding back social expenditures.

Similarly, after they returned to power in 1994 and 1997, respectively, the Swedish Social Democrats and the French Socialists have taken care not to abrogate the law-and-order legislation voted by the conservative governments that preceded them, even though they had promised to do so during their successful electoral campaigns. In response to the alleged upswing of youth delinquency in formerly working-class estates turned to economic fallow by the "modernization" of French capitalism and the retrenchment of the state, the French minister of the interior of a professed Left government could be heard advocating for the reopening of "penal colonies for children" so that "little savages" *(sauvageons)* could be locked up in them. His call was echoed by Left members of parliament who suggested, in an official report commissioned by the prime minister of the same government, that the parents of young delinquents who persist in their errant ways be thrown in prison themselves.[112]

A single quotation from a "social" minister, in charge of health, after he was queried (during the television program *Public* of December 20, 1998) about the government's response to the extended rioting of youths from Toulouse's poor neighborhood of La Reynerie following the killing of one of them by a trigger-happy policeman, provides a verification a fortiori (or is it *per absurdum*?) of the banalization of the penal treatment of social misery and its correlates. After having inventoried for the record the well-known litany of deep causes of this explosion of collective violence, "exclusion from everything you've said, in some ways, from health, from school, from housing, from work," and politely omitting the routine police violence and harassment of younger people of foreign descent in these areas, Bernard Kouchner made this revealing assertion: "One cannot think of resolving this problem *solely* in repressive terms."[113] This statement was confirmed a few days later by his counterpart at the ministry of justice, Elisabeth Guigou, who thought it necessary to declare emphatically before the 1,500 ward secretaries of the Socialist Party gathered at the Mutualité in January 1999, for whom one might have thought that such an argument would go without saying: "One cannot find solutions to delinquency that rely solely on education or on repression. The two must be combined."[114]

The promotion of the police to the front line of the battle against poverty—or is it against the poor?—was, moreover, confirmed by the personal telegram sent to all police staff on the occasion of New Year's Day 1999 by the interior minister upon his return to duty:[115]

> The police were instituted to combat delinquency, the scourge of vice and organized crime. A great deal more is asked of them today: to fight the evil of social exclusion and its destructive effects, to respond to the suffering engendered by idleness, social precariousness, and the feeling of abandonment, to put a check on the will to destroy in order to prove one's existence. This is the watershed where our institutions stand today, the front line where your everyday action is deployed today.

In other words, even though it is not their vocation and they have neither the competencies nor the means for it, the police must henceforth do the work that social workers do not do anymore inasmuch as it is clear that there is not (and will not be) work for everyone. The regulation of perennial poverty through wage labor is thus succeeded by its regulation through the forces of order and the courts.

Just as in December 1995, at the height of popular protests that brought some 2 million people marching in the streets, civic "courage" and political "modernity" were supposed to manifest themselves in support for the Juppé government plan to "downsize" the welfare state in order to "save" the social safety net (tomorrow) by (immediately) generalizing social precariousness, today certain self-proclaimed renovators of public debate—they are just about the same people[116]— are striving to give credit to the notion that progressive daring demands that we embrace the most hackneyed law-and-order clichés, after these have been hastily dabbed with a flashy "made-in-USA" veneer. Thus, to give the moral force of urgency to their appeal for a new offensive (but nonetheless Left) penality, the signers of the infamous call "Republicans, Fear Not!" published by *Le Monde* in September 1998 resort to one of the classic figures of reactionary rhetoric, the "trope of jeopardy," which states in essence: let us hasten to sack a collective good in order to safeguard another that is more threatened still. In the case at hand, let us embrace the "law-and-order" policy implemented in the United States and then in the United Kingdom so as to preserve our democracy under threat and thus launch the "refounding" of the Republic.[117]

> *"To found the Republic anew" requires not an active policy to fight economic insecurity and reduce the social inequalities that have flourished across two decades of almost uninterrupted monetary and budgetary austerity, and the mass unemployment it has spawned, but, much more simply (and economically), a hearty reassertion of state authority, the firm inculcation of school and family discipline, and stringent enforcement of the law, the whole law, and nothing but the law. This is especially true "on the edge of our cities," within those "aberrations" that are the "zones of ethnic settlement" that the article clearly designates as the incubator of the malady. For their residents allegedly suffer first from a deficit, not of jobs and life chances, but of penality, owing to the collapse of the "ancestral respects" devoted in past eras to the (exclusively masculine) figures of order ("the father, the teacher, the mayor, the lieutenant, the shop-floor mate, the party cell secretary") and the "decline of the law in favor of direct action," when it is not in favor of the "law of the underworld" and the "law of the jungle." Régis Debray and his cosignatories thus rehash—apparently without even knowing it—point by point, with a thirty-year lag, the arguments flung by Richard Nixon in the face of the urban riots and protest movements that shook the United States around 1968, which formed the breviary of the social and racial reaction experienced by that country since.[118]*
>
> *Deriding the old-style "justice activists" (which they once were) who, submitting to the "pleasure principle that is the pleasure of principles," behave like "Sisters of Charity" and show an infantile attachment to "the law of good sentiments [which] would dictate prevention without repression," denouncing the recourse to "the SAMU state[119] favored by some of today's Leftists," these advocates for the reinforcement of the penal state in France clamor that one must urgently reestablish "the rule of law" in order eo ipso to allow "access of all to equality." Their reasoning*

presumes that the diligence of the police and the severity of the judges will, by themselves and as it were by magic, open wide the gates to schooling, employment, and civic participation; and that state constraint will restore the legitimacy of a political power that its economic and social policy disqualifies in the eyes of the very citizens whom the penal system must target. They point to the alleged "success of the 'broken-windows' doctrine in New York City," promoted New Jerusalem of the law-and-order religion to which they are exhorting conversion. They peremptorily assert that "it is by tending toward zero tolerance for petty incivility that we will be able tomorrow to resolve large-scale disregard for civic values" and finally tame "savagery in the city." To do this, one must "dare" to make people responsible for their actions and to punish them fearlessly: in short, the state must train *the fractions of the working classes that have fallen back into a kind of state of barbarousness (not to say to the animal level, as suggested by the term "jungle").*

The imperative of responsibility—also imported straight from America: it was the fetish theme of Clinton's campaigns, with his mantra of "opportunity, responsibility, community," and it has already been aped across the Channel by Tony Blair with fair electoral success—is stipulated by way of a psalmody: "making adults responsible for their social conduct"; "making the administrations in charge of the public interest responsible"; "making law-enforcement agencies responsible in the face of daily incivilities" (but not their hierarchy for the abuses, discriminations, and disrespectful treatment that these agencies routinely commit); "making foreigners seeking naturalization responsible" along with "France's international partners" that persist in sending her those immigrants that the country no longer wants (insinuating a causal connection between immigration and crime: it is by mastering the former that one will crush the latter);[120] "making high-school students responsible" by "restoring the basics of discipline everywhere"; and finally, "making minors responsible by lowering the age of penal responsibility" (as in the United States and the United Kingdom, which, not coincidentally, had just passed legislation authorizing the imprisonment of preteens and their arrest for mere "antisocial behavior") on grounds that nowadays one can *"be a lookout at ten, steal a car at thirteen, and kill at sixteen"* (as if there were anything new in that).

These fearless sponsors of the penal (yet *"republican"*) management of poverty solemnly warn that harsh punishment is the only means to make people responsible and to ground institutions, because *"the refusal to punish"* is but *"the first paving stone of hell."* Oblivious to the explosive rise in the number of inmates sentenced for narcotics offenses over the past decade,[121] they assail the alleged leniency of the courts toward the use and trafficking of recreational drugs. They openly deplore the fact that *"unsuspended prison sentences of less than a year are no longer applied in many jurisdictions,"* forgetting (if they ever knew it) that without such a policy of *"penal dualization,"*[122] the carceral population of the European countries would have experienced an increase resembling that of the United States. They feign indignation at the fact that the courts resolve only a small fraction of the cases brought before them—which has always been the case in every country—and surprise at the shortage of resources suffered by the criminal justice system. And, to make their argument more dramatic or seemingly realistic (in the sense of *"Reality TV"*), Debray and his cosignatories pepper their text with ominous references to an American-style drift, with the fearsome fantasy of *"areas of ethnic settlement,"* *"crack in the housing projects,"* and judicial leniency such that *"all offenses,* even the most murderous, *never have any consequences"* (emphasis added).

In truth, there is nothing original in this appeal apart from its claim to intrepidity (its authors write that they are braving the *"intimidation"* and censorship of *"the authoritative thought of prestigious thinkers"*) since it merely echoes aloud what is being hatched in the corridors of state power since the arrival of the *"Plural Left."* It repeats, down to the vocabulary, the slogans that have guided the penal revisionism of the Jospin government from its beginnings. In his inaugural address of June 1997 before Parliament, the new prime minister had elevated *"security"* to the rank of *"paramount duty of the state."* Six months later, the Villepinte Colloquium on *"Safe Cities for Free Citizens"* had made official this promotion of the law-and-order imperative to the rank of priority of governmental action, on a par with the *fight against unemployment (but, curiously, there is no parallel call for applying "zero tolerance" to violations of labor and social law by employers). So it would be a mistake to see in this opinion piece only the expression of the deplorable drift of former leftists and communists who, having grown old and bourgeois, are discovering the virtues of the very authority they held in contempt in their younger days, now that it safeguards their personal comforts. For it is emblematic of the ideological* aggiornamento *of the governmental Left that aims to redefine the perimeter and modalities of state action, in a restrictive direction on the economic and social front, and in an expansive direction in police and penal matters.*

The reasoning of Debray et al. rests on the naive postulate that delinquency is the exception and conformity to the law the rule. In reality, it is exactly the other way around: studies of offending behavior among the youths of European countries, for example, have shown repeatedly that the vast majority of teenagers (between two-thirds and nine-tenths) commit at least one delinquent act in the course of a year (damage to property and vandalism, possession of a weapon, drug use, brawls or riots, and extrafamilial violence).[123] *But, above all, their appeal reveals a stunning, if widespread, ignorance of the urban and penological realities of contemporary France: on the one hand, there is nothing explosive about the so-called explosion of "urban violences" (as shown earlier by trends in official crime statistics) and, on the other hand, the hardening of police and judicial responses that they are clamoring for has already happened, and it has failed to bring in its wake the "republican refoundation" alleged to be its purpose. The carceral population of France has doubled in twenty years, during the very period when the symptoms of the "crisis" of the Republic have proliferated: will it have to double again for the malady to be cured (as was recently proposed in the United States by the fanatics of all-out confinement)?*

The Penal State on Guard

Yesterday, the interior minister, Jean-Pierre Chevènement, asked prefects gathered at Place Beauveau to form "watch committees" *[cellules de veille]* to monitor the most sensitive neighborhoods in matters of urban violence.

In addition to these committees, which will be formed "everywhere where it is necessary," Jean-Pierre Chevènement asked the prefects to ensure "the full and frank cooperation of all law-enforcement agencies" (Public Security, Domestic Information Agency, Criminal Investigation, Border Police, Gendarmerie). They will, moreover, have to "gather, analyze, and make full use of the data collected by these coordinating offices, and to collaborate more closely with state prosecutors to ensure that offenses committed in cases of urban violence receive full criminal prosecution."

—"Brèves" section, *L'Humanité*, February 16, 1999.

The officials of the French governmental Left are not alone in trumpeting the rhetoric of "individual responsibility" and advocating a more generous use of repressive measures against delinquent youth and in awarding themselves at little cost a certificate in penal and moral severity (which allows them to reaffirm in passing their own juridical probity, seriously damaged by multiplying scandals in recent years). Similar measures, lowering the age of criminal responsibility for minors and establishing the joint responsibility of parents in civil and even criminal matters, have recently been discussed by the parliaments of Spain and Italy and are frequently mentioned in the Dutch and German public debate. They are already on the books in England, the bridgehead of the "Americanization" of penal policies in Europe, as attested by the Crime and Disorder Act of 1998, which abolishes *doli incapax* for children between ten and thirteen, institutes curfews for children under ten, and authorizes the placement of preteens as young as ten under probation and in detention starting at twelve on grounds of "antisocial behavior."

It is not by accident that the first prison for children in Europe opened its gates in Kent in spring 1998, under the aegis of a commercial firm and a New Labor government that is locking people up with more zeal than its Conservative predecessors. For England is not content with being the locomotive for "flexibility" on the employment front and the uncontested leader in the campaign for the unilateral economic disarmament of the state through denationalization. It has also converted to privatization on the correctional front: eleven for-profit prisons are now in operation in the United Kingdom and an additional five are about to come on line or are under construction. As in the United States, the detention of illegal immigrants and the transportation of inmates have served, along with the treatment of juvenile delinquency, as beachheads for commercial operators, to whom these missions are now largely subcontracted.[124] And, as in the United States, the directors and top managers of imprisonment firms actively recruit from among senior officials of the country's correctional authority in order to better diffuse inside the state the notion that resorting to the private sector is the ideal means, at once efficient and economical, to pursue the ineluctable expansion of the confinement of poverty.

A new *neoliberal penal common sense* is thus being propagated across Europe—we saw earlier how it crossed the Atlantic through the agency of a network of conservative think tanks and their allies in the bureaucratic, journalistic, and academic fields—articulated around the increased repression of minor offenses, the mounting severity of sentences, the erosion of the specificity of the treatment of juvenile delinquency, the targeting of populations and territories considered "at risk," the deregulation of correctional services, and the redrawing of the division of penal work between the public and private sectors,[125] in perfect harmony with the neoliberal *doxa* in economic and social matters, which it completes and comforts by purging any consideration of a political or civic order to extend the economicist mode of reasoning, the imperative of individual responsibility (whose flip side is collective irresponsibility), and the dogma of the efficiency of the market to the realm of crime and punishment.

As the promised land of the "market evangelists" for two decades, Great Britain has, on the one side, privatized its public services, compressed its social expenditures, and generalized wage-labor precariousness, thenceforth instituted as a veritable norm of employment to which the recipients of the meager public assistance that remains are obliged to conform under the threat of sanction.[126] On the other side, it has significantly hardened its penal policies and expanded recourse to incarceration such that, as in the United States, the budget of the prison service is the public expenditure item that has grown the most since 1979. The carceral population of England and Wales increased slowly under Margaret Thatcher's governments before dropping noticeably from 1990 to 1993 following the Criminal Justice Act of 1991, which was prompted by a string of spectacular carceral revolts. It then swelled suddenly between 1993 and 1998, jumping from under 45,000 to nearly 67,000 in only five years, crossing the mark of

120 inmates per 100,000 inhabitants even as the country's crime rate was steadily decreasing. Over the same period, the number of inmates "contracted out" to the commercial sector jumped from 198 to 3,707 and it is scheduled to double again in the next three years to reach one-tenth of the English carceral "market."[127] At this pace, England will soon catch up with and overtake the United States in the race for carceral inflation and the commercialization of punishment.

Whereas in the United States it is entrepreneurs who supplied the impetus for the resurgence of imprisonment for profit after a half-century of eclipse, in the United Kingdom it is the state that took the initiative as part of a fervent policy of privatization taking on the allure of a crusade. Concretizing the dogma of the superiority of the market in every domain, this policy was propelled by the servile imitation of America, the country pioneering the systematic commodification of public goods under Reagan's command (it was during a study mission to the United States in 1986, at the invitation of Corrections Corporation of America, that Sir Edward Gardiner, the president of the House of Lords Commission on Home Affairs, converted to the virtues of private incarceration). It was further assisted by the work of ideological undermining carried out by neoconservative think tanks (a sensational report by the Adam Smith Institute published in 1987 had recommended ending the "public monopoly" over the provision of "correctional services") and endorsed by the about-face of certain progressive intellectuals (who repeated the error committed by their American counterparts two decades earlier by thinking that any significant prison reform must eventually bring about a strengthening of its rehabilitative component).

The first private prison contracts were thus signed in 1991, without the slightest study having been conducted to buttress the notion, taken to be self-evident, that turning confinement over to the private sector would necessarily translate into a reduction in costs and an improvement in "outputs." In 1992, the Prison Service was even invited to enter competitive bidding for the reopening of the Manchester prison (trashed during the April 1990 riots) so as to demonstrate its capacity to "flexibilize" carceral work—as in Australia, where the introduction of private incarceration in the Province of Queensland in 1989, to the benefit of an Australian subsidiary of Corrections Corporation of America, had the explicit goal of breaking the prison staff union.[128]

When they were in the opposition, the leaders of the Labor Party swore by all the gods that, as soon as they returned to government, they would abolish for-profit imprisonment, on the grounds that "private companies should not make a profit off of state punishment" because "this is a morally repugnant practice." As late as 1994, they promised to bring all the private prisons created under the Tories back into the public fold. But, as early as April 1997, during the electoral campaign that was to open the doors of 10 Downing Street to Anthony Blair, the New Laborites commenced an about-face that would end in a complete alignment on the crime and carceral policy of their Conservative opponents. Jack Straw, a former leftist and future interior minister, promised at first to respect the contracts signed with commercial operators, under the pretext that it would be too costly for the government to denounce them, but as compensation he committed himself to not opening any new private establishment of detention. Hardly a month later, on the morrow of electoral victory, Straw announced to Parliament that it was not possible to "nationalize" Blackenhurst, a private correctional facility in the Midlands whose contract was about to expire. And he promptly invited imprisonment firms to submit their bids for the construction of two new penitentiaries and for the takeover of a third. From "morally repugnant practice," reliance on for-profit prisons has become simply practical and it is now an integral feature of British penal policy, after the fashion of the United States.[129] This newfound "pragmatism" is making possible the addition of some twenty new detention facilities in the coming decade, since the New Labor government is planning on the unprecedented carceral inflation of the past decade to continue unabated.

This is because New Labor has taken over as its own, as well as amplified, the policy of penalization of poverty inaugurated by John Major.[130] And for good reason: it is the indispensable functional complement to the imposition of precarious and underpaid wage labor and to the draconian reduction in social protection that the New Laborites have made the touchstone of their "Third Way" between capitalism and social democracy. Economic deregulation and penal overregulation go hand in hand: *social disinvestment entails and necessitates carceral reinvestment,* which alone is capable of checking the dislocations triggered by the dismantling of the welfare state and the generalization of material insecurity that ineluctably ensues at the bottom of the class structure. All of this augurs well for the future of the four major firms vying for the flourishing private market in the confinement of the poor in England: Group 4, a subsidiary of the Swedish conglomerate Securitas International and the market leader, which counts among its executive officers a former cabinet minister and several former high-ranking officials of the Prison Service who have gone over to for-profit incarceration; United Kingdom Detention Services (UKDS), a joint subsidiary of the U.S. imprisonment giant Corrections Corporation of America and the French institutional catering business Sodexho (which services numerous French prisons placed under semiprivate management opened as part of "Plan 13,000" launched under the Chirac government in 1986); Premier Prisons, born of the alliance of the number two U.S. firm Wackenhut and the English firm Serco, in charge of Gatwick's infamous retention center for foreigners; and Securicor, whose CEO, the brother of a former Tory member of Parliament, enjoys close links to high-ranking members of the Metropolitan Police Department as well as Scotland Yard.

Everything suggests that these firms will cross the Channel, and their American colleagues the Atlantic, as soon as they are given the opportunity to prove that privatizing prisons "pays," as did the privatization of industry, energy, insurance, and banking that preceded it, and above all that it alone is capable of generating and then managing the confinement capacities required to tackle simultaneously the flexibilization of labor and the criminalization of social precariousness.

After Monetary Europe, Police and Penitentiary Europe?

Add to all this the multiplication of specialized operators and contractual schemes aiming to (re)establish "security" (in schools, businesses, neighborhoods, and the city), the proliferation across the Continent of measures intended to preempt or repress breaches of civil norms in public such as municipal decrees prohibiting panhandling and police sweeps against the homeless,[131] the establishment of curfews for minors enforced in a discriminatory manner in dispossessed urban areas (sometimes in total illegality, as in France), the broad deployment of video surveillance in public places and on public transportation, and the popularity enjoyed in advance by "electronic home detention" when there is every indication that it tends to supplement rather than substitute for incarceration, and it becomes clear that these developments are not merely a matter of the "hysterical denial" of the plain impotence of authorities when it comes to crime, which officials concede through their strategies of citizen "responsibilization" and de facto delegation of control over proximate space, as David Garland suggests.[132] They express a deep-seated shift toward the *expansion of the penal treatment of poverty* and the train of disorders and derelictions that, paradoxically, stem precisely from the weakening of the state's capacity for social intervention and the abandonment of its prerogatives in the face of the omnipotent figure of the "market," that is, the unfettered extension of the economic law of the strongest. There are grounds to put forth the hypothesis that this drift toward the police, judicial, and carceral management of urban poverty is all the more probable and pronounced, the more the economic and social policy pursued by the government of the country in question draws its inspiration from neoliberal theories pushing for the "commodification" of social relations, and the weaker the protective capacity of that welfare state to begin with.

It is not by happenstance that, of the large countries of the European Union, England posts the highest incarceration rate (and the rate that has increased the most rapidly over these past several years), the most "deregulated" labor market (whence a record level of poverty and especially of "working poverty"), the deepest social inequalities (which have also risen faster than elsewhere), and the narrowest—as well as the most "Americanized"—system of social protection.[133] It is also not a mere coincidence if the Scandinavian countries, which have best resisted internal and external pressures aiming to dismantle the social state and where institutions of redistribution and collective risk sharing are the most deeply rooted, are also those that confine the least, and where the punitive treatment of social insecurity remains a last resort rather than a first reflex, as attested by the moderate rise in the confined population in Sweden, its near stagnation in Norway and Denmark, and its spectacular fall in Finland (the result of a systematic policy of carceral deflation whereby this country has signaled and solidified its membership in the social-democratic bloc of the Western sphere). Finally, if the Latin countries, Spain, Portugal, and Italy, have also seen their prison population swell abruptly these past few years, it is because they have only recently cut into social assistance programs that were already relatively restrictive, and "modern-ized" their labor market, that is, loosened the rules for layoffs and expanded the conditions for labor exploitation by copying the British (and thus, indirectly, the American) pattern. According to a comparative study focusing on England, Wales, France, Germany, Holland, Sweden, and New Zealand, international differences in incarceration rates and their evolution are not explained by disparities in the crime rates posted by these countries but by differences between their social and penal policies, as well as by the degree of socioeconomic inequality they exhibit.[134]

Everything suggests that an alignment of *social* Europe toward *the bottom,* entailing a further loosening of the political and administrative regulations of the labor market and continued weakening of collective protections against the risks of wage-labor life (unemployment, illness, retirement, poverty), would inescapably be accompanied by an alignment of *penal* Europe toward *the top,* via the generalization of the most severe doctrines and policies pertaining to crime and punishment. The acceleration of monetary integration, leading to the creation of a single currency under a Stability Pact designed to fight inflation by forcing member states to reduce public expenditures and hold wages down, has created a profoundly inhospitable environment for the harmonization of their employment and welfare systems. It fosters the "shift to an American-type economic system where the social safety net is thin and the private insurance sector plays a key role."[135] Such a convergence—of which the diffusion of the most classic law-and-order discourses and measures, wrapped in falsely progressive locutions, among leaders of the European governmental Left is one harbinger—will in due time translate into a vigorous new surge in carceral inflation and a hardening of confinement regimes, under the combined effect of the lack of resources and the repressive drift of the judicial ideologies supposed to justify them, the charge of "laxity" in budgetary matters finding its natural counterpart in denunciations of "leniency" on the policing and punishment front.

This is to say that one must urgently register, opposite the tally of the presumed benefits of the "liberalization" of the wage economy on the European scale, that is, the deregulation of the labor market allowing for increased fragmentation and exploitation of the workforce, the astronomical financial, social, and human costs, nearly always invisible and poorly estimated as they are *diffused or deferred in time,* of the policy of penalization of poverty that is their sociological counterpart at the bottom of the class structure. As Western and Beckett have shown in the case of the United States, the stupendous increase in the population under lock artificially reduces the unemployment rate in the short run by making a significant volume of potential job seekers vanish from the labor-force statistics. But, over the medium and long run, it can only worsen the jobless rate by making those who have sojourned behind bars harder to employ—nay, unemployable in a deskilled labor market that is already overcrowded.[136] One must add to this labor-market impact the destabilizing effects of incarceration on the populations and places most directly put under penal tutelage: the stigmatization and the sense of indignity it carries; the interruption of educational, marital, and occupational trajectories; the destabilization of families and the amputation of social networks; the crystallization of a "culture of resistance" and even defiance of authority in the dispossessed districts where imprisonment is becoming a routine occurrence, even a normal stage in the life course of lower-class young men; and the whole train of pathologies, suffering, and (inter)personal violence commonly associated with passage through the carceral institution.

As the cleanup carriage of social precariousness, the carceral institution does not merely collect and warehouse the (sub)proletarians held as useless, undesirable, or threatening, thus *concealing* deepening poverty and *containing* its most disruptive effects. It also actively contributes to extending and perpetuating the social insecurity and dereliction that feed it and serve as its warrant. A total institution conceived and operated for the poor, and a criminogenic and disculturing milieu shaped by the imperative (and the fantasy) of security, the prison cannot but impoverish those handed over to it and their entourage, by stripping them of the meager resources they possess upon entry, by obliterating under the repellent label of "con" all the statuses liable to confer upon them some socially recognized identity (as son, husband, father, wage earner or unemployed, patient, resident of Marseille or Madrid, etc.), and by thrusting them down into the irresistible spiral of *penal pauperization,* the dark and hidden face of the state's "social policy" toward the dispossessed, normalized by the inexhaustible discourse on "recidivism" and the need to toughen regimes of detention (with the obsessive thematics of "country-club prisons") until they finally prove dissuasive.

The Prison as Poverty Factory

An in-depth field study of seven prisons in France shows that the carceral trajectory of the inmate may be described as a succession of shocks and ruptures governed, on the one hand, by the mandate of internal security of the establishment and, on the other, by the demands and edicts of the judicial apparatus, which combine to propel a programmed descent on the ladder of destitution—a descent that is all the more steep, the more dispossessed the inmate is at the outset.[137] Entry in detention is typically accompanied by the loss of one's job and housing, but also by the partial or total suppression of public aid and other social benefits. This sudden material impoverishment cannot but affect the inmate's family and, in return, fray his ties and weaken his affective relations with those close to him (separation from his partner or wife, "placement" of children with child protective agencies, distancing from friends, etc.). Next comes a series of transfers within the penitentiary archipelago that translate into so much dead time, confiscation or loss of personal possessions, and difficulties in gaining access to the scarce resources of the facility, such as work, job training, and leisure activities.

Finally, whether it be on furlough, on parole, or after discharge, exiting the prison causes a new impoverishment through the expenses it induces (for transportation, clothing, gifts to family and friends, frantic consumption) and because it brutally reveals the poverty that incarceration had temporarily bracketed. "As a closed institution that too often considers the inmate's outside investments as secondary, as a place where the security imperative prevails and that systematically gives priority to the interests of the social body (or the image held of them), which must be protected before the inmate's, the prison actively contributes to rendering precarious the meager assets of a good part of the carceral population and to consolidating temporary situations of poverty."[138]

These field observations on carceral denudement are fully

*confirmed by official correctional statistics: in France 60 percent
of inmates released from jail or prison are jobless, 12 percent are
homeless, and over one-fourth do not have any money at hand—
or, to be more precise, less than a hundred francs (twenty dollars), the threshold below which the correctional administration
acknowledges their status as "indigent" and grants them limited
aid (foreign inmates are even more destitute, with 68 percent,
29 percent, and 30 percent, respectively). Half of them have never
received a visit from a family member or friend during their sojourn behind bars, and nearly one-third have no one waiting for
them as they reenter society. One inmate in three suffers from at
least three of these five handicaps, which makes "reintegration"
a dubious enterprise considering the weakness of the means allocated to supporting them on the outside and the multiple obstacles faced by "ex-cons."*[139]

*But there is worse yet: the impoverishing effects of penal con-
finement are not limited to inmates alone. The prison's perimeter
of influence extends far beyond its walls as it exports its poverty
by destabilizing the families and neighborhoods subjected to its
tropism. The result is that the carceral treatment of poverty continually (re)produces the conditions for its own extension: the
more the poor are locked up, the more they are guaranteed to
remain durably poor, ceteris paribus, and consequently the more
they offer a convenient target for the policy of criminalization of
poverty. The penal management of social insecurity thus feeds on
its own programmed failure.*

No Solidarity for France's Inmates

The United States systematically excludes its 2 million inmates from social
protection and redistribution in the form of welfare, social security, disability, and other government benefits. France does not do much better since its
54,000 detainees and prisoners are largely kept out of the social allowances
programs for which they are eligible on the outside on account of their marginal position on the labor market and the weakness of their savings and
assets (when they have any).

If they can, in the best of cases, continue to collect the guaranteed minimum old-age pension, disability stipends, and widower's allowance (which
obviously is statistically unlikely given their age distribution), French inmates
are barred from the specific solidarity allowance (ASS), single-parent aid

(API), and payments from unemployment insurance (ASSEDIC) even when they have contributed to the latter. And a "perfidious decree"—to use the carefully weighed expression of Jean-Michel Belorgey, the Socialist representative who shepherded the bill that instituted the national guaranteed minimum income plan (RMI) through the National Assembly[140]—sneaked through by the Socialist government of Michel Rocard in December 1988 excludes them from the RMI after the sixtieth day of detention, even though it is well documented that, if there is a population for which pecuniary help and durable support toward social integration are both vital, in the strong sense of the word, it is prisoners.

Remittance of the RMI to inmates who are entitled to it "outside" would have four virtues. First, it would contribute to alleviating the deep class inequalities that stamp the experience of detention and gravely contravene the principle of justice. Second, it would facilitate the maintenance of carceral peace by minimizing the trafficking, racketeering, and violence fueled by the extreme material deprivation of a very large part of the confined population (this is why a great many prison wardens favor it). Thus, it is an open secret among correctional staff and outside service providers that a good number of France's inmates have to prostitute themselves[141] to obtain the necessities of daily life—soap (which is used for bathing, cleaning dishes, and laundry), hygiene and grooming supplies, and cigarettes—or to be able to purchase goods from the prison store *(cantiner)* and improve their diet, or to buy themselves medicines, to not mention correspondence courses, which cost money and are well outside the financial reach of the convicts who need them the most. The state is not content here with depriving inmates of liberty: it also enforces material and moral poverty upon the occupants of jails and prisons.

In the third place, the RMI allowance would help preserve family solidarity by avoiding situations where the inmate suddenly turns into an unbearable financial burden for those close to him. The price of incarceration can indeed prove prohibitive for relatives, as one must add to the loss of the income of the prisoner the considerable expenses that his confinement causes (monies deposited on his account, linens, payments for the canteen, transportation for visits, legal fees and court costs, etc.). Finally, and above all, granting this allowance to those inmates who are eligible for it according to the rules of common law is to mark symbolically that inmates still belong to the community of citizens (or denizens) and to better prepare for their eventual return to society. There exists no juridical justification, and still less any penological rationale, for this destitution of social rights, which is akin to "double sentencing" for nationals—foreigners are already largely excluded from the RMI on the outside.

In any case, *the European penal state is already in the process of being built* in practice, whereas the construction of a continental social state is still stagnating at the level of sketches and pious wishes.

For the Europe of the free circulation of capital, goods, and persons is also the Europe of police, judicial, and correctional cooperation, and this cooperation has greatly intensified in the wake of recent advances in economic and monetary integration.[142] Thus, as described by political scientist Didier Bigo, the networks of informal relations and interpersonal contacts woven during the 1970s within the antidrug groups, the antiterrorism clubs (of Bern, Trevi, Quantico, and Kilowatt), and colloquiums among European police officials were harnessed together and formalized by the Schengen agreements of 1985 and 1990. These agreements have extended the right to cross-border observation and pursuit, assigned liaison officers to the police departments of other national states, and created the "Schengen computerized system" (or SIS, "système informatisé de Schengen"), a data bank located in Strasbourg that contains the files sent by all the signatory countries on persons implicated in serious crimes as well as on foreigners who have been denied visas or admission at their border. The Maastricht Treaty has institutionalized police cooperation in the fight against terrorism, organized crime, cross-border crime, and narcotics. The so-called K-4 Committee, created under the aegis of the Justice and Home Affairs Council by Title VI of the treaty, has also the mission of fostering the harmonization of the policies of member states in the realms of civil and criminal justice, immigration, and the right to asylum.

These accords, conventions, and commissions that are proliferating and operating in the penumbra of the nascent European bureaucratic field have extended the notion of "domestic security" so as to encompass in it the entry and cross-border movements of foreigners from countries outside the Euro-American sphere, who are in effect defined as a menace against the integrity of the territory that these agreements are intended to govern—the "Schengen space" until they cover the totality of the member nations of the Union. The political-administrative coupling "border–crime–immigration" partakes of the demonization of (non Euro-American) foreigners and reinforces the conflation of immigration and insecurity that feeds the xenophobic currents that have swept through most Western European societies over the past decade or so.

The Europol convention under discussion since 1995 will soon result in the establishment of a European Police Bureau, endowed with an independent juridical personality, also headquartered in Strasbourg, that prefigures an eventual federal police on the scale of the European Union. Finally, for two decades already, the heads of the correctional administrations of the member countries of the Council of Europe have been meeting regularly (twice per year lately) within the Council for Penological Cooperation, in order to confront their experiences, define common standards of detention, and harmonize their practices. The creation of the single market in the late 1980s has thus been accompanied by an acceleration of the Europeanization of policing and security, promoted to the rank of "third construction site, admittedly discreet, nay secret, but which is being built up more rapidly and is mobilizing almost as much energy and staff as the building of monetary Europe and military Europe, which are much more media-friendly." And, much as the rise of the penal state in America has diametrically opposite effects at the two ends of the social and ethnoracial hierarchy, the development of policing at a distance and network policing on the European scale opens onto an "era of greater freedom of movement for the majority of citizens while concentrating surveillance on minorities and cross-border flows,"[143] which are in effect subjected to a monitoring that is discriminatory in principle as well as in its modalities.

In this context, the experience of the few countries that, as a result of voluntaristic policies, have acted to deflate or stabilize their carceral population in recent years, in particular by generalizing the use of fines, expanding parole release, and sensitizing judges to the harsh realities of life behind bars, takes on a particular analytic and political value (see Table 5). Thus, between 1985 and 1995, Austria reduced its incarceration rate by 29 percent, Finland by 25 percent, and Germany by 6 percent (before unification). This rate remained stable in Denmark as well

Table 5. Carceral deflation in three European countries, 1983–2000

Country	1983	1990	1997	2000	Change
(West) Germany	62,525	48,548	60,489	NA	–4%
Austria	8,387	6,231	6,954	6,986	–8%
Finland	4,709	3,106	2,798	2,703	–41%
Denmark	3,120	3,213	3,299	3,279	15%

Source: *Statistiques pénales annuelles du Conseil de l'Europe, Enquête 2000* (Strasbourg: Council of Europe, 2001).

as in Ireland. And these movements of carceral depopulation have had no detectable negative impact on the level of crime.[144]

The results achieved by these societies remind us that in penal as in social matters—insofar as one can still distinguish between these two registers of public action in the lowest regions of social and urban space—one always stands within what Marcel Mauss called "the domain of modality." No more than precarious wage labor, carceral inflation is not a natural fate or a calamity preordained by some distant and untouchable divinity: it pertains to cultural preferences and political decisions that need to be subjected to full scrutiny and broad democratic debate. Like every social phenomenon, according to Mauss, it is a "work of collective will, and who says human will says choice between different possible options."[145] It is urgent that these options be clearly identified and evaluated as such, and not selected surreptitiously or (worse) blindly adopted only to be later presented as so many inescapable and irreparable evolutions.

The experience of the United States demonstrates at any rate that one cannot today, any more than at the close of the nineteenth century, separate social policy and penal policy or, to put it summarily, wage work, social work (if it can still be called that), and the police, courts, and prison, without prohibiting oneself from understanding the one and the other as well as their interconnected transformations.[146] For, wherever it manages to become reality, the neoliberal utopia brings in its wake, for the most dispossessed—but also for all those who will sooner or later fall out of the sector of protected employment—not an enhancement of freedom, as its devotees clamor, but its abridgement, nay its suppression, as result of a regression toward a repressive paternalism of another age, that of savage capitalism, but augmented by an omniscient and omnipotent punitive state. The "invisible hand" dear to Adam Smith has indeed returned, but this time it is backed up by an overgrown "iron fist."

America has clearly opted for the criminalization of poverty as a complement to the generalization of wage precariousness and social insecurity. Europe stands at the crossroads, faced with a historic alternative between, on the one side, in the mid-term, the mass confinement of the poor and intensified police surveillance and penal control of the populations destabilized by the revolution in wage work and the weakening of social protection it mandates, and, on the other side, starting today, the *creation of new citizens' rights*—such as a guaranteed minimum income independent of work performance,[147] lifetime education and job training, effective access to housing for all, and universal medical coverage—accompanied by an offensive reconstruction of the social capacities of the state eventually leading to the creation of a European social state worthy of the name. On this choice depends the type of civilization Europe intends to offer its citizens.

Three

The Great Penal Leap Backward: Incarceration in America from Nixon to Clinton

In 1967, as the Vietnam War and race riots were roiling the country, President Lyndon B. Johnson received a report on its judicial and correctional institutions from a group of government experts. The Commission on Law Enforcement and Administration of Justice related that the inmate count in federal penitentiaries and state prisons was slowly diminishing, by about 1 percent per annum.[1] That year, America's penal establishments held some 426,000 inmates, projected to grow to 523,000 in 1975 as a by-product of national demographic trends. Neither prison overcrowding nor the inflation of the population behind bars was on the horizon, even as crime rates were steadily rising. Indeed, the federal government professed to accelerate this downward carceral drift through the expanded use of probation and parole and the generalization of community sanctions aimed at diverting offenders from confinement. Six years later, it was Richard Nixon's turn to receive a report on the evolution of the country's carceral system. The National Advisory Commission on Criminal Justice Standards and Goals noted that the population under lock had stopped receding. Nonetheless, it recommended a ten-year moratorium on the construction of large correctional facilities as well as the phasing out of establishments for the detention of juveniles. It counseled shifting away decisively from the country's "pervasive overemphasis on custody" because it was proven that "the prison, the reformatory, and the jail have achieved nothing but a shocking record of failure. There is overwhelming evidence that these institutions create crime rather than prevent it."[2]

At about the same time, Alfred Blumstein and his associates put forth their so-called homeostatic theory of the level of incarceration in modern societies. According to the renowned criminologist, each country presents not a "normal" level of crime, as Émile Durkheim had proposed a century earlier in his classic theory of deviance, but a constant level of punishment resulting in a roughly stable rate of penal confinement outside of "severely disruptive periods like wars or depressions." When this rate departs from its natural threshold, various stabilizing mechanisms are set into motion: the police, prosecutors, courts, and parole boards adjust their response to crime in a permissive or restrictive direction so as to redraw the boundary of deviant behaviors subjected to penal sanction, adjust sentences, and thereby reduce or increase the volume of people behind bars. The proof for this view was found in time-series analyses of the feeble oscillations of the imprisonment rates revealed by U.S. statistics since the Great Depression and by Canadian and Norwegian statistics since the closing decades of the nineteenth century.[3]

As for the revisionist historians of the penal institution, from David Rothman to Michael Ignatieff by way of Michel Foucault, they substituted a strategic narrative of power for the humanistic trope of enlightened reform and painted imprisonment not merely as a stagnant institution but as a practice in irreversible if gradual decline, destined to occupy a secondary place in the diversifying arsenal of contemporary instruments of punishment. Thus Rothman concluded his historiographic account of the concurrent invention of the penitentiary for criminals, the asylum for the insane, and the almshouse for the poor in the Jacksonian republic by sanguinely asserting that the United States was "gradually escaping from institutional responses" so that "one can foresee the period when incarceration will be used still more rarely than it is today."[4] For Foucault, "the carceral technique" played a pivotal part in the advent of the "disciplinary society," but only inasmuch as it became diffused throughout the "social body as a whole" and fostered the transition from "inquisitory justice" to "examinatory justice." The prison turned out to be only one island among many in the vast "carceral archipelago" of modernity that links into a seamless panoptic web the family, the school, the convent, the hospital, and the factory, and of which the human sciences unwittingly partake: "In the midst of all these apparatuses of normalization which are becoming tighter, the specificity of the prison and its role as hinge lose something of their raison d'être."[5]

Spotlighting this tendency toward the dispersal of social control exercised by the state, the radical sociology of the prison hastened to denounce the anticipated perverse effects of "decarceration." Andrew Scull maintained that the movement to release inmates, from behind the walls of penitentiaries and mental hospitals alike, into the community worked against the interests of deviant and subordinate groups by giving the state license to unload its responsibility to care for them. Conversely, Stanley Cohen warned against the dangers of the new ideology of the "community control" of crime on grounds that diversion from prison at once blurs, widens, intensifies, and disguises social control under the benevolent mask of "alternatives to imprisonment." These academic critiques were echoed for the broader public by such journalistic exposés as Jessica Mitford's portrait of the horrors of America's "prison business" and of the "lawlessness of corrections," leading to the denunciation of further prison building as "the establishment of a form of legal concentration camp to isolate and contain the rebellious and the politically militant."[6]

In short, by the mid-1970s a broad consensus had formed among state managers, social scientists, and radical critics according to which the future of the prison in the United States was anything but bright. The rise of a militant prisoners' rights movement patterned after the black insurgency that had brought down the Southern caste regime a decade earlier, including drives to create inmates' unions and to foster convict self-management, and the spread of full-scale carceral uprisings throughout the United States, followed by their diffusion to other Western societies (Canada, England, France, Spain, and Italy), powerfully reinforced this shared sense of an institution mired in unremitting and irreversible crisis.[7]

The Great American Carceral Boom

Yet nothing could have been further from the truth, as the prison was just about to enter an era not of final doom but of startling boom.

Beginning in 1973, American penal evolution abruptly reversed course and *the population behind bars underwent exponential growth,* on a scale without precedent in the history of democratic societies. On the morrow of the 1971 Attica revolt, acme of a wide and powerful internal movement of protest against the carceral order,[8] the United States sported a rate of incarceration of 176 per 100,000 inhabitants—two to three times the figure for the major European countries. By 1985, this rate had doubled to reach 310 before doubling again over the ensuing decade to pass the 700 mark in mid-2000 (see Table 6). To gauge how extreme this scale of confinement is, suffice it to note that it is about 40 percent higher than South Africa's at the height of the armed struggle against apartheid and six to twelve times the rate of the countries of the European Union, even though the latter have also seen their incarceration rate rise rapidly over the past two decades. During the period 1985–95, the United States amassed nearly 1 million more inmates at an infernal pace of an additional 1,631 bodies per week, equivalent to incorporating the confined population of France every six months. As of 2000, when runaway growth finally appeared to taper off, the population held in county jails, state prisons, and federal penitentiaries had reached 1,931,000 people and crossed the 2-million milestone if one reckons juveniles in custody (109,000).

There are three types of carceral establishments in the United States. The 3,300 city and county jails house suspects brought in by the police, awaiting arraignment or trial, as well as convicts

Table 6. Growth of the carceral population of the United States, 1975–2000

	1975	1980	1985	1990	1995	2000
County jails	138,800	182,288	256,615	405,320	507,044	621,149
Federal and state prisons	240,593	315,974	480,568	739,980	1,078,357	1,310,710
Total	379,393	498,262	737,183	1,145,300	1,585,401	1,931,850
Growth index	100	131	194	302	418	509

Source: Bureau of Justice Statistics, *Historical Corrections Statistics in the United States, 1850–1984* (Washington, D.C.: U.S. Government Printing Office, 1986), and Bureau of Justice Statistics, *Prison and Jail Inmates at Midyear 2000* (Washington, D.C.: U.S. Government Printing Office, 2001).

in transit between facilities or sanctioned by terms of confine-
ment inferior to one year. The 1,450 state prisons of the fifty
members of the Union hold felons sentenced to terms exceeding
one year, while those convicted under the federal penal code are
sent to one of the 125 federal prisons, irrespective of the length
of their sentence. Each sector possesses its own enumeration sys-
tem, which explains discrepancies in the data over time (includ-
ing when they come from the same source). This census excludes
establishments for juveniles, military prisons (which held 2,400
inmates at end of 2000), facilities run by the Immigration and
Naturalization Service (8,900), prisons in U.S. overseas territo-
ries (16,000), and jails on Native American reservations (1,800).
It also omits police lockups, which are more numerous than jails
(in 1993, 3,200 police departments operated one or more such
facilities with an average capacity of ten detainees).[9]

One might think that after fifteen years of such frenetic growth
American jails and prisons would reach saturation and that certain of
the homeostatic mechanisms postulated by Blumstein would kick in.
Indeed, by the early 1990s, federal penitentiaries were officially operating at 146 percent of capacity and state prisons at 131 percent, even
though the number of establishments had tripled in thirty years and
wardens had taken to systematically "double-bunking" inmates. In
1992, forty of fifty states and the District of Columbia were under court
order to remedy overpopulation and stem the deterioration of conditions of detention on pain of heavy fines and prohibitions on further incarceration. So much so that many jurisdictions took to hastily releasing
thousands of nonviolent inmates to disgorge their facilities and that over
50,000 convicts sentenced to terms exceeding one year were consigned
to county facilities in 1995 for want of space in state prisons.

But America's carceral bulimia did not abate: at the end of the
single year 1995, as Clinton prepared to campaign for reelection on
a platform of "community, responsibility, and opportunity" but-
tressed by the "end of Big Government," an additional 107,300 found
themselves behind bars, corresponding to an extra 2,064 inmates per
week.[10] Eight states had seen their carceral population grow by more
than 50 percent between 1990 and 1995: Arizona, Wisconsin, Georgia,
Minnesota, Mississippi, Virginia, North Carolina, and Texas, which

Table 7. States leading carceral expansion, 1993

State	State and federal prisons	County jails	Total incarcerated	Incarceration rate per 100,000 residents
California	119,951	69,298	189,249	607
Texas	71,103	55,395	126,498	700
New York	64,569	29,809	94,378	519
Florida	53,048	34,183	87,231	636
Ohio	40,641	11,695	52,336	473
Michigan	39,529	12,479	52,008	550
France	—	—	51,457	84
Georgia	27,783	22,663	50,446	730
Illinois	34,495	14,549	49,044	420
Pennsylvania	26,050	19,231	45,281	376
United States	948,881	459,804	1,408,685	546

Note: States are ranked by total incarcerated population.
Sources: For city and county jails, Bureau of Justice Statistics, *Jail and Jail Inmates, 1993–94* (Washington, D.C.: U.S. Government Printing Office, 1995). For federal and state prisons, Bureau of Justice Statistics, *Prisoners in 1993* (Washington, D.C.: U.S. Government Printing Office, 1994). For state populations, estimates by the U.S. Census Bureau available online.

held the national record with a doubling in a short five years. As early as 1993, six states each counted more inmates than France (see Table 7). California, with 32 million inhabitants, confined nearly as many as the eleven largest continental countries of the European Union put together. Georgia, with a mere 7 million residents, had more inmates than Italy with 50 million.

And this is but the emerging point of the American penal iceberg, for these figures do not take into account offenders placed on probation or released on parole after having served the greater part of their sentence (typically, 85 percent by virtue of federal "truth-in-sentencing" mandates). Now, their numbers far surpass the inmate count and they too increased steeply following the penal turnaround of the mid-1970s. Between 1980 and 2000, the total number of persons on probation leaped from 1.1 million to 3.8 million, while those on parole shot from 220,000 to nearly 726,000. As a result, *the popu-*

Table 8. Population under correctional supervision in the United States, 1980–2000 (in thousands)

Year	Probation	Jail	Prison	Parole	Total
1980	1,118	184	320	220	1,842
1985	1,969	257	488	300	3,013
1990	2,670	405	743	531	4,350
1995	3,078	507	1,078	679	5,343
2000	3,840	621	1,312	726	6,467

Source: Bureau of Justice Statistics, *Correctional Populations in the United States, 2000* (Washington, D.C.: U.S. Government Printing Office, 2002), 2.

lation placed under correctional supervision approached 6.5 million at the end of this period, as against 4.3 million ten years earlier and under 1 million in 1975.

These 6.5 million individuals represent 3 percent of the country's adult population and one American male in twenty (Table 8). Breaking that figure down by ethnicity reveals that one black man in nine today is under criminal oversight. We will indeed see later that the massive and rapidly growing overrepresentation of African Americans at all levels of the penal system expresses the new role that the latter has assumed in the panoply of instruments of ethnoracial domination since the ghetto uprisings of the 1960s.

A Correctional Marshall Plan

Another reliable indicator of the stupendous prosperity of the penal economy of the United States in the past two decades: the "corrections" rubric in the country's budget soared from $9 billion in 1982 to $54 billion in 1999. It now consumes fully one-third of direct public expenditures devoted to crime control of $160 billion, behind $70 billion for the police and well ahead of the $36 billion allotted to the courts. For the first time in modern American history, local governments spend more on criminal justice than they do on education, since 1977 in the case of cities and since 1982 as concerns counties. And this gap has been growing since crime control budgets at all levels have risen faster than other public expenditures: in 1995, in spite of several years of steadily declining crime rates, the states were set to augment their corrections outlays by an average of 8 percent per year, as against a 4.3 percent increase for schools and 2.1 percent for the main assistance program for destitute households, Aid to Families with Dependent Children.[11] Between 1977 and 1999, total state and local government funds for all functions rose by 400 percent; education budgets grew by only 370 percent, hospitals and health care by 418 percent, while corrections exploded by 946 percent.

The result of this priority given to penal over social functions is that incarceration has overtaken the two main programs of assistance to the poor in the nation's budget (see Table 9). In 1980, the United States spent three times more on Aid to Families with Dependent Children and food stamps taken together than it did on operating its jails and prisons ($11 billion plus $10 billion versus $7 billion); in 1985, these three programs received each the same sum of about $13 billion; ten years later, on the eve of the abolition of "welfare as we know it" on account of its excessive drain on the government's coffers, incarceration surpassed AFDC by 130 percent and food stamps by 70 percent. Yet there is scarcely any mention in the official debate on crime of the burden that an out-of-control correctional system places on taxpayers. Worse yet, on the heels of the most costly criminal justice package ever voted in world history, the Omnibus Crime Control Act of 1994, Congress passed the 1995 No Frills Prison Act, which compels states to apply "truth-in-sentencing" provisions (on pain of losing federal funds earmarked for prison construction) requiring that all convicts serve at least 85 percent of their sentence before being eligible for parole release, thereby guaranteeing massive across-the-board increases in correctional expenditures for years to come.

Table 9. Comparative evolution of correctional and public aid budgets, 1980–95 (in billions of current dollars)

	1980	1982	1984	1986	1988	1990	1992	1993	1995
Corrections (state and federal)	6.9	9.0	11.8	15.8	20.3	26.1	31.5	31.9	46.2
Aid to Families with Dependent Children	10.9	12.1	13.4	14.3	15.5	17.1	20.4	20.3	19.9
Food stamps	9.6	11.7	13.3	13.5	14.4	17.7	24.9	26.3	27.4

Sources: Kathleen Maguire and Ann L. Pastore, *Sourcebook of Criminal Justice Statistics, 1996* (Washington, D.C.: Bureau of Justice Statistics, 1997), 3; Lea Gifford, *Justice Expenditures and Employment in the United States, 1995* (Washington, D.C.: Bureau of Justice Statistics, November 1999), 8; and Committee on Ways and Means, *1996 Green Book* (Washington, D.C.: U.S. Government Printing Office, 1997), 459, 861, 921.

The same disproportionate expansion in favor of penal functions has affected county and state employment: while the staff devoted to social services and education has stagnated or decreased over the past two decades, the American crime-fighting machine doubled its personnel to 2.2 million in 1999, including 717,000 in correctional administrations, taking in an annual payroll of some $8 billion.[12] Fourteen states and the District of Columbia now have more than 13 percent of their employees in the justice system (in Florida, Nevada, and the District of Columbia, this share approaches one in five). To say the least, the doctrine of "small government" and the policy of downsizing public employment have not applied to penal confinement, whose unit cost has also risen steadily. In 1996, operating expenditures for state prisons came to $20,142 per inmate after a 20 percent increase in a decade in constant dollars,[13] with most large states of the East and Midwest falling in the $20,000 to $30,000 range and Southern states lagging noticeably behind—seven of the eight states with annual costs inferior to $14,000 per inmate were located in the South, led by Alabama with a measly $7,987. Given that staff salaries and wages consume about half of prison operating expenses, these regional disparities are explained primarily by lower pay and by the much higher inmate-to-staff ratio common in the South: in 1998, Alabama had one correctional employee for every 7 prisoners compared to one for 3.8 for California and one for 2.6 in Michigan and Minnesota.

"Government recognizes that it cannot allow the growth rate in its corrections budgets to continue at the pace of recent history. The private sector is the best way to constrain this growth. We save money on the front end, then hold increases to a minimum. At CCA, we understand the enormous opportunity this presents for our future."[14] As this address to investors by the chief executive officer of Corrections Corporation of America indicates, the mad dash to mass imprisonment into which the United States has thrown itself has spawned *a new and thriving industry, private incarceration,* whose growth and profit rates rivaled those of the leading sectors of the national economy at the height of the mid-1990s boom. Two forces have combined to foster the resurgence of for-profit imprisonment a half-century after the banning of the Southern convict-lease system, the one ideological and the other material.

The first force is the ascendancy of the doctrine of privatization orchestrated by neoconservative think tanks and widely relayed by the mainstream media and the established parties. Whether to care for orphans, to deliver health and social services, or to supply housing for the poor, since Ronald Reagan successive governments have consistently turned to firms and charitable organizations to carry out public missions. This "new bipartisan consensus on market principles as the template for social policy"[15] was extended to encompass corrections under the press of the second factor of material expediency. For counties and states simply did not have the capacity to contain the onrushing flood of inmates they unleashed: they possess neither the fiscal and human resources nor the bureaucratic agility to finance, design, build, and staff the thousands of additional cells they have needed every year.[16] So they turned to specialized firms that promised to deliver facilities in short order while trimming the costs of confinement by 10 to 20 percent per head, thanks to their ready access to the bond market, the low wages and paltry benefits they provide their guards (who, unlike their colleagues in the public sector, are not unionized), and their license to circumvent cumbersome bureaucratic regulations. As a result, in just over a decade, privately built and operated facilities went from nonexistent to forming an integral and seemingly irreversible component of the U.S. carceral system, extending across all security levels and present in two dozen states, where they contribute up to one-fourth of total capacity: "A critical mass has been reached in terms of prison and inmates numbers and percentages, custodial responsibilities as manifested by security ratings, participating states, and commercial maturity. In addition, the financing arrangements tie governments in private sector participation in ways that would be difficult to unscramble."[17]

Aside from supplying the gamut of goods and services required for operating a custodial facility (furniture, food, maintenance, health care, safety and surveillance, communication systems, etc.) as well as correctional services (such as education, drug treatment, and psychological counseling), which have long been largely contracted out to the commercial sector, by the late 1990s a dozen firms divided up the fast-growing market for the financing, construction, and management of private establishments of detention. In 1997, there were still only about one hundred of them, distributed across nineteen states, but they were spreading at vertiginous speed. From zero in 1983 at the founding of the Correctional Corporation of America, the number of "private beds" in the United States escalated to 15,000 in 1990 before surpassing 85,000 in 1997, corresponding to some 6 percent of the country's carceral population (and equal to the inmate count of Spain and Italy put together). That year, one-fourth of the 100,000 new beds put "on line" by the country's correctional system came from the private sector. With revenues doubling every two years and a seemingly infinite supply of new bodies to warehouse, it is no wonder that the top managers of the major corrections firms were unanimous in predicting that their market share would at least triple over the ensuing decade.[18] The facilities director for the fourth-largest enterprise in the industry commented in 1998:

> The era of prejudice against private prisons is behind us. More and more states are looking at privatization without that sort of prejudice, because it's been around long enough now, where there was a really big "wait-and-see" attitude, and some states were very reluctant. But once privatization proved to be a viable alternative to the states, then more and more states are doing it too. And it's less expensive than the public sector to do it this way. . . .
> *So this movement of opposition to the privatization of prisons is behind us?*
> It's dying. And that's spilling over into the juvenile field too: more and more states and counties are looking into privatization in the juvenile area.

With 26 federal prisons and 96 state penitentiaries under construction in 1996, the financing of carceral building has become one of the most profitable sectors in the bonds market. This was not lost on the big Wall Street brokerage firms, such as Goldman Sachs, Smith Barney Shearson, Prudential-Bache, and Merrill Lynch, which sank $2 to $3 billion dollars per year into it during the 1990s.[19] The siting of penitentiaries has, by the same token, turned into a potent tool for regional economic development. Towns in declining mono-industrial regions and remote rural areas in particular have scrambled to entice state officials and private operators to locate a prison in their midst: they appeared to be recession-proof "industries" with few negative externalities and the guarantee of perennial employment, business, and tax receipts.[20] A large-scale market in the import-export of inmates has even emerged, as correctional operators in areas with available beds court jurisdictions with a surplus of bodies desperate for room in which to lock them. As of 2000, some 15,000 inmates were kept in facilities outside their state of conviction. The deep crisis that shook up the private incarceration industry in the wake of the bursting of the stock-market and technology "bubble" in 2000 has stopped its runaway growth, but it has failed to significantly curtail its role in the punitive economy of the country.

The Crime–Incarceration Disconnect

How are we to explain this "great leap backward" of the American carceral apparatus when all the observers of the penal scene agreed in forecasting its downturn—if not, for the boldest of them, its extinction—only a quarter of a century ago? The official doctrine on the matter, diffused conjointly by state managers, elected officials, and the media, is that it is a response to the relentless growth of crime, and especially violent crime (that is, offenses against persons as distinct from offenses against property). After the aborted "War on Poverty" of the 1960s, the U.S. government decided to wage a "War on Crime" and devoted the necessary means to it.[21] This endeavor was supported by a public that has been increasingly and intensely concerned about its safety as crime intensified and diffused throughout society. But there is a catch: this commonsense argument is directly contradicted by all the available data, provided that one examines them closely.

First, with few exceptions, well localized in time and space, crime rates have not increased but have *stagnated and then declined* over the past three decades. Next, the vast majority of new convicts thrown behind bars over the years have not been dangerous and hardened criminals but small-time, *nonviolent offenders*. And, finally, contrary to the obsessive drumbeat of the media, which have made commercial hay out of the daily spectacle of criminal violence, most Americans have had little reason to live in terror of anonymous physical aggression for the latter remains strongly concentrated in social and physical space.[22]

As Figure 4 shows, the gross volume of crimes and misdemeanors committed in the United States remained roughly constant and then declined during the period corresponding to the steep takeoff of the carceral population. From 1973 to 1982, in good years and bad, about 40 million Americans were victims of criminal offenses. By 1992 this

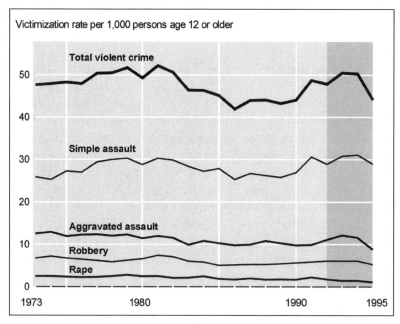

Figure 4. Trends in violent criminal victimization in the United States, 1973–95. *Source:* Bureau of Justice Statistics, *Criminal Victimization in the United States, 1975–1995* (Washington, D.C.: U.S. Government Printing Office, 1997).

figure had fallen to about 35 million—and this decline has accelerated since then to a low of 25 million in 2000. A close reading of the findings of the National Crime Victimization Survey confirms the drop in major criminal infractions and directly refutes the idea that the explosion of incarceration results from an upsurge in crime rates.[23] Thus, among offenses against persons, the frequency of robberies declined between 1974 and 1978 before rising until 1981; it then headed down again from 1981 to 1985 before slowly increasing until 1994—all without leaving a narrow range of between 200 and 250 incidents per 100,000 residents. The rate for aggravated assaults receded markedly from 1974 until the mid-1980s—just when the prison boom was getting under way—before stabilizing and then climbing back to its initial level from 1990 to 1993; it then fell sharply to reach its lowest point in twenty-three years. Constant from 1977 to 1979 after a three-year rise, the probability of being a victim of assault has declined without interruption since; today it is at the same level as at the end of the 1960s.

According to the Federal Bureau of Investigation's annual *Uniform Crime Report,* the murder and nonnegligent manslaughter rate fluctuated between 8 and 10 per 100,000 inhabitants between 1975 and 1995 without showing any particular trend in either direction. To be sure, the number of murders recorded by the FBI exceeded 23,300 in 1994, as against 20,700 eight years earlier, but as a proportion of the country's population their occurrence was virtually unchanged. And, again, since 1995 the murder rate has declined markedly to close in on 5 per 100,000 in 2000 (corresponding to 12,943 victims). As for offenses concerning property (burglary, simple theft, and auto theft), their frequency went down uniformly and continuously from 1974 to 1995, with the exception of the period 1985 to 1990 for motor vehicle theft. Overall, the victimization rate for property crime in the United States dropped steadily from 540 for 1,000 households in 1974 to 385 for 1,000 in 1995, and it has continued to recede in the years since to sag below 200 in 1999.[24]

Finally, during the 1980s the expression "random violence" became a staple of public discourse about crime and served as blanket justification for the hardening of penal responses. A succession of media panics about "drive-by shootings" and freeway violence, "wilding" and stalking, kids and guns, carjackings, gang initiations, and so-called sexual predators nourished the collective sense, cemented by the discourse of officials and official criminologists, that violent crime had become pandemic, predatory, and unpredictable, and was spiraling out of control. In 1994, the Federal Bureau of Investigation accompanied the release of its latest installment of the *Uniform Crime Report* with this alarming note: "Every American now has a realistic chance of murder victimization in view of the random nature that crime has assumed."[25] Yet the very data that the FBI compiles directly refutes this notion by displaying the obdurate social and geographic patterning of serious offenses against persons. The perennial variables of race, class, sex, and residence have never ceased to determine gaping disparities in chances of victimization. Thus, between 1975 and 1995, the murder rate of whites remained consistently one-sixth that of blacks (it fluctuated between a low of 4.8 and a high of 6.3 per 100,000 while the figures for blacks ranged from 27.7 to 39.3). Throughout that period, the incidence of homicide for white females over twenty-five years of age remained extremely low, oscillating between 2.6 and 3.3 per 100,000—and in the large majority of cases they were killed by lovers and spouses (typically of the same ethnicity), not by strangers. In 1995, the frequency of robberies in the suburbs was one-third that in cities; the robbery rate for suburban white females was 2.0 per 1,000 persons ages twelve and over compared to 24.6 for black men in urban centers. At the height of the fear of lethal violence from anonymous black men in public space, widely perceived as the modal crime risk, only 699 of 4,954 white victims had been killed by black assailants, representing a mere 3 percent of the 22,434 homicides recorded that year.[26]

Now, there was a spectacular and abrupt upsurge in murders between 1985 and 1993, but there was nothing "random" about it: it concerned essentially unemployed young black men in the poor neighborhoods of big cities, both as perpetrators and as victims. In the dilapidated perimeter of the dark ghetto, the withdrawal of the wage-labor economy combined with the retrenchment of the welfare state to produce inordinately high rates of interpersonal violence fueled by the informalization of the economy, the homogenization of the social structure dominated by dispossessed households, and the waning of communal organizations liable to supply resources and stabilize life strategies. Where the booming crack trade became the leading employment sector for youth from the black subproletariat, violent crime became pandemic, tearing further at the local social and economic fabric.[27] But this lethal burst was well circumscribed within the racialized urban core and sharply divergent from the general tendency of criminality in the rest of the population and country, even as it dominated the media and public perception.

If the number of inmates has grown fivefold since the mid-1970s even as crime rates failed to increase and then curved downward sharply after 1993, it is because recourse to incarceration was vastly expanded and intensified. Over the years, the authorities have applied *penal confinement with growing frequency and severity to all* misdemeanants, petty or not, and criminals, violent or not, and with a zeal inversely proportional to the seriousness of the offense. Proof: the share of convicts for violent crimes among admissions to state prisons dwindled from 50 percent in 1980 to less than 27 percent by 1990, while the weight of those sentenced for narcotics violations swelled from 7 to 31 percent. Every year since 1989, convicts put under lock for property and drug offenses have been *twice as numerous as those confined for violent crimes* (see Figure 5). In 1997 for instance, 100,200 convicts entered the gates of state prisons to serve time for a felony against persons; but 102,600 new inmates were admitted for narcotics violations and an additional 94,700 joined them for having committed a property offense. The prison "class of 1997" counted more burglars than robbers (39,300 versus 30,600), more thieves than criminals found guilty of aggravated assault (23,500 for larceny/theft plus 6,999 for vehicle theft versus 29,800), and nearly four times more convicts for public-order offenses than murderers (35,700 versus 9,100).[28]

In 1992, at the acme of America's carceral boom, the typical inmate entering a state correctional facility was a man under thirty years

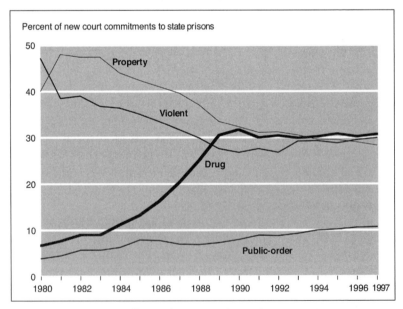

Figure 5. Most serious offense of convicts admitted to state prisons, 1980–97. *Source:* Bureau of Justice Statistics, *Correctional Population of the United States, 1997* (Washington, D.C.: U.S. Government Printing Office, 1997), 13.

of age (53 percent of admissions) of African-American origin (nearly 54 percent) who had not finished high school (for two-thirds of them), put under lock for a *nonviolent offense in over seven cases in ten*. Of the 27 percent walking in through the gates for having committed a violent crime that year, 11 percent had been convicted of aggravated assault and 7 percent of simple assault, as against 5 percent for sexual crimes and only 3.5 percent for homicide.[29] These tendencies were particularly pronounced in the states that top the carceral charts. Of every 100 people sentenced to prison in Texas in the early 1990s, 77 were convicted of four lesser categories of infractions: possession and transport of drugs (22 and 15 percent, respectively) and burglary and theft (20 percent each). Furthermore, over half of those sentenced for narcotics offenses had been caught for simple possession of *less than one gram* of drugs. California quadrupled its prison population between 1980 and 1993; 76 percent of that growth was due to the incarceration of nonviolent offenders. This disproportion was even more glaring in federal penitentiaries, where 94 percent of the 40,000 new inmates admitted in the course of a year during that period entered for nonviolent crimes.[30]

In short, American jails and prisons are overflowing with convicts who would not have been thrown behind bars thirty years ago and who, moreover, would not be rotting there if the public were better informed about the realities of the country's penal policy.[31] What changed during the intervening decades, then, is not the frequency and character of criminal activity but the *attitude of the society and the responses of the authorities toward street delinquency* and its principal source, urban poverty concentrated in the big cities. Since the turnabout of the mid-1970s, the carceral system of the United States serves not only to repress crime: it also has as its mission to bolster the social, racial, and economic order via the punitive regulation of the behaviors of the populations prone to visible and offensive deviance because they are relegated to the bottom of a polarizing class and caste structure. The prison has been called upon to contain the disorders generated by the rising tide of dispossessed families, street derelicts, unemployed and alienated youths, and the desperation and violence that have accumulated and intensified in the segregated urban core of the metropolis as the "safety net" of the U.S. semi-welfare state was torn and desocialized wage labor in the low-wage service sectors became the normal horizon of work for the deskilled fractions of the postindustrial working class.[32]

The Demise of Rehabilitation and the Politicization of Crime

Three causal series have telescoped to make imprisonment America's punishment of choice and to produce the unparalleled carceral hyperinflation the country has witnessed from the Nixon presidency to the second Clinton administration. The first includes a string of *changes internal to the criminal justice system* tied to the demise of rehabilitation as the operant correctional philosophy and the correlative *deautonomization of penal professionals* leading to a brutal hardening and acceleration in the mode of sentencing. The second entails the accelerating *politicization and media exploitation of crime,* which are the obverse, active side of the process whereby criminal punishment came to be driven by extrajudicial purposes and interests. The third entwines changing penal policy with the *collapse of the dark ghetto* after the wave of riots of the 1960s. For clarity's sake, each is discussed in turn here, but it must be stressed that these three sets of factors worked dynamically in tandem with one another.

Hegemonic in the United States since the interwar period, the idea that imprisonment aims to reform the criminal with a view toward his eventual reintegration into society was abruptly discredited in the 1970s by the unexpected convergence of critiques from the Right and the Left.[33] Conservatives have long held that the primary mission of the prison is to punish and not to rehabilitate: believing that society is composed of two distinct types of individuals—honest citizens ("the innocent") and intrinsically bad deviants ("the wicked")—they contend that incarceration must first of all serve to protect the former by consigning the latter between four walls as long as possible.[34] The novelty to come out of the 1960s was that this retrograde vision of the prison found powerful reinforcement in the progressive critique for which rehabilitation is but a sham and the modulation of punishment an illegitimate exercise in state power. The supporters of "decarceration," sociologists and criminologists of radical persuasion, argued that educational measures and treatment programs served mostly to legitimate a "total institution" (to use Erving Goffman's characterization) that, by definition, corrodes those who are entrusted to it. And they attacked head-on the adjustment of penal sanctions to the individual characteristics of perpetrators implemented under the regime of "indeterminate sentencing" on grounds that it gravely disadvantages convicts issued from the lower regions of social space, that is, poor people and African Americans.

Under the system of "indeterminate sentencing" introduced in the 1920s and prevalent until the mid-1970s, the criminal courts condemned an offender to a term of confinement defined by broad parameters (e.g., between two and eight years), while the length of the sentence served was set later by a parole board in response to the inmate's behavior and perceived progress toward "rehabilitation." The progressive reformers of the 1970s denounced the hypocrisy of such an offender-centered "correctional" paradigm; to avoid rampant discrimination in the administration of justice, they recommended that the discretionary authority of magistrates and parole boards be curtailed and that penalties be set a priori within strict brackets based essentially on the nature of the offense. They were aware that their demand for such a system of "determinate sentencing" risked lending credibility to the diametrically opposed proposals of the partisans of an extension of the carceral apparatus. But any reform seemed to them preferable to a penal status quo deemed intolerable by the libertarian yardstick of the 1960s and theories inspired by antipsychiatry.[35] And they counted on politicians recoiling from the exorbitant cost of imprisonment to turn eventually toward "intermediate" or community sanctions. It is an understatement to say that their expectations were cruelly disappointed. Historian David Rothman, who actively participated in this campaign of denigration of the rehabilitation model, draws up its miserable balance sheet in these terms:

> The reformers proved wrong on all counts. Determinate sentences were introduced in the 1980s, both in the federal system and in roughly one-third of the states. But, apart from a few jurisdictions (most notably Minnesota), sentencing guidelines have increased the time served, had relatively little impact on [socioracial] disparity in sentences, promoted prison overcrowding, and reduced the importance of judges in sentencing by enhancing the discretion of prosecutors. The distaste for rehabilitation has contributed as well to making prisons warehouses. If educational and training programs are mischievous and futile, why should the state spend money on them?[36]

This shift of penal philosophy is well illustrated by the changing contents and tone of the run-of-the-mill teaching literature on the prison. A typical "reader in penology" from the late 1960s portrays the penitentiary as a "complex organization" geared to the task of "people-changing" and devotes its core chapters to "the therapeutic function of prisons." Even as it inadvertently recognizes that "most of the 'techniques' used in 'correcting' criminals have not been shown to be either effective or ineffective and are only vaguely related to any reputable theory of behavior or criminality," the book *Prison within Society* confidently asserts that "the only means by which society can achieve its desired protection is a resocialization of the deviant which leads to his reintegration into society. Mere imprisonment can provide only a short-term protection at best and may in the long run compound the danger from which society seeks some relief."[37] Thirty years later, a standard textbook on crime and punishment aimed at the booming market in criminal justice training centers on "why prisons are built when they are, where they are, and administered as they are." Its only discussion of offender treatment is to review the special management problems posed inside custodial facilities by "specific inmate groups, from mentally ill offenders to those suffering from AIDS, to female inmates and gang members," not to mention the correctional staff. *Incarcerating Criminals* (the shift in title wording speaks volumes) addresses the question of offender employment, for instance, only *intra muros,* first as a means for "reducing the strain that correctional expenditures have placed on state budgets" and, second, as way of reducing idleness and violence; the question of postdetention employment is never considered. This is because

> [v]ery few Americans today voice the inspiring, enriching motivations behind incarceration that our predecessors held. We approach prisons today with expectations that are minimal—we demand that these institutions keep them away from us, for as long as possible and as inexpensively as possible. Time in prison has become the metric through which effective response to crime is measured, and we demand more time for more offenders. We are impatient with the numerous community-based alternatives to prison that were pursued in previous decades, because anything that is an alternative to or in lieu of the "real" penalty of incarceration represents a "slap on the wrist" and an evasion of legitimate punishment.[38]

The second engine of American carceral inflation is the *mutation of the political and media uses of criminality* in reaction to the protest movements of the 1960s and the ramifying social changes they ushered in. To curb the popular unrest provoked by the Vietnam War and the sweeping mobilization of blacks for civic equality that toppled Jim Crow in the South and overran the ghetto in the North, conservative politicians, Republicans and Democrats alike, pounced upon the "problem" of urban turmoil and made the "war on crime" their main bulwark against the (modest) expansion of the welfare state required to reduce both crushing poverty and abysmal racial inequality.[39] Introduced during the 1968 presidential campaign by Richard Nixon, who borrowed it from the political notables of the segregationist South, the repressive theme of "law and order" offered a new proving ground for the restoration of government authority. It furnished an electoral leitmotif that was all the more valued as it made it possible to express in an apparently civic idiom—ensuring the safety and tranquillity of the citizenry—the rejection of black demands and thereby to exorcise the menacing specter of "integration," which was accepted in principle but rejected in fact, as indicated by the mass migration of whites to the sheltered space of the suburbs and their abandonment of urban public institutions, from school and housing to hospitals and parks.

The success of this moral panic around criminality conflated with challenges to the racial order stems from the structural complicity that developed on this count over the years between the political field, the journalistic field, and the field of penal institutions, whose autonomy was drastically curtailed and whose functioning was increasingly subjected to the rhythms and dictates of electoral and media competition. At first, fighting crime was the rallying cry of politicians anxious to reassure white, middle-class voters from suburban zones frightened by turmoil in the "unheavenly city" (which they had just fled by the millions) and at the same time opposed to welfare policies and affirmative action, which they viewed as undue favors accorded to the blacks responsible for the urban riots that rocked the 1960s.[40] But, under pressure from the media and its relentless logic of the "sound bite" and constant search for spectacular news liable to boost ratings, the necessity of being "tough on crime" swiftly came to be imposed on all politicians, as well as on prosecutors and judges whose positions are elective and for whom the suspicion of laxity soon amounted to an occupational death sentence.[41]

For, in the meantime, crime had also become the darling subject of journalists. Crime allows the media to produce low-cost shows of morality that appeal to common sentiments and thus to preserve or conquer market shares by pandering to the morbid fascination of the public for violence. As a result, crime stories invaded the front page of newspapers and the television screen to the saturation point, even as the incidence of violent offenses was stagnating and then declining in the country. Between 1989 and 1993, the number of such reports on the nightly news of the three major national networks (ABC, CBS, and NBC) quadrupled to reach 1,632, or nearly five per evening, despite the drop in most offending rates. So much so that the Center for Media and Public Affairs wondered about the onset of "drive-by journalism." Crime rates continued to decrease rapidly for six years; yet in 1999 these three leading news outlets still broadcast an astounding 1,613 crime reports, keeping crime the first news topic (tied with the raging war in Kosovo at 1,615), with one-third of all stories devoted to murders (amounting to four times the score for Clinton's impeachment trial).[42]

In short, a crime wave did hit the United States after the 1980s, but it was a cultural wave generated by the media's increasing fascination with and market-driven use of criminal violence as cheap raw materials for "infotainment" and even entertainment. By the mid-1990s, "reality crime shows" had become a staple of television programming, with *America's Most Wanted* and *Unsolved Mysteries* vying for viewers with *Cops, Crimewatch Tonight,* and *Rescue 911.* These lurid shows consistently depicted crime as more frequent and more violent than it really is.[43] The wide diffusion of footage of police operations and videos of live crime scenes, typically involving the forcible arrest of dark-skinned young men in poor neighborhoods, cemented the association between dangerousness and blackness, and fueled a culture of vilification of criminals that harnessed underlying antiblack animus. It will come as no surprise that the shared obsession of the media and politicians with crime was met with the enthusiasm of those in charge of the country's penal institutions. Attorneys general, state correctional administrations, police departments, guards unions, and business lobbies connected to the prison sector: all concurred in seeing and portraying "crime control" as a national priority that should brook no hesitation and no limitation. For it is above all a priority tailor-made to justify the boundless expansion of their staff, budgets, and prerogatives.

The de-autonomization of the penal field and the politicization-mediatization of the crime question stand in a dialectical relation of mutual reinforcement. The more the question of crime is posed in dichotomous moral terms geared to electoral games in the public sphere, the less relevant the empirical knowledge produced by experts and the technical constraints faced by correctional administrators become to the conduct of penal policy. Conversely, as the authority of penal professionals is eroded and disregarded, moral entrepreneurs in journalism and politics can shape the mission of the police, courts, and prisons to suit their own agendas and interests, thereby under-cutting attempts to reestablish a prospective rationale for imprisonment going beyond retribution and neutralization.[44] The result of this collusive triangular relationship between the political, media, and penal fields has been the proliferation of repressive laws—California voted more than a thousand in fifteen years—that extend recourse to imprisonment, lengthen the duration of sentences inflicted and served, stipulate mandatory minimum sanctions for a wide range of offenses, and go so far as to impose life imprisonment for the third violent crime or felony, a measure sold to the electorate with help of the catchy baseball expression "Three Strikes and You're Out."

The Color of Punitiveness

Two deep-seated trends have struck observers of the contemporary penal scene in the United States. First, the percentage of prison inmates convicted for drug-related offenses soared from 5 percent in 1960 to 9 percent in 1980 to nearly one-third in 1995. During the same period, the share of African Americans among admissions to federal and state penitentiaries nearly doubled, with the result that for the first time in national history black convicts make up a majority of entering cohorts (55 percent in 1995), even though African-American men compose under 7 percent of the country's adult population. The concurrence of these two tendencies points to the third major cause of the quadrupling of the incarcerated population in the United States in twenty years: *the penal system has partly supplanted and partly supplemented the ghetto* as a mechanism of racial control, after the latter revealed itself unsuited to keeping the black urban (sub)proletariat consigned to the place assigned to it in the new American social space emerging from the upheavals of the 1960s and the accelerating restructuring of the metropolitan economy.[45]

It is true that blacks have been overrepresented in American penitentiaries throughout the twentieth century for two main reasons. The first is that they commit proportionately more crimes than whites, owing to differences in class composition and socioeconomic stability between the two communities (one African American in three lived below the official poverty line in 1993 as against one Euro-American in ten) and to the extreme levels of residential segregation inflicted upon them in the large cities. Douglas Massey has shown how the "hypersegregation" of blacks combines with their high poverty rate to create a unique "ecological niche" that is exceptionally conducive to the development of criminal activities and interpersonal violence.[46] This explains why urban blacks are the primary perpetrators but also the main victims of violent crime. But the share of African Americans among individuals arrested by the police for the four most serious offenses against persons (murder, rape, robbery, aggravated assault) decreased from 51 percent in 1973 to 43 percent in 1996.[47] So, if the ethnic composition of the prison population tracked trends in criminal violence, it should have *whitened* over the past quarter-century, and not blackened as it did.

This points to the second reason for the stupendous rise of incarceration among blacks, independent from rates of offending: the preferential enforcement of those laws most likely to lead to the arrest and prosecution of poor African Americans. True, discrimination in sentencing remains a reality at the final stage of the criminal justice process: controlling for prior record, seriousness of offense, and for indirect effects of race, blacks are more likely to receive a sanction of penal confinement than whites.[48] But such discrimination clearly has not *increased* since the mid-1970s and so it cannot account for the spectacular worsening of "racial disproportionality" in prison admission in the recent period. The latter suggests that a new relationship has been established between imprisonment and the caste division that underlies the structure of U.S. society since the uprisings that shook the ghetto.

The black–white gap has deepened rapidly in the course of the last two decades, to the point where the incarceration rate of African Americans is nearly eight times that of their compatriots of European stock. This sudden and accelerating "darkening" of the carceral stock is directly connected to the onset of the latest "War on Drugs" launched with gusto by Ronald Reagan and amplified by Bush and Clinton.[49] This policy has served as a cover for a veritable police and penal guerrilla campaign against sellers of narcotics and other street operators and, by extension, for the punitive containment of the residents of the dispossessed black urban neighborhoods in which they congregate. Following the economic decay and collapse of public institutions in the inner city, ghetto dwellers have been suspected of deviating from national cultural norms and accused of adopting those "antisocial behaviors" alleged by the pseudoscientific discourse on the "underclass" to be the cause of social dislocations in the metropolis.[50] Putting them under the tutelage of the penal apparatus at once extends and intensifies the paternalistic oversight already imposed on them by social services, first under the aegis of "welfare" and later under the plank of "workfare." In addition, it makes it possible to exploit—and to feed—the latent racial hostility of the electorate and its scorn for the poor for maximum media and political returns.[51]

Far from hunting down the scourge wherever it strikes, starting with prosperous white suburbs, downtown business districts, and university campuses, the federal antidrug campaign has concentrated squarely on the declining dark ghetto. As a result, the arrest rate of blacks for narcotics violations shot up tenfold in ten years to peak at 1,800 per 100,000 by 1989, while the same rate for whites fluctuated between 220 and 250 per 100,000 (although the incidence of drug consumption is nearly identical in the two communities). As a result, the number of African Americans caught in the snares of the penal apparatus exploded, and with it the litany of deleterious consequences for their employment prospects and family life: if one adds those on probation and parole to jail detainees and prison inmates, about half of young African Americans in the big cities are currently under criminal justice supervision, so much so that a deep *structural and functional symbiosis has emerged between the collapsing ghetto and the booming prison.* The two institutions interpenetrate and complement each another in that both ensure the confinement of a population stigmatized by its ethnic origin and deemed superfluous both economically and politically.[52]

Upon a painstaking examination of the relations between racial division, crime, and punishment in America, legal scholar Michael Tonry asserts that the architects of the War on Drugs were fully cognizant of what they were doing:

> They knew that drug use was falling among the vast majority of the population. They knew that drug use was not declining among the disadvantaged members of the urban underclass. They knew that the War on Drugs would be fought mainly in the minority areas of American cities and that those arrested and imprisoned would disproportionately be young blacks and Hispanics.[53]

One is thus led to conclude that the "War on Drugs" expresses the will to penalize poverty and to contain the assortment of "pathologies" associated with it, either by hemming it at the core of the crumbling ghetto or, when these secondary effects spill over its scorned perimeter, by damming it inside the prisons to which the racialized urban core is now symbiotically joined. Beyond that, the functional coupling of the penal apparatus and the black ghetto fits with the onset of a "new penology" whose aim is neither to avert criminal activity nor to reintegrate offenders into society once they have served their sentences, but merely to isolate populations viewed as posing a threat to the sociomoral order and to durably warehouse away their most recalcitrant members.[54]

Historical and comparative studies concur to demonstrate that the level of incarceration in a given society bears no relation to its crime rate: it is at bottom an expression of cultural stands and political choices. On this account, the carceral hyperinflation that the United States has experienced from Nixon to Clinton is revealing: it constitutes, as it were, the hidden face of the American "social model," premised on the unfettered reign of the market, a categorical welfare state that buttresses labor discipline, and the continued sociospatial isolation of African Americans. Indeed, the grotesque overdevelopment of the penal sector in the past three decades emerges as the necessary counterpart to the shriveling of the welfare sector, and the joining of the remnants of the dark ghetto with the penitentiary as the logical complement to the policy of criminalization of poverty pursued by the country's authorities. As in other societies, the discourses that seek to connect crime and punishment in America have no validity other than ideological. Far from accounting for the country's great carceral leap backward, they partake of the social construction of a hypertrophic and hyperactive penal state that constitutes without contest one of the most unforeseen and cruelest historical experiments of the democratic era.

Afterword

A Civic Sociology
of Neoliberal Penality

This book is an exercise in *civic sociology,* that is, an effort to deploy the tools of social science to engage in, and bear upon, a current public debate of frontline societal significance.[1] The topic of the debate is the *rising role of the prison and the punitive turn in penal policy* discernible in most advanced societies during the closing two decades of the twentieth century and since. The initial target was France and its neighbors, as eager importers of the crime-control categories, slogans, and measures elaborated during the 1990s in the United States as vehicles for that country's historic shift from the social-welfare to the penal management of urban marginality. The aim was to circumvent the dominant policy and media discourse fostering the diffusion of this new punitive *doxa* and to alert European scholars, civic leaders, and the interested citizenry to the shady springs of this diffusion, as well as to the dire social consequences and political dangers of the growth and glorification of the penal wing of the state. When I wrote this book, I did not expect to venture further into what was then for me a novel and unfamiliar terrain of inquiry. I had brought the criminal-justice apparatus into my analytic ambit because of its stupendous growth in and aggressive deployment around the imploding black ghetto in the United States after the ebbing of the civil rights movement, and I firmly intended to return to issues of urban inequality and ethnoracial domination.[2] But two unexpected developments prodded me to pursue this line of research and intellectual activism.

The Global Firestorm of "Law and Order": A Field Report

The first is the unusual reception of the book, first in France and then in the countries that quickly translated it, traversing the borders separating scientific scholarship, citizen militancy, and policy making. The second is the fact that the twofold thesis it puts forth—that a new "punitive common sense" forged in the United States as part of the attack on the welfare state is rapidly crossing the Atlantic to ramify throughout Western Europe, and that this dissemination is not an internal response to the changing incidence and profile of crime but an offshoot of the external spread of the neoliberal project—received spectacular prima facie validation when *Les Prisons de la misère* was published in a dozen languages within a few years of its release. This impassioned foreign reaction afforded me the opportunity to travel across three continents to test practically the pertinence of its arguments. It enabled me to verify that the global popularity of the "New York model" of policing, incarnated by its erstwhile chief William Bratton and the mayor who had hired (and fired) him, Rudolph Giuliani, is indeed the tip of the iceberg of a larger revamping of public authority, one element in a broader stream of transnational policy transfer encompassing the flexible reorganization of the low-wage labor market and the restrictive revamping of welfare into workfare after the pattern provided by the post-Fordist and post-Keynesian United States.[3] A selective recounting of the meteoric trajectory of the original edition of *Prisons of Poverty* across spheres of debate and national frontiers can help us better discern the stake of the intellectual discussion and political struggles it joins, which concerns not so much crime and punishment as the *reengineering of the state* to promote, then respond to, the economic and sociomoral conditions coalescing under hegemonic neoliberalism.

From the outset the book crossed the borders between academic, journalistic, and civil spheres. In France, *Les Prisons de la misère* was literally launched from the heart of the carceral institution: on a gray and cold afternoon in November 1999, I presented the fruits of my investigations live on Canalweb and Télé La Santé, the internal tele-vision station run by the inmates of the jail of La Santé in Paris, and then debated them again late into the night with the full staff and recruits of the national training school for correctional personnel in their jam-packed cafeteria just outside the city. Within weeks, the dis-cussion extended to major media outlets and to academic and activist venues as diverse as the École normale supérieure in Paris and the annual fair of the Trotskyist party Lutte Ouvrière; the Maison des Sciences de l'Homme in Nantes and a *débat de bar* staged by the Greens in Lyon; the National Center for Scientific Research and the École de la magistrature (France's academy for judges); and public meet-ings across the country variously sponsored by Les Amis du Monde Diplomatique, Amnesty International, Attac, the Ligue des droits de l'homme, Raisons d'Agir, Genepi (a national student outfit running prison teaching programs), local universities and neighborhood as-sociations, several political parties, and one of the country's major Masonic lodges. A daylong public meeting on "The Penalization of Poverty," organized at the Maison des syndicats in my hometown of Montpellier in May 2000, exemplified this spirit of open and vigorous discussion by bringing together social scientists, lawyers and magis-trates, and activists and union representatives spanning the educa-tional, health, social-welfare, youth-justice, and correctional arms of the state.[4] Soon *Les Prisons de la misère* was adapted for theater (and played onstage at the Rencontres de la Cartoucherie in June 2001); its arguments inserted in documentary movies; and its text excerpted in academic anthologies, libertarian fanzines, and government publica-tions. And I was asked by the International Labor Organization to present it at the Forum 2000 of the United Nations in Geneva, where representatives from several countries pressed me to travel to their lands to engage the policy discussion there.

It was difficult to decline these invitations as, within months, the book was translated and released in a half-dozen countries, triggering a deluge of calls from universities, human rights centers, city and regional governments, and the gamut of professional and political or-ganizations eager to debate its implications in nations as far and wide as Italy and Ecuador, Canada and Hungary, and Finland and Japan (it is now in print in nineteen languages). On the Iberian Peninsula, *Les Prisons de la misère* was swiftly translated into not only Spanish but also Catalan, Galician, and Portuguese. In Bulgaria, my translator was invited to present the book's arguments on national television since I could not make the trip to Sofia to do so myself. In Brazil, the launch of *Prisões da miseria,* sponsored by the Instituto Carioca de Criminologia and the criminal law program at Universidade Candido Mendes, featured a debate with the minister of justice and a former governor of the state of Rio de Janeiro and was covered by the leading national newspapers (perhaps intrigued by the title I had given my address: "Does the Brazilian Bourgeoisie Wish to Reestablish a Dictatorship?").[5] Within weeks the book's thesis was invoked by journalists, scholars, and lawyers as well as cited in a Supreme Court decision. In Greece, the book's release anchored a two-day conference co-sponsored by the French embassy in Athens on "The Penal State in the United States, France, and Greece," bringing together social scientists, jurists, historians, justice officials, and an assortment of reporters. In Denmark, a progressive association of social workers sponsored the publication of *De fattiges fængsel* as scholarly ammunition to resist the bureaucratic drift toward the punitive supervision of the poor by their profession. In Turkey, prior to its release in a legal edition, the book circulated via the country's school for police directors in an unauthorized translation produced by a commissioner, who had read it while pursuing his sociology studies in France, until it was brought out in a legal edition.

But it is the visit that I made to Argentina in April of 2000 that best revealed just how raw a sociopolitical nerve the book had hit. This was the first time I had set foot in that country; I had no prior knowledge of its police, justice, and correctional institutions and traditions; yet it was as if I had formulated an analytic framework designed to capture and clarify current Argentinian developments. Landing in Buenos Aires in the final stretch of a heated municipal election campaign in which the candidates of Left and Right had both made combating crime with U.S.-inspired methods their top priority, just one month after the global apostle of *"tolerancia zero,"* William Bratton, had flown in to preach his policing gospel, I was caught in the eye of an intellectual, political, and media storm. In ten days, I gave twenty-nine talks to academic and activist audiences, consultations with government officials and legal experts, and interviews to the gamut of print, television, and radio outlets. By the end of the week I was getting stopped on the streets of Buenos Aires by passersby anxious to ask further questions about *Las Cárceles de la miseria*. It was, both then and now in retrospect, a surreal experience captured in part by this field report sent to a correspondent in the United States on April 26, 2000, at 1:46 a.m. from the Ayacucho Hotel:

> I started at 8:30 a.m. with a short interview on a national commercial radio with a star radio personality. Then off to the Ministry of the Interior, where I had a 2.5-hour session with the top advisors to the ministers of justice and of the interior (police), seven of them total, six of whom had clearly read the book (one of them cover to cover and scribbled throughout), a session concluded by the ceremonial signing of two copies dedicated to the two ministers. . . . From there we jetted to a bookstore-bar where I heard myself sounding a clarion "call to Argentine women to resist zero tolerance and the penal state" in an interview with *Luna*, a glitzy women's magazine (the Argentine cousin of *Cosmopolitan*). . . .
>
> For distraction we went to visit several bookstores where *Cárceles de la miseria* was prominently displayed in windows and on tables, and where I collected the effusive greetings and admirative thanks of the store-owners. One of them runs a radio show, so I gave yet another impromptu interview on the spot for future play. At 5 p.m., after a brief rest, we drove off to *La Nación* (the equivalent of *Le Monde*) for another long interview (and another lengthy photo session: I have had more photos of me taken in three days than in the previous three decades), in which I brashly equated zero tolerance with the return of dictatorship over the poor. Through the day I kept getting more political and more assertive.
>
> By 7 p.m. I was completely exhausted but the main event was just coming up: a public lecture and debate at the Centro Cultural Ricardo Rojas, broadcast on cable TV, with the country's leading legal scholar of prisons, the director of the national corrections administration (could you imagine this in the United States?), the head of the sociology department at UBA [Universidad de Buenos Aires], and an "expert in security" who is also chief advisor to the left candidate in the upcoming municipal elections after the said candidate, Anibal Ibarra, opted out of the debate because the mounting rumor among journalists and politicos (which could hurt him at the polls) is that "Caballo [the rightist candidate] runs with Bratton [who came here twice earlier this year to peddle his wares], and *Ibarra runs with Wacquant*"! (As I write this, I find it hard to believe I'm not making it up.) Add to this that the chief Justice in charge of all judges and prosecutors for the province of Buenos Aires showed up and pleaded with me to travel to La Plata (the regional

capital) tomorrow to give a special presentation to the full assembly of magistrates of the state.

The auditorium was packed to the rafters, hot, sweaty, with maybe three hundred people in a room designed for half that many, sitting on the floor, in the aisles, in the wings, standing pressed like sardines along the walls. I feared I was going to zonk out. But in a near unconscious state I gave a completely improvised talk. The atmosphere was electric. . . . Then the debate went on till eleven, periodically turning into a verbal mêlée with everybody shouting and flailing wildly (which, I'm told, is the typical pattern of Argentine discussions: *es la pasión*), with moving questions about police violence from people who had been tortured, or about the "disappeared" and state corruption (a problem that I proposed to tackle by taking politicians at their word and applying "zero tolerance" to cases of official graft and fraud), after which I was mobbed by the crowd, requests for autographs of the book, and more questions one on one.

When I finally managed to extricate myself from the crowd, and I thought I was going to pass out right there and then from exhaustion, tension, and heat, I was whisked off to a TV studio in the same building to do one more interview for the television channel run by that cultural center. And I don't mention that I had a full-page interview, "La globalización es un invento norteamericano," in today's *Página 12*, the main Left daily, and that, while I was talking, I also appeared on television at 10 p.m. on the public affairs show of [leading political journalist] Horacio Verbitsky. Word came late that the Ministry of Justice has requested that I give another presentation to their full staff. Tomorrow I have seven more interviews scheduled and a public lecture on "The Cunning of Imperialist Reason." My publisher is pressing me to scrap my meager one day of rest in Uruguay (just across the Río Plata, which I've so far successfully resisted) to try and cram a dozen more requests for interviews.

The point of this recapitulation is emphatically not to suggest that the foreign reception of *Prisons of Poverty* provides an apt measure of its analytic merits, but to give an idea of the wide diffusion and fiery fever that the phenomenon it tracks evinces in the political, journalistic, and intellectual fields of First and Second World societies. A firestorm of "law and order" has indeed been raging across the globe, which has transformed public debate and policy on crime and punishment in ways that no observer of the penal scene could have foreseen a dozen years before. The reason behind the unusual international *engouement* for the book was the same as in France: in all these countries, the mantras of "zero tolerance" policing and "prison works,"

lionized by U.S. officials and showcased by the Giuliani–Bratton duet
as the cause for the seemingly miraculous crime drop in New York,
were being hailed by local officials. Everywhere politicians, of the
Right *and more significantly of the Left,*[6] were vying to import the
latest American methods of law enforcement presented as the panacea
for curing urban violence and assorted dislocations, while skeptics
and critics of these methods were scouring for theoretical arguments,
empirical data, and civic firebreakers with which to thwart the adoption of punitive containment as a generalized technique for managing
rampant social insecurity.

Plumbing the "Washington Consensus" on Crime Fighting

The swift international diffusion of *Les Prisons de la misère* turned into
an unplanned experiment in the politics of social-scientific knowledge.
It disclosed that, whereas I had aimed my analytic sights at the core
of the European Union, the model of the link between neoliberalization and punitive penality sketched in it was even more pertinent to the
periphery of the Old World caught in the throes of the post-Soviet conversion and to the countries of the Second World saddled with a history
of authoritarianism, a hierarchical conception of citizenship, and mass
poverty backed by steep and rising social inequalities, where the penalization of poverty is guaranteed to have calamitous consequences.

From this angle, the societies of Latin America that had engaged
in precocious experimentation with radical economic deregulation
(that is, reregulation in favor of multinational firms) and then fallen
under the tutelage of the international financial organizations enforcing monetarist dogmas offered a most propitious terrain for the
adoption of harsh versions of penal populism and the importation
of American crime-fighting stratagems. Put in capsule form: the ruling elites of the nations seduced—and subsequently transformed—by
the "Chicago Boys" of Milton Friedman in the 1970s were bound to
become infatuated with the "New York Boys" of Rudy Giuliani in the
1990s, when the time came to deal with the ramifying consequences
of neoliberal restructuring and to face the endemic social instability
and broiling urban disorders spawned by market reform at the bottom of the dualizing class structure. It is not by happenstance that
Chile, which was first to embrace the policies dictated by the "money

doctors" from the University of Chicago[7] and soon became the continent's leading incarcerator, saw its imprisonment rate zoom from 155 per 100,000 in 1992 to 240 per 100,000 in 2004, while Brazil's rate jumped from 74 to 183 and Argentina's from 63 to 140 (with Uruguay caught between, soaring from 97 to 220).[8] Throughout the continent there is not only an acute public fear of festering urban crime, which has increased alongside socioeconomic disparities in the wake of the return to democratic rule and the social disengagement of the state, and intense political concern for the management of problem territories and categories; there is also a common set of punitive solutions—the broadening of police powers and prerogatives centered on street offenses and narcotics infractions, the acceleration and hardening of judicial processing, the expansion of the warehousing prison, and the normalization of "emergency penality" applied differentially across social and physical space[9]—*inspired or legitimated by nostrums coming from the United States,* thanks to the diligent action abroad of American diplomats and justice agencies, the targeted activities of U.S. think tanks and their local allies, and the thirst of foreign politicians for law-enforcement mottos and measures enwrapped in the *mana* of America.[10]

In the Southern Hemisphere as in Western Europe, the role of think tanks has been pivotal to the diffusion of aggressive penality "made in USA." In the 1990s, the Manhattan Institute spearheaded a successful transatlantic campaign to alter the parameters of British policy on poverty, welfare, and crime. A decade later, it developed the Inter-American Policy Exchange (IAPE), a program designed to export its favorite crime-fighting strategies to Latin America as part of a neoliberal policy package comprising "business improvement districts," school reform through vouchers and bureaucratic accountability, government downsizing, and privatization. Its chief envoys were none other than William Bratton himself, his former NYPD assistant William Andrews, and George Kelling, the celebrated coinventor of the "broken windows theory." These missionaries of "law and order" traveled south to meet with the police chiefs and mayors of big cities but also with governors, cabinet members, and presidents. Backed by the permanent office of the IAPE in Santiago de Chile, they propagandize through local right-wing think tanks, branches of the American Chamber of Commerce in the country, and business organizations and wealthy patrons, delivering lectures, offering policy consultations, and even participating in civic rallies—Kelling once made a noted speech in Buenos Aires to some ten thousand Argentines gathered in Luna Park to protest the escalating crime rate.[11] When necessary, the IAPE bypasses the national level and works with regional or municipal opponents of the central government to promote its pro-market and policing remedies. This is the case in Venezuela, where leftist President Hugo Chávez wishes to fight crime by reducing poverty and inequality, while his political adversaries, such as the mayor of Caracas, share the Manhattan Institute's view that it is criminals who are responsible for crime and that the mission to suppress them falls solely on the forces of order.

"CONFERENCES IN LATIN AMERICA"
(excerpt from a Manhattan Institute brochure)

The Manhattan Institute has found partnering with local think tanks in Latin America to hold conferences an effective way to introduce ideas and create enthusiasm. However, the ultimate goal of our work is not simply to hold conferences, but to build long-term working relationships to help leaders in these countries develop practical crime-fighting, school-building, and government-reform programs. For that reason each of our conferences is arranged to include several days of smaller working seminars and one-on-one meetings with government officials and opinion leaders. . . .

Venezuela: In September 2000, former New York City Police Commissioner and Senior Fellow of the Institute Bill Bratton, Senior Fellow George Kelling, and Carlos Medina visited Caracas, Venezuela. Their trip was organized by the think tank CEDICE, the Venezuela-American Chamber of Commerce, and the new Mayor of Caracas Alfredo Pena. It included a major conference entitled "Restoring Order and Reducing Crime in Our Communities" that was attended by over 500 people and a smaller seminar with all the business leaders of Caracas entitled "Improving Commercial Spaces—Business Improvement Districts." The visit also included meetings with the mayors of the five largest municipalities in Caracas, the Attorney General Javier Elechiguerra, the Chiefs of the Metropolitan Police Force and the Municipal Police Force, and U.S. Ambassador Donna Hrinak.

Mexico: In May 2000, George Kelling visited Mexico City and gave the keynote address before 5,000 people at a major Mexico Unido Contra la Delincuencia conference. All three major presidential candidates were in attendance and George Kelling met privately with the presidential candidate Vicente Fox, who has used his ideas as the basis for his proposed

public safety agenda. Dr. Kelling also spoke at a conference at the Instituto
Ludwig Von Mises. Finally, U.S. Ambassador Jeffrey Davidow hosted a lunch
at his residence to discuss solutions for Mexico's escalating crime problem that
included a dozen high-ranking government officials such as the Governor of
the State of Queretaro, Ignacio Loyola; the Governor of the State of Nuevo
Leon, Fernando Canales Clariond; and the Secretary for Public Safety for
Mexico City, Alejandro Gertz Manero.

The Manhattan Institute translates its reports, policy briefs, and
media articles supporting its vision into Spanish and Portuguese, and
distributes them to opinion makers throughout South America. It also
brings Latin American officials to New York City in batches for field
visits, training sessions, and intensive indoctrination into the virtues
of small (social and economic) government and astringent law enforcement (for lower-class crime). This policy evangelism has "spawned
a whole generation" of Latin American "politicians for whom the
Manhattan Institute is the equivalent of an ideological Vatican,"[12] and
its bifurcated conception of the role of the state sacrosanct: laissez-
faire and enabling at the top, intrusive and disabling at the bottom.
These politicians are keen to apply inflexible law enforcement and
expanded incarceration to safeguard the streets and tame the disorders that roil their cities, notwithstanding the rampant corruption of
the police, the procedural bankruptcy of the criminal courts, and the
vicious brutality of jails and prisons in their home countries, which
ensure that *mano dura* strategies routinely translate into escalating
fear of crime, violence, and "extralegal detention and punishment for
minor offenses, including the military-style occupation and collective
punishment of entire neighborhoods."[13]

Remarkably, the magnetism of U.S.-style penality and the political proceeds they promise are such that elected leaders throughout
Latin America have continued to press for punitive responses to street
crime even as Left parties have ascended to power and turned the region into "an epicenter of dissent from neoliberal ideas and resistance
to U.S. economic and political dominance."[14] This is well illustrated
by the ceremonial signing by Andrés Manuel López Obrador, the progressive mayor of Mexico City, of a $4.5 million contract (paid for by
a consortium of local businessmen headed by Latin America's richest
man, Carlos Slim Herú) with the consultancy firm Giuliani Partners

to apply its "zero tolerance" magic potion to the Mexican capital, in spite of the glaring unsuitability of its standard measures at ground level.[15] One example: efforts to eliminate street vendors and windshield wipers (most of them children) through assiduous police intervention are bound to fail given their sheer numbers (in the tens of thousands) and the central role they play in the informal economy of the city, and therefore in the reproduction of lower-class households whose electoral support López Obrador needs. Not to mention that the Mexican police themselves are deeply engaged in informal trades of every kind, legal and illegal, needed to supplement their famine-level wages. But no matter: in Mexico City as in Marseille or Milan, what counts is less to adopt realistic strategies for reducing crime than *to stage the resolve of the authorities* to attack it head on so as to ritually reassert the fortitude of the ruler.

The international reaction to *Prisons of Poverty* and criminal-justice developments over the past decade in countries as varied as Sweden, France, Spain, and Mexico, have confirmed not only that Brattonmania has gone (nearly) global, but that the dissemination of "zero tolerance" partakes of a broader international traffic in policy formulas that binds together market rule, social retrenchment, and penal enlargement.[16] The "Washington consensus" on economic deregulation and welfare retraction has in effect *extended to encompass punitive crime control* in a pornographic and managerialist key, as the "invisible hand" of the market calls forth the "iron fist" of the penal state. Their matching geographic and temporal pattern of propagation corroborates my central thesis that the surge and exaltation of the police, courts, and prisons in First and Second World societies over the past two decades are integral to the neoliberal revolution. When and where the latter advances unfettered, the deregulation of the low-wage labor market necessitates the restrictive revamping of welfare to impress precarious work on the postindustrial proletariat. Both, in turn, trigger the activation and enlargement of the penal wing of the state, first, to curtail and contain the urban dislocations caused by the spread of social insecurity at the foot of the class and spatial hierarchy and, second, to restore the legitimacy of political leaders discredited by their acquiescence to, or embrace of, the impotence of Leviathan on the social and economic fronts.[17] *A contrario*, where neoliberalization has been thwarted on the employment and welfare

172 *Afterword: A Civic Sociology of Neoliberal Penality*

tracks, the push toward penalization has been blunted or diverted, as indicated, for instance, by the stubborn deafness of the Nordic countries to the sirens of "zero tolerance" (notwithstanding their greater zeal in sanctioning narcotics infractions and drunken driving over the past decade)[18] and the resulting stagnation or modest increases of their prison populations even as national concern for and anxiety over crime have mounted.

Learning from the Travels and Travails of Neoliberal Penality

Accordingly, *Prisons of Poverty* proposes that we need to supplement, nay supplant, the *evolutionary* models that have dominated recent theoretical debates on penal change in advanced society with a *discontinuist and diffusionist* analysis tracking the circulation of punitive discourses, norms, and policies elaborated in the United States as constituent ingredients of the neoliberal government of social inequality and urban marginality.

In Jock Young's vision of the "exclusive society" and in David Garland's account of the "culture of control," as in the latest Eliasian, neo-Durkheimian, and neo-Foucauldian conceptions of penality,[19] contemporary shifts in the political reconfiguration of crime and punishment result from reaching a *societal stage*—late modernity, postmodernity, the risk society—and emerge endogenously in response to rising *criminal* insecurity and its cultural reverberations *across social space*. In the model adumbrated in the present book (and revised in subsequent publications), the punitive turn of public policy, applying to *both social welfare and criminal justice*, partakes of a political project that responds to rising *social* insecurity and its destabilizing effects in the *lower rungs* of the social and spatial order. This project involves the retooling and redeployment of the state to buttress marketlike mechanisms and discipline the new postindustrial proletariat while restraining the internal disruptions generated by the fragmentation of labor, the retrenchment of social protection schemes, and the correlative shakeup of the established ethnic hierarchy (ethnoracial in the United States, ethnonational in Western Europe, and a mix of the two in Latin America).[20] But the crafting of the new Leviathan also registers the external influences of political operators and intellectual entrepreneurs engaged in a multilayered campaign of ideological marketing across national boundaries in matters of capital/labor, welfare, and law enforcement. Even as neoliberalism is from its inception a multi-sited, polycentric, and geographically uneven formation,[21] at century's turn this campaign to revamp the triadic nexus of state, market, and citizenship from above had a nerve center located in the United States, an inner ring of collaborating countries acting as relay stations (such as the England in Western Europe and Chile in South America), and an outer band of societies targeted for infiltration and conquest.

With precious few exceptions, American students of punishment have ignored the foreign ramifications of the police, justice, and carceral schemas forged by the United States in reaction to the breakup of the Fordist–Keynesian compact and the collapse of the black ghetto— when they have not denied them.[22] Yet reckoning with this cross-border dissemination, which has brought to European shores not only zero-tolerance policing but also youth night curfews and electronic monitoring, boot camps and pretrial "shock incarceration," plea bargaining and mandatory minimum sentences, sex-offender registries and the diversion of juveniles into adult justice, is key to elucidating the analytics and politics of neoliberal penality. First, it reveals the direct connections between market deregulation, welfare curtailment, and penal expansion by spotlighting their joint or sequential diffusion across countries. It is telling, for example, that the United Kingdom adopted first the policy of flexible labor governance and then the compulsory workfare blueprint pioneered by the United States before it imported the latter's aggressive crime-control idiom and programs suited to dramatizing the reborn moral stringency and penal severity of the authorities.[23]

Next, tracking the international circulation of U.S. penal formulas helps us avoid the conceptual trap of American exceptionalism as well as hazy disquisitions on "late modernity" by pointing to the mechanisms propelling the growth of the penal state—or to the institutional obstacles and vectors of resistance to it, as the case may be— in a spectrum of societies subjected to the same political-economic tropism. It invites us to envision the rise of the penal state in United States not as an idiosyncratic case but as a particularly *virulent case*, owing to a host of factors that combine to facilitate, accelerate, and intensify the punitive containment of social insecurity in that society: among them, the fragmentation of the bureaucratic field, the strength of moral individualism supporting the mantric principle of "individual responsibility," the generalized degradation of labor, the high levels of both class and ethnic segregation, and the salience and rigidity of racial division making lower-class blacks in the crumbling inner city propitious targets for converging campaigns of welfare contraction and penal escalation.[24]

Lastly, there is a looping, retroactive relationship between local (city or regional), national, and international policy innovation and emulation, such that tracing the globalization of "zero tolerance" and "prison works" provides a fruitful avenue for dissecting the processes of selection and translation of penal notions and measures across jurisdictions and levels of government that usually go unnoticed or unanalyzed inside a given country. It also offers novel insights into the fabrication of the reigning neoliberal vulgate that has everywhere transformed political debates via the planetary spread of the folk concepts and concerns of U.S. policy makers and scholars: by exporting its penal theories and policies, America institutes itself as the barometer of no-nonsense crime control around the world and effectively legitimizes its vision of law enforcement by universalizing its particularities.[25]

As the first book-length study of the transnational diffusion of U.S.-style penality at century's close, *Prisons of Poverty* anticipated the burgeoning of the field of police and justice "policy transfer."[26] As such, it is an oblique contribution to research on the globalization of crime and justice from the punishment side, but one that goes against the grain of globalization studies insofar as it insists that what appears as a blind and benign drift toward planetary convergence, putatively fostered by the technological and cultural unification of the world polity, is actually a stratified process of *differential and diffracted Americanization,* fostered by the strategic activities of hierarchical networks of state managers, ideological entrepreneurs, and scholarly marketers in the United States and in the countries of reception. It is also a call for students of policy migration on the world stage to bring the penal domain into their purview, alongside economic and welfare policies, and to heed the driving role played by think tanks and heteronomous scholarly disciplines and academics in the international peregrinations of public policy formulas.[27]

The travels of *Prisons of Poverty* across national borders, like the sweep of the punitive wave it follows around the globe, taught me that the diffusion of neoliberal penality is not only more advanced but also more diversified and more complex than portrayed in the book. Just as there are varieties of capitalism, there are many paths down the road to market rule, and thus many possible routes to the penalization of poverty. Penalization assumes a multiplicity of forms, not limited to incarceration; it percolates through and operates with variable effects in the different subsectors of the police, justice, and carceral apparatuses; it extends across policy domains, intruding into the provision of other public goods such as health care, child assistance, and housing; and it commonly evokes reticence, often meets with resistance, and sometimes triggers vigorous counterattacks.[28] Moreover, the material and discursive components of penal policy can become decoupled and journey separately, leading to the hyperbolic accentuation of the symbolic mission of punishment as vehicle for categorization and boundary drawing. All of which called for amending and elaborating the rudimentary model of the nexus of neoliberalism and punitive penality sketched in *Prisons of Poverty*.

This is the task undertaken in *Punishing the Poor: The Neoliberal Government of Social Insecurity*.[29] This book breaks with the standard parameters of the political economy of punishment by bringing developments in welfare and criminal justice into a single theoretical framework equally attentive to the instrumental and expressive moments of public policy. It deploys Pierre Bourdieu's concept of "bureaucratic field" to show that changes in social and penal policies in advanced society over the past quarter-century are mutually linked; that stingy "workfare" and generous "prisonfare" constitute a single organizational contraption to discipline and supervise the poor under a philosophy of moral behaviorism; and that an expansive and expensive penal system is not just a consequence of neoliberalism—as argued in the present volume—but an *integral component of the neoliberal state* itself. The contemporary travails of penality turn out to partake of a broader reengineering and remasculinizing of the state that have rendered obsolete the conventional scholarly and policy separation between welfare and crime. The police, courts, and prison are not mere technical implements whereby the authorities respond to crime—as in the commonsensical view enshrined by law and criminology—but core political capacities through which the Leviathan both produces and manages inequality, marginality, and identity. This spotlights the need to develop a political sociology of the return of the penal state to the forefront of the historical stage at the start of the twenty-first century, an intellectual project to which *Prisons of Poverty* is both a prelude and an invitation.

Notes

1. How America Exports Its Penal Common Sense

1. On the social conditions and mechanisms of cultural diffusion of this new planetary vulgate, whose fetish-terms, seemingly shot up out of nowhere, are nowadays everywhere—"globalization" and "flexibility," "multiculturalism" and "communitarianism," "ghetto" or "underclass," and their "postmodern" cousins: identity, minority, ethnicity, fragmentation, etc.—see Pierre Bourdieu and Loïc Wacquant, "On the Cunning of Imperialist Reason," *Theory, Culture, & Society* 16.1 (February 1999 [1998]): 41–57, and idem, "Neoliberal Newspeak," *Radical Philosophy* 105 (January 2001): 2–5.

2. Régis Debray, Max Gallo, Jacques Juillard, Blandine Kriegel, Olivier Mongin, Mona Ozouf, Anicet LePors, and Paul Thibaud, "Républicains, n'ayons pas peur!" *Le Monde,* September 4, 1998, 13 (the sheer number and supposed or proclaimed dispersal of the signatories across the political spectrum aim to give the appearance of neutrality, and thus of reason, to the position advocated). One could cite here any number of similar pronouncements by left-leaning French public figures, such as this one by historian Maurice Agulhon, characteristic of this penal drift to the point of caricature: "On problems of public order, the Left got on the wrong track thirty or forty years ago. The current evolution, nonetheless, goes in the right direction, as witnessed by the statements of [Prime Minister Lionel] Jospin, who had the courage to say that the notion of order is not in itself a reactionary notion.... It is a matter of returning to this *elementary common sense* of which leftist infatuations, which I shared in my time, somehow made us lose sight"; cited by Hugues Jallon and Pierre Mounier, "Les fous de la République," *Les Inrockuptibles* 178 (December 16, 1998): 25, emphasis added.

3. These regions, however, have the excuse of rates of violent crime comparable or superior to that of the United States, and, for some of them, of their direct economic

and diplomatic subordination to the United States. Such is the case with Mexico, which has to writhe before the U.S. Congress each winter to prove that it is waging the "War on Drugs" ordered by its "Big Brother of the North" with zeal and determination. The deleterious impact of U.S.-style police and penal policies on formerly authoritarian countries of the Second World is discussed in Loïc Wacquant, "Towards a Dictatorship over the Poor? Notes on the Penalization of Poverty in Brazil," *Punishment & Society* 5.2 (April 2003): 197–205.

4. The same would apply to other areas of "policy transfer" such as monetary (de)regulation, welfare, labor markets, health, and education, all of which have witnessed intense one-way traffic across the Atlantic in the past decade.

5. On this crucial distinction between the "empirical" individual (or institution) encountered in reality and the "epistemic" individual (or institution) constructed by and for purposes of sociological explanation, see Pierre Bourdieu, *Homo Academicus* (Cambridge: Polity Press, 1988 [1984]), 21–35.

6. For an analysis of the institution of a transnational corporate law market fostering the universalization of the Anglo-American model of economic (de)regulation that has a paradigmatic value in this domain, see Yves Dezalay, *Marchands de droit. La restructuration de l'ordre juridique international par les multinationales du droit* (Paris: Arthème Fayard, 1992). The worldwide exporting of U.S. electoral marketing is dissected by Fritz Plasser and Gunda Plasser, eds., *Global Political Campaigning* (Westport, Conn.: Praeger, 2002), 15–105; and the international proliferation of "think tanks" by Diane Stone, Andrew Denham, and Mark Garnett, eds., *Think Tanks across Nations* (Manchester: Manchester University Press, 1999).

7. Loïc Wacquant, "L'ascension de l'État pénal en Amérique," *Actes de la recherche en sciences sociales* 124 (September 1998): 7–26; and in this book, 58–79, for a synopsis of the major components of the great U.S. "carceral boom."

8. On this subject, read the useful overview by Steven Donziger, *The Real War on Crime* (New York: Basic Books, 1996), 63–98.

9. See especially James A. Smith, *The Idea Brokers: Think Tanks and the Rise of the New Policy Elite* (New York: Free Press, 1991), and the benign insider view of David Ricci, *The Transformation of American Politics: The New Washington and the Rise of Think Tanks* (New Haven: Yale University Press, 1994).

10. Charles Murray, *Losing Ground: American Social Policy, 1950–1980* (New York: Basic Books, 1984).

11. Chuck Lane, "The Manhattan Project," *New Republic*, March 25, 1985, 14–15.

12. A methodical refutation of the empirical claims of *Losing Ground* is in William Julius Wilson, *The Truly Disadvantaged: The Inner City, the Underclass, and Public Policy* (Chicago: University of Chicago Press, 1987).

13. George Gilder, *Wealth and Poverty* (New York: Basic Books, 1981), and idem, "Blessed Are the Money-Makers," *Economist*, March 7, 1981, 87–88. An excellent analysis of the return of this antediluvian conservative discourse on poverty in the 1980s, and the inability of the "liberal" vision to check it, is Michael B. Katz, *The Undeserving Poor: From the War on Poverty to the War on Welfare* (New York: Pantheon, 1989), 137–84.

14. Charles Murray, *In Pursuit of Happiness and Good Government* (New York: Simon and Schuster, 1988). A decade later, no doubt disappointed by the fiasco of his philosophical sortie, Murray reiterated his arguments in a pamphlet titled *What It Means to Be a Libertarian: A Personal Interpretation* (New York: Broadway Book, 1998).

15. Charles Murray and Richard Herrnstein, *The Bell Curve: Intelligence and Class Structure in American Life* (New York: Free Press, 1994), 167, 251, 253, and 532–33.

For a devastating and definitive critique of *The Bell Curve,* based on a correct(ed) analysis of the same survey data that leads to diametrically opposed conclusions, see Claude Fischer et al., *Inequality by Design: Cracking the Bell Curve Myth* (Princeton, N.J.: Princeton University Press, 1996). The purely ideological character of Murray and Herrnstein's theses on crime-related matters emerges from the statistical replication carried out by Francis T. Cullen, Paul Gendreau, G. Roger Jarjoura, and John Paul Wright, "Crime and the Bell Curve: Lessons from Intelligent Criminology," *Crime and Delinquency* 43.4 (October 1997): 387–411.

16. Several accounts of the Manhattan Institute's rise on the public scene describe Rudolph Giuliani furiously filling his notepad at these conferences and report the regular presence of his advisers at the major meetings held there. The mayor himself has publicly acknowledged his "intellectual" debt to the institute on several occasions.

17. George Kelling and Catherine Coles, *Fixing Broken Windows: Restoring Order and Reducing Crime in Our Communities* (New York: Free Press, 1996); the original article that is extended and illustrated by the book is James Q. Wilson and George Kelling, "Broken Windows: The Police and Neighborhood Safety," *Atlantic Monthly* (March 1982): 29–38. If this "commonsense theory" is true, one wonders why it took more than fifteen years for anyone to realize it.

18. For an incisive theoretical and empirical critique of "broken windows" and its application to New York City, read Bernard E. Harcourt, "Reflecting on the Subject: A Critique of the Social Influence Conception of Deterrence, the Broken Windows Theory, and Order-Maintenance Policing New-York Style," *Michigan Law Review* 97.2 (November 1998): 291–389. For a thorough refutation based on methodical field observation of Chicago neighborhoods that finds the relationship between public disorder and crime to be spurious, see Robert J. Sampson and Stephen W. Raudenbush, "Systematic Social Observation of Public Spaces: A New Look at Disorder in Urban Neighborhoods," *American Journal of Sociology* 105.3 (November 1999): 603–51. Ralph Taylor has shown, in the case of Baltimore, that changes in levels of street disorder, housing dilapidation and physical decay, and racial composition of the neighborhoods do not in themselves cause rises in the local incidence of crime, whereas sustained economic decline does. See Ralph B. Taylor, *Breaking Away from Broken Windows: Baltimore Neighborhoods and the Nationwide Fight against Crime, Fear and Decline* (Boulder, Colo.: Westview Press, 2001).

19. William Bratton, "Cutting Crime and Restoring Order: What America Can Learn from New York's Finest," *Heritage Lecture n. 573* (Washington, D.C.: Heritage Foundation, 1996), and idem, "The New York City Police Department's Civil Enforcement of Quality of Life Crimes," *Journal of Law and Policy* 3 (1995): 447–64; see also "Squeegees Rank High on Next Police Commissioner's Priority List," *New York Times,* December 4, 1993.

20. William Bratton and William Andrews, "What We've Learned about Policing," *City Journal* 9.2 (summer 1999): 14–27.

21. For a critical yet succinct presentation of these three models of "police reform" recently in competition in the United States, and how they have all been appropriated by the "most repressive police tradition," see Jean-Paul Brodeur, "La police en Amérique du Nord: des modèles aux effets de mode?" *Les Cahiers de la sécurité intérieure* 18.2 (spring 1997): 182.

22. "NYPD, Inc.," *Economist* 7925 (July 20, 1995): 50, and "The C.E.O. Cop," *New Yorker* 70 (February 6, 1995): 45–54.

23. Figures on budget and staffing come from *Citizen's Budget Commission–*

Annual Report (New York: October 1998); the police-to-population is from Harcourt, "Reflecting on the Subject," 333–34.

24. Judith A. Greene, "Zero Tolerance: A Case Study of Police Policies and Practices in New York City," *Crime and Delinquency* 45.2 (April 1999): 171–87.

25. The number of murders in New York had already fallen by half between 1990 and 1994 (when Bratton took up his post), from a peak of 2,300 to under 1,200, and the number of property crimes by 25 percent. The same abrupt decline in most crime categories was also observed in Canada after 1990, without it being attributable to any police innovation or increased penal sanctions (the prison population of Canada went down throughout the 1990s).

26. William W. Bratton with Peter Knobler, *Turnaround: How America's Top Cop Reversed the Crime Epidemic* (New York: Random House, 1998). Bratton received a $375,000 advance to "write" this panegyric on his own life with the collaboration of Knobler, a journalist specializing in schmaltzy biographies of stars of sports and politics (among his other books are the "autobiographies" of basketball player Kareem Abdul-Jabbar and the ex-governor of Texas, Ann Richards). After his firing in March 1996, Bratton became vice chairman of Boston-based First Security Services Corp. before moving to the Carco Group Inc., a Saint James security services firm, in early 1998.

27. Published as "Making America's Cities Great Places to Live," *Civic Bulletin* (the Manhattan Institute's newsletter) 17, April 1999, 2.

28. The account that follows is based on a survey of the research literature and governmental publications, a close tracking of the international press, and personal communication with researchers in the different countries concerned (England, Germany, Austria, Italy, Brazil, and Argentina).

29. In 1993, the year when Rudolph Giuliani became mayor, New York ranked 87th out of 189 cities listed (by decreasing order) on the crime scale of the FBI. In 1999, it was perched in 140th place.

30. Henry McLeish, "Zero Tolerance Will Clean Up Our Streets," *Scottish Daily Record & Sunday Mail,* February 10, 1999. On this theme of the "responsibilization" of citizens and (geographic or ethnic) "communities" in the struggle against crime, see David Garland, "Les contradictions de la société punitive: le cas britannique," *Actes de la recherche en sciences sociales* 124 (September 1998): 56–59, and Adam Crawford, *The Local Governance of Crime: Appeals to Community and Partnership* (Oxford: Clarendon Press, 1997).

31. "The Polish are particularly active in organized car theft; prostitution is dominated by the Russian mafia, drug criminals most often come from southeastern Europe or black Africa. . . . We should no longer be so timid toward the foreign criminals we catch. For whomever violates our law of hospitality, there is only one response: out!—and fast" (Gerhard Schröder, campaign remarks made in July 1997, as reported in *Le Monde,* January 28, 1999). The case of Germany is interesting because it illustrates a process common to various countries on the European continent: Germany imports the made-in-USA doctrines on law and order both directly from the United States (Bratton's tour of the country in 1998) and, at the same time, through the intermediary of the other "trading posts" of U.S. security ideology (the envious emulation of Tony Blair's Britain and the ambivalent interest in Gabriele Albertini's Milan).

32. On the social foundations of the new, expansive discourses and policies on security in Italy, see Alessandro De Giorgi, *Zero Tolleranza. Strategie e pratiche della società di controllo* (Rome: Derive Approdi, 2000); for a close-up study of the trans-

formation of the tactics and role of policing in the maintenance of urban order, Salvatore Palidda, *Polizia Postmoderna. Etnografia del nuovo controllo sociale* (Milan: Feltrinelli, 2000).

33. The quote from Bratton is in "'Tolerancia cero' para Buenos Aires: Bill Bratton, el creador de la reforma de seguridad de Nueva York vino a trabajar en un proyecto similar para Nueva Dirigencia," *La Nación* 17 (January 2000). I spent nine days in Argentina in April 2000, during which I was able to measure firsthand the fascination bordering on obsession of the Argentine media and political class with New York–style policing techniques and slogans (see my account in the Afterword). On the export to South America of neoliberal penality by the "New York Boys" of Giuliani two decades after the "Chicago Boys" had experimented with neoliberal economic policies on that continent, see Loïc Wacquant, "Mister Bratton Goes to Buenos Aires: Prefacio a la edición para América Latina," in *Cárceles de la miseria* (Buenos Aires: Ediciones Manantial, 2000), 11–17.

34. "Lawsuit Seeks to Curb Street Crimes Unit, Alleging Racially Biased Searches," *New York Times,* March 9, 1999.

35. "Those NYPD Blues," *U.S. News and World Report,* April 5, 1999. According to the statistics of the New York Police Department, street stops aimed at the interdiction of weapons lead to twenty-nine arrests for every person actually carrying a weapon, a ratio vastly superior to the police norm in other cities (ten arrests for every armed target).

36. Greene, "Zero Tolerance," 171–87.

37. Attorney General, *The New York City Police Department's "Stop and Frisk" Practices: A Report to the People of the State of New York from the Office of the Attorney General* (New York: Civil Rights Bureau, 1999), 9.

38. "Cop Rebellion against Safir: 400 PBA Delegates Vote No Confidence, Demand Suspension," *New York Daily News,* April 14, 1999.

39. "Poll in New York Finds Many Think Police Are Biased," *New York Times,* March 16, 1999.

40. New York City Police Department, *Statistical Report: Complaints and Arrests* (Office of Management Analysis and Planning, Crime Analysis Unit, 1994 to 1998).

41. "Crackdown on Minor Offenses Swamps New York City Courts," *New York Times,* February 2, 1999.

42. Malcolm Feeley has shown that, for lower-class Americans who commit minor misdemeanors and crimes, the true penal sanction resides less in the legal penalty inflicted upon them as the outcome of judicial processing than in this processing itself, that is, the disdainful and chaotic treatment they receive at the hands of the courts and its ancillary economic, social, and moral costs (Malcolm Feeley, *The Process Is the Punishment: Handling Cases in a Lower Criminal Court* [New York: Russell Sage Foundation, 1979], 199–243).

43. Keith Dixon, *Les Évangélistes du marché. Les intellectuels britanniques et le néolibéralisme* (Paris: Raisons d'agir Éditions, 1998). They were later joined by Demos, the official "think tank" of Blair's team, which defends similar (nay, identical) theses from "across" the political divide.

44. "I arrived in Great Britain earlier this year, a visitor from a plague area come to see whether the disease is spreading" (Charles Murray, *The Emerging British Underclass* [London: Institute of Economic Affairs, 1990], 25). On the origins and social uses of the pseudoconcept of "underclass," which came into circulation in several European countries in the late 1990s, see Loïc Wacquant, "L'‘underclass' urbaine dans

l'imaginaire social et scientifique américain," in Serge Paugam, ed., *L'Exclusion. L'état des savoirs* (Paris: La Découverte, 1996), 248–62.

45. Murray, *The Emerging British Underclass,* 41 and 45.

46. Frank Field, MP, "Britain's Underclass: Countering the Growth," in ibid., 58 and 59.

47. "Get the Poor off Our Over-Taxed Backs," *Guardian,* September 17, 1994, 29.

48. "Britain's Poor a Growing Threat to Society," *Times of London,* May 4, 1990.

49. "Get the Poor off Our Over-Taxed Backs."

50. Charles Murray in Ruth Lister, ed., *Charles Murray and the Underclass: The Developing Debate* (London: Institute of Economic Affairs, 1996), 127.

51. "Get the Poor off Our Over-Taxed Backs."

52. Ibid. One notes the parallel with the lament of Debray et al. ("Républicains, n'ayons pas peur!"), for whom penal laxity poses a similar threat to the Republic in France. Murray's rhetoric is premised on a dichotomous opposition between "the New Victorians" (a term designating the middle and upper classes who are allegedly rediscovering the virtues of work, abstinence, and patriarchal domesticity) and "the New Rabble" composed of the dregs of society, mired in promiscuity, the refusal of (underpaid) work, and predatory crime. This sociological balderdash, the American–British version of a certain French discourse on the "social divide" (the *fracture sociale* famously ballyhooed by Jacques Chirac during the 1995 presidential race to give a semblance of "social" contents to his campaign), was repeated ad lib as is in the *Sunday Times* and several other British dailies (e.g., "Britain Split as Underclass Takes Root alongside 'New Victorians,'" *Sunday Times,* May 22, 1994).

53. Lawrence Mead, ed., *From Welfare to Work: Lessons from America* (London: Institute of Economic Affairs, 1997). The title needs no comment.

54. Lawrence Mead, *Beyond Entitlement: The Social Obligations of Citizenship* (New York: Free Press, 1986), 24, 13, and 84.

55. Lawrence Mead, *The New Politics of Poverty: The Nonworking Poor in America* (New York: Basic Books, 1992), 239 and passim. For a pointed critique of the manifold paralogisms that underlie Mead's arguments, read Michael B. Katz, "The Poverty Debate," *Dissent* (autumn 1992): 548–53. One notes in passing that the advocates of the police treatment of street-level poverty make the same criticism of the "sociologism" that is guilty in their eyes of insisting that crime has social rather than individual causes.

56. Lawrence Mead, ed., *The New Paternalism: Supervisory Approaches to Poverty* (Washington, D.C.: The Brookings Institution, 1997), 21–22, and idem, "Telling the Poor What to Do," *Public Interest* 132 (summer 1998): 97–112. Note that Mead is careful to *not* say that paternalism serves the *freedom* of the poor as it does that of "others": as with children (and, in another era, slaves), their freedom must be curtailed for their own good.

57. The preface to the collection edited by Mead, *The New Paternalism,* signed by Michael Armacost, chairman of the Brookings Institution, the "progressive" think tank (it is close to the "New Democrats") that financed and published this research, opens with these lines, which speak volumes about the integration of social and penal policies targeted at the (sub)proletariat: "American social policy is becoming more paternalistic. Traditionally, social programs gave benefits to people, but recently government has sought to supervise the lives of the poor who become dependent on it, *either through welfare or the criminal justice system*" (vii, emphasis added).

58. Mead, ibid., 22. For a definitive empirical refutation of this personal mythology of the racial mixing of poor populations in urban America, see Douglas Massey and

Nancy Denton, *American Apartheid* (Cambridge: Harvard University Press, 1993), and Robert Bullard, J. Eugene Grigsby, and Charles Lee, eds., *Residential Apartheid: The American Legacy* (Los Angeles: CAAS Publications, 1994).

59. Frank Field had anticipated the imminent importation and adoption of the Murray–Mead themes in his own book *Losing Out: The Emergence of Britain's Underclass* (Oxford: Basil Blackwell, 1989), whose title is an obvious takeoff on *Losing Ground*.

60. Mead, *From Welfare to Work*, 127.

61. Lawrence Mead, "The Debate on Poverty and Human Nature," in S. Carlson-Thies and J. Skillen, eds., *Welfare in America: Christian Perspectives on a Policy in Crisis* (Cambridge: William Eerdmans Publishing Co., 1996), 215–16, 238, 241–42.

62. As in 1989 and 1994, the *Sunday Times* generously accorded several full pages to a two-part article by Charles Murray that gave the views of the "visitor from America" an instant national visibility that no lifelong British student of crime and punishment has ever enjoyed, even though Murray's simplistic and sophomoric statements are based on no original research: they are a mere rehash of well-worn works by leading ultraconservative criminologists and crime ideologues such as James Q. Wilson and John DiIulio. We reach here the limit of pure *ideological marketing work* aiming to sell a conservative pig in a sociological poke.

63. For a dismantling of this "Case for More Incarceration" presented by U.S. Attorney General William Barr in 1992 as part of the federal campaign to push states to boost their prison population, read Donziger, *The Real War on Crime*, 75–76.

64. Charles Murray, ed., *Does Prison Work?* (London: Institute of Economic Affairs, 1997), 26.

65. Norman Dennis et al., *Zero Tolerance: Policing a Free Society* (London: Institute of Economic Affairs, 1997), xii.

66. David Downes, "Toughing It Out: From Labour Opposition to Labour Government," *Policy Studies* 19. 3/4 (winter 1998): 191–98.

67. Dennis et al., *Zero Tolerance*. Tony Blair's statement is reported by the *Guardian* of April 10, 1997. (I am grateful to Richard Sparks, professor of criminology at Keele University, Staffordshire, for the valuable information he supplied on these developments.)

68. "Towards Zero Tolerance," *Times Literary Supplement* 4919, July 11, 1997, 25. The same article offers an enthusiastic advertisement for a germane book by Roy Ingleton titled *Arming the British Police: The Great Debate* (London: Frank Cass Publishers, 1997) (traditionally, police officers in the UK do not bear weapons).

69. At the Villepinte Colloquium "Safe Cities for Free Citizens" at which Lionel Jospin's government announced its penal turnaround, the interior minister drew this audacious parallel between education policy and police policy: "Giving free rein to my imagination, I would gladly imagine, following the example of the 'Universities 2000' plan, a five-year 'Neighborhood Security 2002' plan to accelerate the building of police stations in the difficult neighborhoods" (Colloquium proceedings, available from the archives at the interior ministry's Internet site: www.interieur.gouv.fr).

70. Institut des Hautes Études de la Sécurité Intérieure, *Guide pratique pour les contrats locaux de sécurité* (Paris: La Documentation française, 1997), 318 and 320. "Local Security Contracts" are compacts signed with the central state through which municipalities plan, promote, and implement proactive anticrime measures.

71. The expressions in quotation marks are those of Beaumont and Tocqueville, "Le système pénitentiaire aux États-Unis et son application en France," in Alexis de Tocqueville, *Œuvres complètes*, vol. 4, *Écrits sur le système pénitentiaire en France et à l'étranger*, ed. Michelle Perrot (Paris: Gallimard, 1984), 11.

72. That is to say, in the present conjuncture in France (spring 1999), to attract the voters of the National Front, particularly those left disoriented by the party's abrupt splintering in December 1998. This is the banal explanation for the sudden acceleration of the measures announced by the Jospin government to "reestablish" (republican) order and to "reconquer" the *banlieues*—another term borrowed from the military language of the American state and its "War on crime," which suggests that these outer-city areas have been "invaded" by an enemy (immigrants). This is also the reason behind the sudden about-face of the same prime minister in favor of the increased use of penal means in the treatment of juvenile delinquency, catapulted to the rank of priority for state action, even though a close-up examination of the existing statistics published in the official report on the question submitted to the government (which neither its authors nor its sponsors seem to have taken the trouble to read attentively) demonstrates that the physiognomy of French juvenile delinquency has hardly changed in recent years, contrary to media and political hype (cf. the appendix by criminologist Bruno Aubusson de Cavarlay, "Statistiques," in Christine Lazerges and Jean-Pierre Balduyck, *Réponses à la délinquance des mineurs. Mission interministérielle sur la prévention et le traitement de la délinquance des mineurs* [Paris: La Documentation française, 1998], 263–91; also idem, *La Mesure de la délinquance juvénile* [Paris: CESDIP, 1998]). I return to this point later in this chapter.

73. Sophie Body-Gendrot, Nicole Le Guennec, and Michel Herrou, *Mission sur les violences urbaines, Rapport au Ministre de l'intérieur* (Paris: La Documentation française, 1998). The bureaucratic invention of the notion of "urban violences" (the plural is essential to its attraction) as part of a strategy of reconversion and legitimation of police work in the area of domestic surveillance is recounted by Laurent Bonelli, "Renseignements généraux et violences urbaines," *Actes de la recherche en sciences sociales* 136–37 (March 2001): 95–103.

74. Lazerges and Balduyck, *Réponses à la délinquance des mineurs,* 433–36.

75. Ibid., 435.

76. William Ruefle and Kenneth Mike Reynolds, "Curfews and Delinquency in Major American Cities," *Crime and Delinquency* 41.3 (July 1995): 347–63; Craig Hemmens and Katherine Bennett, "Juvenile Curfews and the Courts: Judicial Response to a Not-So-New Crime Control Strategy," *Crime and Delinquency* 45.1 (January 1999): 99–121; and Tony Jeffs and Mark K. Smith, "'Getting the Dirtbags off the Streets': Curfews and Other Solutions to Juvenile Crime," *Youth & Policy* 53 (summer 1996): 1–14.

77. The IHESI is a state institute that conducts training seminars and "studies" on security and law-enforcement issues and policies. It is placed under the aegis not of the Ministry of Research but of the Ministry of the Interior (as part of its law-enforcement division); its works pertain to bureaucratic propaganda but aim to look like scholarly research.

78. Julien Damon, review of William Bratton and Peter Knobler, *Turnaround: How America's Top Cop Reversed the Crime Epidemic* (1997), *Les Cahiers de la sécurité intérieure* 34 (1998): 263–65. For a stinging analysis of the "authoritarian and racist technocratism" of which Bratton's pseudo-autobiography is the expression, read Helmut Otner, Arno Pilgram, and Heinz Steinert, eds., *Die Null-Lösung: Zero-Tolerance-Politik in New York—Das Ende der urbanen Toleranz?* (Baden-Baden: Nomos Verlag, 1998).

79. Sébastian Roché, *Sociologie politique de l'insécurité* (Paris: Presses Universitaires de France, 1997) (with the snappy subtitle "Urban violence, globalization, in-

equalities" and the dramatic query on the back cover: "Cities have been the cradle of civilization, will they be its grave?"), and Sébastian Roché and Jean-Louis Schlegel, *La Société d'hospitalité* (Paris: Éditions du Seuil, 1999).

80. In a book written in collaboration with Ronald Reagan's former secretary of education, with the most sensationalist title (and militaristic rhetoric) imaginable: William J. Bennett, John J. DiIulio, and John P. Walters, *Body Count: Moral Poverty . . . and How to Win America's War against Crime and Drugs* (New York: Simon and Schuster, 1996). DiIulio was later briefly in charge of Faith-Based Initiatives to combat poverty in the first Bush White House.

81. Sébastian Roché, "'Tolérance zéro': est-elle applicable en France?" *Les Cahiers de la sécurité intérieure* 34.4 (winter 1998): 217, 222, 225, 227, emphasis added.

82. "Que sais-je?" (What do I know?) is a high-prestige series published by Presses Universitaires de France consisting of short volumes reputed to provide the best up-to-date scientific information on a given topic.

83. Alain Bauer and Xavier Raufer, *Violences et insécurités urbaines,* Collection "Que sais-je?" no. 3421, updated edition (Paris: Presses Universitaires de France, 1999), 62–65, emphasis in the original.

84. Institut des Hautes Études de la Sécurité Intérieure, *Guide pratique pour les contrats locaux de sécurité,* 133–34.

85. Cf. Kenneth Clark, *Dark Ghetto: Dilemmas of Social Power* (New York: Harper and Row, 1965); Loïc Wacquant and William Julius Wilson, "The Cost of Racial and Class Exclusion in the Inner City," *The Annals of the American Academy of Political and Social Science* 501 (January 1989): 8–25; Joan Moore and Raquel Pinderhughes, eds., *In the Barrios: Latinos and the Underclass Debate* (New York: Russell Sage Foundation, 1993); William Julius Wilson, *When Work Disappears* (New York: Knopf, 1996).

86. Wesley G. Skogan, *Disorder and Decline: Crime and the Spiral of Decay in American Neighborhoods* (Berkeley: University of California Press, 1990). For a critical analysis of Skogan's thesis, see Loïc Wacquant, "Désordre dans la ville," *Actes de la recherche en sciences sociales* 99 (September 1993): 79–82.

87. Sophie Body-Gendrot, *Les Villes face à l'insécurité. Des ghettos américains aux banlieues françaises* (Paris: Bayard Éditions, 1998) (*banlieue* designates stigmatized areas of poverty in the French urban periphery; it is here roughly equivalent to "inner city"). According to the law of the genre, the book mixes scientific works (to give authority to its pronouncements) and journalistic reporting (to be accessible to decision makers and the media), as attested by the motley mix of its references, which have Jean Baudrillard rubbing shoulders with William Julius Wilson, articles from *Science* with *International Herald Tribune* pieces, quick "interviews" with judges, fiery editorials from the Parisian newsmagazine *Le Nouvel Observateur,* and pamphlets by former members of the Reagan administration.

88. The advertising copy communicated by the publisher at the book's launching asks the question more abruptly still: "Between the French *banlieues* and the American ghettos, *convergences exist:* a rise in youth delinquency, drugs, fighting among gangs, etc. For all that, can the policies of massive incarceration that have been *successfully* adopted in the United States be applied in France?" (emphasis added).

89. Page numbers in this section refer to Bruno Aubusson de Cavarlay, "Statistiques," in Lazerges and Balduyck, *Réponses à la délinquance des mineurs,* 263–91.

90. Lionel Jospin, "Lettres de mission," in Lazerges and Balduyck, *Réponses à la délinquance des mineurs,* 9.

91. The total absence of statistics on these phenomena did not prevent an editor of *Libération* (January 7, 1999) from writing with admirable self-assurance: "The situation that has been created on certain urban fringes is unprecedented, in the proportion of young people implicated, in the degree of violence that they exhibit, but also in the precociousness with which they move toward committing misdeeds."

92. "La loi Guigou adoptée en première lecture," *Libération*, March 27–28, 1999.

93. Jean-Pierre Chevènement, the minister in charge of police, had previously commissioned Body-Gendrot to write a "Report on Urban Violences" and the Interministerial Agency for City Policy financed the "mission" of a few weeks that allowed her to "live some field experiences in the sensitive neighborhoods of the United States" *[sic]* (Body-Gendrot, *Les Villes face à l'insécurité*, 14).

94. See Loïc Wacquant, "'A Black City within the White': Revisiting America's Dark Ghetto," *Black Renaissance–Renaissance Noire* 2.1 (fall–winter 1998): 141–51.

95. As Katherine Beckett showed in the case of the United States in her book *Making Crime Pay: Law and Order in Contemporary American Politics* (New York: Oxford University Press, 1997).

96. Body-Gendrot, *Les Villes face à l'insécurité*, 346, 332, 320–21, emphasis added. The work closes on this moving envoi, where moralizing lyricism vies with magazine politology, and which no minister of urban affairs would repudiate, even one belonging to the Socialist Party: "Let the police be placed at the service of the residents, let the school be a focus of neighborhood life, let elected officials deploy citizens' innovations, let the fight against crime become also the business of the inhabitants, and one sees another horizon dawn in the City." In other words, when life in the city is good, it will be jolly good. (A twin paragraph appears as the conclusion of the "Field Monographs Abroad" that adorn the official report of the *Mission sur les violences urbaines*, 136.)

97. "La loi Guigou adoptée en première lecture," *Libération*, March 27–28, 1999.

98. "L'argument sécuritaire l'a emporté à propos de la comparution immédiate," *Le Monde*, March 27, 1999.

99. John Williamson, "What Washington Means by Policy Reform," in John Williamson, ed., *Latin American Adjustment: How Much Has Happened?* (Washington, D.C.: Institute for International Economics, 1990). On the construction of this notion at the intersection of the academic and bureaucratic fields, see the provocative article by Yves Dezalay and Bryant Garth, "Le 'Washington consensus': contribution à une sociologie de l'hégémonie du néolibéralisme," *Actes de la recherche en sciences sociales* 121–22 (March 1998): 2–22.

2. From Social State to Penal State

1. One illustration among countless others: the leaflet of the German Ministry of Finance justifying Chancellor Schröder's brusque turn toward neoliberalism in the summer of 1999 (entailing the reduction of public expenditures by €16 billion, the lowering of personal income taxes, the freezing of pensions, the deregulation of employment, and the shrinking of social protection) has as its epigram this heartfelt cry from Mark Wössner, the CEO of the media conglomerate Bertelsmann: "A little bit of America, that's the path to follow for greater economic prosperity in Germany."

2. See Lawrence Mishel and John Schmidt, *Beware the U.S. Model: Jobs and Wages in a Deregulated Economy* (Washington, D.C.: Economic Policy Institute, 1995), and Charles Noble, *Welfare as We Knew It: A Political History of the American Welfare State* (New York: Oxford University Press, 1997), especially "Backlash," 105–35.

3. Doug Henwood, "Booming, Borrowing, and Consuming: The U.S. Economy in 1999," *Monthly Review* 51.3 (July–August 1999): 120–33.

4. Lee Rainwater and Timothy M. Smeeding, *Doing Poorly: The Real Income of American Children in Comparative Perspective* (Syracuse, N.Y.: Maxwell School of Citizenship and Public Affairs, Luxembourg Income Study Working Paper no. 127, 1995); and Laurence Mishel, Jared Bernstein, and John Schmidt, *The State of Working America, 1996–1997* (New York: M. E. Sharpe, 1997), 304–7.

5. On this "reform," the single most regressive piece of social legislation promulgated by a democratic government in the past half-century, see Loïc Wacquant, "Les pauvres en pâture: la nouvelle politique de la misère en Amérique," *Hérodote* 85 (spring 1997): 21–33, and the stern indictment by Nobel Prize economist Robert Solow, *Work and Welfare* (Princeton, N.J.: Princeton University Press, 1998).

6. Marion Nestle, "Hunger in America: A Matter of Policy," *Social Research* 66.1 (spring 1999): 257–79; Peter K. Eisinger, *Toward an End to Hunger in America* (Washington, D.C.: Brookings Institution, 1998); Olveen Carrasquillo et al., "Trends in Health Insurance Coverage, 1989–1997," *International Journal of Health Services* 29.3 (1999): 467–83; and James Wright, Beth Rubin, and Joel Devine, *Beside the Golden Door: Policy, Politics, and the Homeless* (New York: Aldine de Gruyter, 1998).

7. These figures and those in the preceding paragraph are taken from the important article by Richard Freeman, "Le modèle économique américain à l'épreuve de la comparaison," *Actes de la recherche en sciences sociales* 124 (September 1998): 36–48, and idem, "Rising Economic Disparity: Achilles' Heel of the American Economy," in *The Growth of Income Disparity in the United States* (Washington, D.C.: National Policy Association, 1998).

8. Martina Morris and Bruce Western, "Inequality in Earnings at the Close of the Twentieth Century," *Annual Review of Sociology* 25 (1999): 623–57, and Sarah Anderson et al., *A Decade of Executive Excess* (Washington, D.C.: Institute for Policy Studies, 1999), 3 and 8. Anderson and her collaborators compute that, if the average worker's wages had merely *risen* as fast as the pay of CEOs over the last decade, today the typical U.S. worker would be earning over $110,000 annually and the hourly minimum wage would exceed $22 (as against $5.15 in reality).

9. David Chalmers, *And the Crooked Places Made Straight: The Struggle for Social Change in the 1960s* (Philadelphia: Temple University Press, 1991), and James T. Patterson, *Grand Expectations: The United States, 1945–1974* (New York: Oxford University Press, 1996), esp. 375–406 and 637–77.

10. Calvert Dodge, ed., *A Nation without Prisons* (Lexington, Mass.: Lexington Books, 1975). On these debates, consult Norval Morris, *The Future of Imprisonment* (Chicago: University of Chicago Press, 1974), and Franklin Zimring and Gordon Hawkins, *The Scale of Punishment* (Chicago: University of Chicago Press, 1991), chapter 1.

11. Alexis de Tocqueville, *Œuvres complètes*, vol. 4, *Écrits sur le système pénitentiaire en France et à l'étranger*, ed. Michèle Perrot (Paris: Gallimard, 1984).

12. Unless otherwise indicated, I rely, for all these statistics, on various publications of the Bureau of Justice Statistics of the U.S. Department of Justice (especially its periodic reports on *Correctional Populations in the United States* (Washington, D.C.: U.S. Government Printing Office), available online at www.ojp.usdoj.gov/bjs.

13. See Bureau of Justice Statistics, *Criminal Victimization in the United States, 1973–1995* (Washington, D.C.: U.S. Government Printing Office, 1997). For a more detailed examination, see Loïc Wacquant, "Crime et châtiment en Amérique de Nixon à Clinton," *Archives de politique criminelle* 20 (spring 1998): 123–38, and Alfred

Blumstein, "U.S. Criminal Justice Conundrum: Rising Prison Populations and Stable Crime Rates," *Crime and Delinquency* 44.1 (January 1998): 127–35.

14. "Index crimes" include the property crimes of burglary, larceny-theft, and car theft, as well as the "violent crimes" of homicide and nonnegligent manslaughter, forcible rape, robbery, and aggravated assault; see Bureau of Justice Statistics, *Sourcebook of Criminal Justice Statistics 1999* (Washington, D.C.: U.S. Government Printing Office, 2000), 528, table 6.43.

15. Christopher Mumola and Allen Beck, *Prisoners in 1996* (Washington, D.C.: Bureau of Justice Statistics, 1997), 4–6, and David Greenberg and Valerie West, *The Persistent Significance of Race: Growth in State Prison Populations, 1971–1991* (New York: New York University, Department of Sociology, 1999).

16. For a field vignette on daily life in the Los Angeles County Jail, see Loïc Wacquant, "La colonie pénitentiaire," *Les Inrockuptibles* 178 (December 1998): 58–60.

17. Bureau of Justice Statistics, *Correctional Populations in the United States, 1997* (Washington, D.C.: U.S. Government Printing Office, 1997); and Vincent Schiraldi, Jason Ziedenberg, and John Irwin, *America's One Million Nonviolent Prisoners* (Washington, D.C.: Justice Policy Institute, 1999).

18. Caroline Wolf Harlow, *Profile of Jail Inmates 1996* (Washington, D.C.: Bureau of Justice Statistics, 1998).

19. James Austin and John Irwin, *It's about Time: America's Imprisonment Binge* (Belmont, Calif.: Wadsworth, 1997), 33.

20. Ibid., 54–55.

21. See Michael Tonry and Kate Hamilton, eds., *Intermediate Sanctions in Overcrowded Times* (Boston: Northeastern University Press, 1995), and Joan Petersilia, ed., *Community Corrections: Probation, Parole, and Intermediate Sanctions* (New York: Oxford University Press, 1997).

22. Diana Gordon describes this synergy very effectively in *The Justice Juggernaut: Fighting Street Crime* (New Brunswick, N.J.: Rutgers University Press, 1991).

23. Bureau of Justice Statistics, *Survey of State Criminal History Information Systems, 1997* (Washington, D.C.: U.S. Government Printing Office, 1999).

24. Two-thirds of employers of low-wage labor are opposed in principle to hiring an applicant with a criminal record, whereas two-thirds are open to taking on board an applicant who has been unemployed for more than a year, and one-half would give a job to a candidate with no work experience (Larry Holzer, *What Employers Want: Job Prospects for Less-Educated Workers* [New York: Russell Sage Foundation, 1996], 45–62).

25. Joan Petersilia, "Parole and Prisoner Reentry in the United States," in Michael Tonry and Joan Petersilia, eds., *Prisons* (Chicago: University of Chicago Press, 1999), 479–529.

26. Malcolm Feeley and Jonathan Simon, "The New Penology: Notes on the Emerging Strategy of Corrections and Its Implications," *Criminology* 30.4 (November 1992): 449–74, and Jonathan Simon, *Poor Discipline: Parole and the Social Control of the Underclass, 1890–1990* (Chicago: University of Chicago Press, 1993).

27. Steven Donziger, *The Real War on Crime* (New York: Basic Books, 1996), 48–51; Camille Graham Camp and George M. Camp, *The Corrections Yearbook 1998* (Middletown, Conn.: Criminal Justice Institute, 1998), 86–87.

28. If one takes into account the employees of private correctional facilities (which include some 14,000 guards), corrections vaults ahead of Kelly Services to take third place behind Manpower Incorporated and Wal-Mart.

29. The share of corporate taxes in federal tax revenues has been halved in three decades, from 23 percent in 1960 to 10 percent in 1995; that year private firms paid a mere 23 percent of their profits in taxes as against 50 percent in 1958. The effective tax rate for the richest 1 percent Americans went down from 35.5 percent to 29.3 percent between 1977 and 1992, while it remained constant for the bottom 80 percent of households (Nancy Folbre, *The New Field Guide to the U.S. Economy* [New York: New Press, 1995], 51–53).

30. Donziger, *The Real War on Crime,* 48. This trade-off is particular costly in Southern states, which have the highest incarceration rates and the biggest correctional budgets (relative to state expenditures) in the country, while their public education systems literally crumble under the weight of decaying infrastructure, insufficient staff, and underperforming teachers and students.

31. Robert Gangi, Vincent Shiraldi, and Jason Ziedenberg, *New York State of Mind? Higher Education vs. Prison Funding in the Empire State, 1988–1998* (Washington, D.C.: Justice Policy Institute, 1998), 1.

32. The penal philosophy dominant today in the United States may be summed up by this expression, in wide currency among correctional officials: "To make prisoners smell like prisoners" (Wesley Johnson et al., "Getting Tough on Prisoners: Results from the National Corrections Executive Survey, 1995," *Crime and Delinquency* 43.1 [January 1997]: 25–26). Whence the reintroduction of corporal punishments and assorted measures designed to humiliate: breaking rocks and cleaning ditches in chain gangs, ankle shackles, striped uniforms, "navy crew" haircuts, the suppression of coffee and cigarettes, and the prohibition of pornographic magazines, weightlifting, personal clothing, Christmas packages, and so on.

33. Michelle Gaseau and Carissa B. Caramanis, "Success of Inmates Fees Increases Their Popularity among Prisons and Jails," *Corrections Network* (online journal), October 1998.

34. Daniel Burton-Rose, Dan Pens, and Paul Wright, eds., *The Celling of America: An Inside Look at the U.S. Prison Industry* (Monroe, Maine: Common Courage Press, 1998), 102–31.

35. Camille Graham Camp and George M. Camp, eds., *The Corrections Yearbook 2001* (Middletown, Conn.: Criminal Justice Institute, 2001), 116–17.

36. Kerry L. Pyle, "Prison Employment: A Long-term Solution to the Overcrowding Crisis," *Boston University Law Review* 77.1 (February 1997): 151–80.

37. For a historical survey of private imprisonment in the United States, see Alexis M. Durham, "Origins and Interest in the Privatization of Punishment: The Nineteenth and Twentieth Century American Experience," *Criminology* 27.1 (1989): 43–52.

38. This growth came to a grinding halt in 2000 due to a combination of three factors: the bursting of the stock market bubble that had fed speculative involvement in incarceration, the sharp slowdown in carceral expansion, and a series of widely publicized scandals tainting the image of the major firms.

39. The data in this paragraph come from four days of field observation and interviews with officials and firm representatives I conducted at the CCA meetings in Orlando in August 1997.

40. Eric Lotke, "The Prison-Industrial Complex," *Multinational Monitor* 17.11 (November 1996): 22.

41. A study of 60 large private prisons covering half of the national market found that for-profit operators received significant subsidies in 17 of 19 states. Fully 78 percent of the establishments built by Corrections Corporation of America and 69

percent of those operated by Wackenhut Corrections Corporation were subsidized. Remarkably, not a single local government had conducted a rigorous impact study documenting the supposed economic benefits of this government support. See Phil Mattera and Mafruza Khan, *Jail Breaks: Economic Development Subsidies Given to Private Prisons* (Washington, D.C.: Institute on Taxation and Economic Policy, 2001).

42. This estimate is high because it merges "Anglo" whites and persons of Hispanic origin, thus mechanically boosting the rate for "whites" of European origin, and increasingly so over time, since Latinos are the category whose incarceration rate has increased the fastest in recent years.

43. This is the title of the book by Jerome Miller, *Search and Destroy: African-American Males in the Criminal Justice System* (New York: Cambridge University Press, 1997).

44. Human Rights Watch, *Punishment and Prejudice: Racial Disparities in the War on Drugs* (New York: Human Rights Watch, 1999), 34.

45. Michael Tonry, *Malign Neglect: Race, Crime and Punishment in America* (New York: Oxford University Press, 1995), 105, and idem, "Racial Politics, Racial Disparities, and the War on Crime," *Crime and Delinquency* 40.4 (October 1994): 475–94.

46. Loïc Wacquant, "Inside the Zone: The Social Art of the Hustler in the Black American Ghetto," *Theory, Culture & Society* 15.2 (May 1998): 1–36; Philippe Bourgois, "Just Another Night in a Shooting Gallery," *Theory, Culture & Society* 15.2 (May 1998): 37–66; and William M. Adler, *Land of Opportunity: One Family's Quest for the American Dream in the Age of Crack* (New York: Atlantic Monthly Press, 1995).

47. Gangi, Shiraldi, and Ziedenberg, *New York State of Mind?* 3.

48. William J. Chambliss, "Policing the Ghetto Underclass: The Politics of Law and Law Enforcement," *Social Problems* 41.2 (May 1994): 177–94, and Martin Gilens, "Racial Attitudes and Opposition to Welfare, *Journal of Politics* 57.4 (November 1995): 994–1014.

49. David Rothman, *The Discovery of the Asylum: Social Order and Disorder in the New Republic* (Boston: Little, Brown, 1971), 254–55.

50. Marta Nelson, Perry Dees, and Charlotte Allen, *The First Month Out: Post-Incarceration Experiences in New York City* (New York: Vera Institute, 1999).

51. Bruce Western and Katherine Beckett, "How Unregulated Is the U.S. Labor Market? The Penal System as a Labor Market Institution," *American Journal of Sociology* 104.4 (January 1999): 1030–60.

52. Sidra Lea Gifford, *Justice Expenditures and Employment in the United States, 1999* (Washington, D.C.: Bureau of Justice Statistics, 2002), 7. This gives the United States 24 correctional employees per 10,000 residents in full-time equivalents, compared to 4 per 10,000 for France (24,220 staff), 5 for Spain (22,035), and 8 for England and Wales (41,065), according to data from *Statistique pénale annuelle du Conseil de l'Europe, Enquête 2000* (Strasbourg: Council of Europe, 2001), 47.

53. Western and Beckett, "How Unregulated Is the U.S. Labor Market?" 1031.

54. Jamie Peck and Nikolas Theodore, "The Business of Contingent Work: Growth and Restructuring in Chicago's Temporary Employment Industry," *Work, Employment & Society* 12.4 (1998): 655–74, and Kathleen Barker and Kathleen Kristensen, eds., *Contingent Work: American Employment Relations in Transition* (Ithaca, N.Y.: Cornell University Press, 1998).

55. For a compressed historical and conceptual elaboration on the coupling be-

tween (hyper)ghetto and prison after the ebbing of the civil rights movement, see Loïc Wacquant, "The New 'Peculiar Institution': On the Prison as Surrogate Ghetto," *Theoretical Criminology* 4.3, special issue on "New Social Studies of the Prison" (2000): 377–89.

56. Kerner Commission, *The Kerner Report. The 1968 Report of the National Advisory Commission on Civil Disorders* (New York: Pantheon, 1989 [1968]); Thomas Byrne Edsall and Mary D. Edsall, *Chain Reaction: The Impact of Race, Rights, and Taxes on American Politics* (New York: W. W. Norton, 1991); and Fred R. Harris and Lynn Curtis, eds., *Locked in the Poorhouse: Cities, Race, and Poverty in the United States* (Lanham, Md.: Rowman & Littlefield, 1998).

57. Armond White, *Rebel for the Hell of It: The Life of Tupac Shakur* (London: Quartet Books, 1997; 2d ed. New York: Thunder's Mouth Press, 2002).

58. Michael B. Katz, *In the Shadow of the Poorhouse: A Social History of Welfare in America,* expanded edition (New York: Basic Books, 1996), chapter 11; and Joel Handler and Yeheskel Hasenfeld, *We the Poor People: Work, Poverty, and Welfare* (New Haven: Yale University Press, 1997).

59. E. Fuller Torrey, "Jails and Prisons: America's New Mental Hospitals," *America Journal of Public Health* 85.12 (December 1995): 1611–13.

60. J. Robert Lilly and Paul Knepper, "The Corrections-Commercial Complex," *Crime and Delinquency* 39.2 (April 1993): 150–66; Eric Schlosser, "The Prison-Industrial Complex," *Atlantic Monthly* 282 (December 1998): 51–77; and Eve Goldberg and Linda Evans, *The Prison Industrial Complex and the Global Economy* (Boston: Kersplebedeb, 1998). A trove of activist writings, calls, and information on the topic is the site www.prisonsucks.com run by the Prison Policy Initiative (based in Northampton, Massachusetts).

61. See, for example, Elihu Rosenblatt, ed., *Criminal Injustice: Confronting the Prison Crisis* (Boston: South End Press, 1996), esp. 13–72; Angela Davis and A. F. Gordon, "Globalism and the Prison-Industrial Complex: An Interview with Angela Davis," *Race and Class* 40.2/3 (1999): 145–57; and Rose Braz et al., "Overview: Critical Resistance to the Prison-Industrial Complex," introduction to a symposium on "The Prison-Industrial Complex," *Social Justice* 27.3 (fall 2000): 1–5.

62. Loïc Wacquant, "De l'État charitable à l'État pénal: notes sur le traitement politique de la misère en Amérique," *Regards sociologiques* 11 (1996): 30–38.

63. In fiscal 2001, UNICOR, the Federal Prison Industries program, employed 22,600 inmates to produce a variety of goods (law-enforcement uniforms and kevlar helmets, bedding and draperies, office furniture, laundry services, bindery, vehicular repair, electronics recycling, etc.) sold to the government for a turnover of $583 million. Despite financial subsidies, a captive market (two-thirds of sales are to the Defense Department), and inmate wages averaging a paltry 23 cents to $1.15 an hour, the program turned up a negative cash flow of $5 million (Federal Bureau of Prisons, *UNICOR 2001 Annual Report* [Lexington, Ky.]).

64. Goldberg and Evans, *The Prison Industrial Complex and the Global Economy,* 5.

65. Zimring and Hawkins, *The Scale of Imprisonment,* 173.

66. Malcolm Feeley and Edward L. Rubin, *Judicial Policy Making and the Modern State: How the Courts Reformed America's Prisons* (New York: Oxford University Press, 1998).

67. Jordan B. Glaser and Robert B. Greifinger, "Correctional Health Care: A Public Health Opportunity," *Annals of Internal Medicine* 118.2 (January 1993): 139–45.

68. André Kuhn, "Populations carcérales: Combien? Pourquoi? Que faire?" *Archives de politique criminelle* 20 (spring 1998): 47–99; see also Pierre Tournier, "The Custodial Crisis in Europe, Inflated Prison Populations and Possible Alternatives," *European Journal of Criminal Policy and Research* 2.4 (1994): 89–110; and the periodic reports in the *Bulletin d'information pénologique* of the Council of Europe (from which the 2000 figures are drawn).

69. Administration Pénitentiaire, *Rapport annuel d'activité 1996* (Paris: Ministère de la Justice, 1997), 14.

70. Pierre Tournier, "La population des prisons est-elle condamnée à croître?" *Sociétés et représentations* 3 (November 1996): 321–32.

71. Thierry Godefroy, *Mutation de l'emploi et recomposition pénale* (Paris: CESDIP, 1998), 16–17. See also Thierry Godefroy and Bernard Laffargue, *Changements économiques et répression pénale* (Paris: CESDIP, 1995).

72. The RMI, to consider only this program, which is emblematic of the new politics of poverty set up in France in the late 1980s, has experienced vigorous growth: in ten years, the number of beneficiaries has multiplied by 2.8 to reach 2 million and its budget has increased fivefold.

73. Georg Rusche and Otto Kirchheimer, *Punishment and Social Structure* (New York: Columbia University Press, 1939; reprinted by Transaction Press, 2003), and Theodore Chiricos and Miriam A. Delone, "Labor Surplus and Punishment: A Review and Assessment of Theory and Evidence," *Social Problems* 39.4 (1992): 421–46. See also David E. Barlow, Melissa Hickman Barlow, and Theodore G. Chiricos, "Long Economic Cycles and the Criminal Justice System in the U.S.," *Crime, Law and Social Change* 19.2 (March 1993): 143–69, and the counterargument for the prevalence of political variables put forth by David Jacobs and Ronald E. Helms, "Toward a Political Model of Incarceration: A Time-Series Examination of Multiple Explanations for Prison Admission Rates," *American Journal of Sociology* 102.2 (September 1996): 323–57.

74. Sonja Snacken, Kees Beyens, and Hilde Tubex, "Changing Prison Populations in Western Countries: Fate or Policy?" *European Journal of Crime, Criminal Law, and Criminal Justice* 3.1 (1995): 18–53, esp. 28–29.

75. Bruno Aubusson de Cavarlay, "Hommes, peines et infractions," *Année sociologique* 35 (1985): 293. Setting aside the legal designation of the offense committed, time in prison strikes "nearly one in two among the jobless, one in seven for workers, one in thirty among employers; the ratio for fines is the obverse" (ibid., 291–92).

76. The proportion of jobless inmates in France was estimated as follows: according to figures from the National File of Prisoners, 26 percent of those whose employment situation could be determined declared themselves unemployed (18 percent had held a job before and 6 percent had never worked); if one makes the conservative hypothesis that the 40 percent of inmates whose job status was "undetermined" were unemployed in the same proportion of one-fourth, that gives at least another 10 percent jobless inmates, to which one can add a portion of the 5 percent of "others, students, military, housewives," for a low estimate exceeding 35 percent. If half of the "undetermined" were jobless, the rate would approach 50 percent (these data were communicated to me by Annie Kensey, demographer with the French Administration pénitentiaire, to whom I am grateful). A qualitative survey conducted in Provence-Alpes-Côte d'Azur lends support to this estimate: it found that one-half of the inmates in this region were jobless at the time of their entry into jail (Jean-Paul Jean, "L'inflation carcérale," *Esprit* 215 [October 1995]: 117–31).

77. Rod Morgan, "Imprisonment: Current Concerns and a Brief History since 1945," in *The Oxford Handbook of Criminology* (Oxford: Oxford University Press, 1997), 1161.

78. David J. Smith, "Ethnic Origins, Crime, and Criminal Justice in England and Wales," in Michael Tonry, ed., *Ethnicity, Crime, and Immigration: Comparative and Cross-National Perspectives* (Chicago: University of Chicago Press, 1997), 101–82.

79. Hans-Jörg Albrecht, "Ethnic Minority, Crime and Criminal Justice in Germany," in Tonry, *Ethnicity, Crime, and Immigration,* 87.

80. Josine Junger-Tas, "Ethnic Minorities and Criminal Justice in the Netherlands," in Tonry, *Ethnicity, Crime, and Immigration,* 257–310.

81. Fabienne Breton, Anabelle Rihoux, and François de Coninck, "La surpopulation et l'inflation carcérales," *La Revue Nouvelle* 109.4 (April 1999): 48–66.

82. The most insidious of these are not the shrill and paranoid delusions of the representatives of the National Front during their electoral meetings, whose excessive and hate-filled tenor "republicans" at heart are unanimous in deploring, but the soft-spoken discourses that are held *within the state apparatus,* for example, in the National Assembly, courteously, between reasonable and respectable people, with all the juridical euphemisms and oratorical denegations that make for the charm—and the force—of official language (as shown by Charlotte Lessana, "La loi Debré: la fabrique de l'immigré," *Cultures et conflits* 31.32 [fall–winter 1998]: 125–59).

83. Pierre Tournier, "La délinquance des étrangers en France: analyse des statistiques pénales," in Salvatore Palidda, ed., *Délit d'immigration/Immigrant Delinquency* (Brussels: European Commission, 1996), 158.

84. According to the ideal-typical distinction introduced by Claude Faugeron, "La dérive pénale," *Esprit* 215 (October 1995): 132–44.

85. The term *double peine* refers to the fact that foreigners can be and frequently are sanctioned twice by French (and other European) law: first by incarceration for the specific crime they committed, and second by banishment from the national territory *after* they have served their sentence via administrative decree or judicial sanction (often executed in violation of the European Convention on the Rights of Man).

86. Jean-Pierre Perrin-Martin, *La Rétention* (Paris: L'Harmattan, 1996), and, for a comparison between France, the United Kingdom, and Germany, as well as with the United States, see the issue of *Culture et conflits* 23 (1996) devoted to the theme "Circuler, enfermer, éloigner: Zones d'attente et centres de rétention des démocraties occidentales."

87. Laurence Vanpaeschen et al., *Les Barbelés de la honte* (Brussels: Luc Pire, 1998); Fabienne Brion, "Chiffrer, déchiffrer: Incarcération des étrangers et construction sociale de la criminalité des immigrés en Belgique," in Palidda, *Délit d'immigration/ Immigrant Delinquency,* 163–223.

88. Salvatore Palidda, "La construction sociale de la déviance et de la criminalité parmi les immigrés: le cas italien," in Palidda, *Délit d'immigration/Immigrant Delinquency,* 231–66.

89. Literally, "justice with forty gears," implying grossly unequal treatment at the hands of the penal system for different social categories and infractions. Longwy is a formerly monoindustrial town in the northeastern region of Lorraine plagued by high rates of long-term unemployment following the collapse of the steel industry in the 1970s.

90. Didier Bigo, *L'Europe des polices et la sécurité intérieure* (Brussels: Éditions

Complexe, 1992), and idem, "Sécurité et immigration: vers une gouvernementalité de l'inquiétude?" *Cultures et conflits* 31.32 (fall–winter 1998): 13–38.

91. On this process of the criminalization of immigrants, see the comparative works assembled by Allesandro Dal Lago, ed., *Lo straniero e il nemico* (Genoa: Costa e Nolan, 1998), and the issue of *Actes de la recherche en sciences sociales* 19 (September 1999) devoted to "Délits d'immigration."

92. Nils Christie, "Suitable Enemy," in Herman Bianchi and René van Swaaningen, eds., *Abolitionism: Toward a Non-Repressive Approach to Crime* (Amsterdam: Free University Press, 1986).

93. The notion of "sub-white" is borrowed from the sociologist Andréa Réa, who himself borrows it from the French rap band IAM: "Le racisme européen et la fabrication du 'sous-blanc,'" in Andréa Réa, ed., *Immigration et racisme en Europe* (Brussels: Éditions Complexe, 1998), 167–202.

94. Nils Christie, *Crime Control as Industry: Towards Gulags, Western Style,* 2d expanded edition (London: Routledge, 1994), 69; also, on the British case, Steven Box, *Recession, Crime, and Punishment* (London: Macmillan, 1987), esp. chapter 4, "The State and 'Problem Populations.'"

95. Christie, *Crime Control as Industry,* 66–67, for Norway; figures on the other European countries are taken from *Statistique pénale annuelle du Conseil de l'Europe, Enquête 1997* (Strasbourg: Council of Europe, 1999).

96. Pierre Tournier, *Inflation carcérale et surpeuplement des prisons* (Strasbourg: Council of Europe, 2000), tables 1.1, 2.3, and 4; also Vivien Stern, "Mass Incarceration: 'A Sin against the Future'?" *European Journal of Criminal Policy and Research* 3 (1996): 9–12, on prison overcrowding and its consequences in Italy, Greece, and Holland.

97. Maud Guillonneau, Annie Kensey, and Philippe Mazuet, "Densité de population carcérale," *Cahiers de démographie pénitentiaire* 4 (September 1997): 1–4.

98. Administration Pénitentiaire, *Rapport annuel d'activité 1996,* 113.

99. Rod Morgan, "Tortures et traitements inhumains ou dégradants en Europe: quelques données, quelques questions," in Claude Faugeron, Antoinette Chauvenet, and Philippe Combessie, eds., *Approches de la prison* (Brussels: DeBoeck Université, 1997), 323–47. See also the account of the Committee for the Prevention of Torture's field visits written by the committee's first president, the jurist Antonio Cassese, *Inhuman States: Imprisonment, Detention, and Torture in Europe Today* (Cambridge: Polity Press, 1996; originally published in Italian as *Umano–Disumano,* 1994).

100. This diversity is underscored by Claude Faugeron, ed., *Les Politiques pénales* (Paris: La Documentation française, 1992); see also John Muncie and Richard Sparks, eds., *Imprisonment: European Perspectives* (New York: St. Martin's Press, 1991). The growth of the population behind bars is not exclusive, for example, of the wider use of judicial arbitration and mediation as well as efforts at decriminalization (de jure or de facto), or increased individualization in the administration of sentences. Penal policies are no more monolithic than social policies, and their evolution synthesizes divergent, indeed contradictory, tendencies.

101. In France, for example, "if the emphasis is still put, in official discourse, on the mission of rehabilitation of the correctional administration, in practice it is always the mission of seclusion that predominates" (Anne-Marie Marchetti, "Pauvreté et trajectoire carcérale," in Faugeron, Chauvenet, and Combessie, *Approches de la prison,* 197). On the hardening of penal policies in France, Belgium, England, and Holland, see Snacken, Beyens, and Tubex, "Changing Prison Populations in Western Countries," 34–36.

102. René van Swaaningen and Gérard de Jonge, "The Dutch Prison System and Penal Policy in the 1990s: From Humanitarian Paternalism to Penal Business Management," in Vincenzo Ruggiero, Mick Ryan, and Joe Sim, eds., *Western European Penal Systems: A Critical Anatomy* (London: Sage, 1995), 24–45. A similar drift is observed in the case of Sweden, another perennial model for a penality with a human face (cf. Karen Leander, "The Normalization of the Swedish Prison," in ibid., 169–93).

103. David M. Downes, *Contrasts in Tolerance: Post-war Penal Policy in the Netherlands and England and Wales* (Oxford: Clarendon Press, 1988).

104. This process of "penalization of the social" is particularly visible in the Belgian case, owing to the weak legitimacy of the central political power and the devolution to the local and regional levels of competencies pertaining to collective protection, the conjunction of which has fostered rapid punitive escalation. See Yves Cartuyvels and Luc Van Campenhoudt, "La douce violence des contrats de sécurité," *La Revue nouvelle* 105 (March 1995): 49–56; Yves Cartuyvels, "Insécurité et prévention en Belgique: les ambiguïtés d'un modèle 'global-intégré' entre concertation partenariale et intégration verticale," *Déviance et société* 20.2 (1996): 162–93; and Philippe Mary, ed., *Travail d'intérêt général et médiation pénale. Socialisation du pénal ou pénalisation du social?* (Brussels: Bruylant, 1997).

105. According to the information first reported in *Le Monde,* July 15, 1999, and verified with documents supplied by the Collectif informatique, fichiers et citoyenneté.

106. One discovers in passing that the management of files on illegal immigrants was quietly computerized in October 1997 without anyone knowing exactly what data are kept in electronic form, for how long, and for what precise purposes.

107. For this purpose, one can point to the long-standing American precedent: in the United States, the linking of the files of public aid offices, Medicaid, taxes (on income and property), and Social Security, has been mandated since 1984 by the Budget Deficit Reduction Act as a condition for the federal allocation of welfare funds to the states (Gary T. Marx, *Undercover: Police Surveillance in America* [Berkeley: University of California Press, 1988], 210).

108. "Interconnexion des fichiers: les nouveaux alchimistes," *Hommes et libertés* 102 (1999): 16.

109. See, respectively, Onderzoekscommissie, *Het Recht op Bijstand* [The Right to Assistance] (The Hague: VUGA, 1993); Paola Bernini and Godfried Engbersen, "Koppeling en uitsluiting: over de ongewenste en onbedoelde gevolgen van de koppelingswet" [Connection and Exclusion: The Undesirable and Unintended Consequences of the File Connection Act], *Nederlands Juristenblad* 74 (1998): 65–71.

110. Radboub Engbersen, *Nederland aan de monitor* (Utrecht: Dutch Institute for Care and Welfare, 1997).

111. Michel Foucault, "'Omnes et singulatim': vers une critique de la raison politique," in *Dits et écrits,* vol. 4 (Paris: Gallimard, 1994 [1981]), 134–61.

112. The report in question is Christine Lazerges and Jean-Pierre Balduyck, *Réponses à la délinquance des mineurs. Mission interministérielle sur la prévention et le traitement de la délinquance des mineurs* (Paris: La Documentation française, 1998).

113. The minister of health went on: "But I remind you that we have made security, this *citizen's security,* one of the beacons, in any case one of the main lines, of public policy—Lionel Jospin has spoken about this often. Here we need to see that security is guaranteed, but it will not be truly guaranteed—the prime minister has said this often, but let us repeat it—unless one understands what is going on. One must understand. *These are not our enemies*" (TF1 Transcription Service, emphasis

added). One would need to inquire into the novel uses of the qualifier "citizen's," which, in the varied domains where it is applied nowadays, aims to give a democratic and progressive coloring to measures that are fundamentally inegalitarian in their implementation and outcomes, if not their intentions—in this case, the differential allocation of police forces "to the benefit" of the urban areas that disproportionately bear the impact of the retreat of the economic and social state. (Along these lines, one possible French translation of the Anglo-American term "workfare" would be *salariat citoyen,* insofar as its justification is to bring welfare recipients into the civic community of wage earners, albeit precariously employed.)

114. "Mme Guigou estime qu'il faut combiner répressif et éducatif" (Mrs. Guigou Deems That Education and Repression Must Be Combined), *Le Monde,* January 19, 1999. For a party claiming to be Left, education is the natural alibi to justify the extension of the means and prerogatives of the penal apparatus in the management of poverty. In fact, the education invoked here has nothing in it that is "preventative" (except of an eventual repeat offense), for it intervenes *after* the sentencing of delinquent youths, under judicial supervision. A genuine measure of prevention would be a matter for the ministry of education, provided *prior* to the commission of unlawful acts. But that would require far larger budgetary investments for much smaller media profits.

115. Reported in *Libération,* January 4, 1999, 2, and in other media outlets, as interior minister Jean-Pierre Chevènement resumed his duties after an extended medical leave, following a miraculous recovery from a coma suffered a few months earlier during routine surgery.

116. Julien Duval, Christophe Gaubert, Dominique Marchetti, and Fabienne Pavis, *Le "Décembre" des intellectuels français* (Paris: Raisons d'agir Éditions, 1998).

117. Régis Debray, Max Gallo, Jacques Juillard, Blandine Kriegel, Olivier Mongin, Mona Ozouf, Anicet LePors, and Paul Thibaud, "Républicains, n'ayons pas peur!" *Le Monde,* September 4, 1998, 13 (the phrases in quotation marks in the next paragraphs are excerpted from this text). On the trope of "jeopardy," see Albert Hirschmann, *The Rhetoric of Reaction: Perversity, Futility, Jeopardy* (Cambridge: Harvard University Press, 1991).

118. Nixon himself had borrowed this "law-and-order" rhetoric from politicians of the segregationist South, who invented it to better discredit and quell the demand of African Americans for civil rights during the preceding decade.

119. SAMU is the acronym for France's national service for emergency medical assistance, run by some hundred hospital-based centers, created in 1968, and reorganized in 1986.

120. "Is it surrendering to the siren calls of racism to observe that the neighborhoods that top the list for problems of violence are the same ones where illegal immigration is the most widespread (due to poverty and unemployment)?" Régis Debray et al. ask with feigned candor, to ensure that the readers understand who the main troublemakers are. One cannot but answer in the affirmative here, considering that this "observation" pertains to pure phantasmal projection: first, there exists no reliable statistic on *illegal* immigration (and still less data by town or geographic district) because the phenomenon by definition escapes official measurement; second, the maps of urban poverty and immigration in France do not overlap with each other, no more than they overlap with the map of delinquency and violence. According to data from the National Institute of Economic and Statistical Information (INSEE), the neighborhoods with the most deteriorated housing and the poorest population are

neither the most "colored" with immigrants (illegal or otherwise) nor those sporting the highest crime rates (Noëlle Lenoir et al., *Bilan-Perspectives des contrats de plan de Développement Social des Quartiers* [Paris: La Documentation française, 1989], and Organization for Economic Cooperation and Development, *An Explanatory Quantitative Analysis of Urban Distress in OECD Countries* [Paris: OECD, 1997]).

121. Convicts for drug-related offenses make up the largest offense category behind bars (at 20 percent) and their share of the carceral population has increased continuously for the past fifteen years. See Annie Kinsey and Philippe Mazuet, "Analyse conjoncturelle de la population détenue," *Cahiers de démographie pénitentiaire* 3 (May 1997): 4.

122. Hilde Tubex and Sonja Snacken, "L'évolution des longues peines de prison: sélectivité et dualisation," in Faugeron, Chauvenet, and Combessie, *Approches de la prison*, 221–44.

123. Josette Junger-Tas et al., *Delinquent Behavior among Young People in the Western World: First Results of the International Self-Report Delinquent Study* (Amsterdam and New York: Kugler, 1994), and Martin Killias, "La criminalisation de la vie quotidienne et la politisation du droit pénal," *Revue de droit Suisse* 114 (1995): 369–449.

124. Mick Ryan, "Prison Privatization in Europe," *Overcrowded Times* 7.2 (April 1996): 16–18, and "Analysis: Private Prisons," *Manchester Guardian*, August 26, 1998. In the United Kingdom as in the United States, since its legal differentiation at the close of the nineteenth century the treatment of juvenile delinquency has been largely turned over to private or semiprivate operators.

125. Wolfgang Ludwig-Mayerhoffer, "The Public and Private Sectors in Germany: Rethinking Developments in German Penal Control," *International Journal of the Sociology of Law* 24 (1996): 273–90.

126. Nick Cohen, *Cruel Britannia* (London: Verso, 1999).

127. Prison Service, *Research Report No. 5* (London, July 1998), and Morgan, "Imprisonment," 1137–94.

128. Douglas McDonald, "Public Imprisonment by Private Means: The Re-Emergence of Private Prisons and Jails in the United States, the United Kingdom, and Australia," *British Journal of Criminology* 34, special issue (1994): 29–48.

129. Brian Williams, "The U.S. New Right and Corrections Policy: The British Example," *The Social Worker/Le Travailleur social* 64.3 (fall 1996): 49–56.

130. The leading scholar of the "penal climate" of the United Kingdom characterizes the repressive drift of the past decade as "a return to the severe attitude that underlay the core of penal ideology (and poverty legislation) in the nineteenth century" (Richard Sparks, "Penal 'Austerity': The Doctrine of Less Eligibility Reborn?" in Rod Matthews and Paul Francis, eds., *Prison 2000* [London: Macmillan, 1996]: 74). This regression toward Victorian penality accompanies social regression and feeds off the collective sentiment of anxiety and resentment caused by the deterioration of living conditions and life chances among the working class and the spectacular increase in inequalities.

131. Just when the offense of panhandling was erased from the new criminal code in 1994, unlawful municipal decrees aimed at repressing it mushroomed, at the urging of both Right and Left mayors. See Julien Damon, ed., *Les SDF* (Paris: La Documentation française, 1996), 20–21, and idem, "La grande pauvreté: la tentation d'une rue aseptisée," *Informations sociales* 60 (1997): 94–101.

132. David Garland, "The Limits of the Sovereign State: Strategies of Crime Control in Contemporary Society," *British Journal of Criminology* 36.4 (autumn 1997): 415–71, and "Les contradictions de la société punitive: le cas britannique," *Actes de la recherche en sciences sociales* 124 (September 1998): 49–67. As Claude Faugeron notes, in most Western European societies, "the penal, more and more, sports a polyvalent character and assumes the shape of a device for managing individual and social risks," and, within the range of penal responses, "the prison represents a mandatory reference," and a priority, such that it tends to become "the habitual mode for treating social disorders" ("La dérive pénale," 133 and 144).

133. According to Robert Walker, England is now closer to the categorizing and stigmatizing "welfare" system of the United States than the near-universal social-protection schemes of Western European countries ("The Americanization of British Welfare: A Case-Study of Policy Transfer," *Focus* 123 [1998]: 12–21). See also Simon Deakin and Hannah Reed, "River Crossing or Cold Bath? Deregulation and Employment in Britain in the 1980s and 1990s," in Gøsta Esping-Andersen and Marino Regini, eds., *Why Deregulate Labor Markets?* (London: Sage, 2000), 115–47.

134. Warren Young and Mike Brown, "Cross-National Comparisons of Imprisonment," in Michael Tonry, ed., *Crime and Justice: A Review of Research* (Chicago: University of Chicago Press, 1993), 1–49. According to research by David Greenberg, international disparities in incarceration rates are explained jointly by the degree of economic inequality and the capacity of the national political institutions ("Punishment, Division of Labor, and Social Solidarity," paper presented at the World Congress of the International Sociological Association, July 1998).

135. Paul Teague, "Monetary Union and Social Europe," *Journal of European Social Policy* 8.2 (May 1998): 136.

136. Bruce Western, Katherine Beckett, and David Harding, "Le marché du travail et le système pénal aux Etats-Unis," *Actes de la recherche en sciences sociales* 124 (September 1998): 27–35; and Western and Beckett, "How Unregulated Is the U.S. Labor Market?"

137. Anne-Marie Marchetti, *Pauvretés en prison* (Ramonville Saint-Ange: Cérès, 1997), esp. 129–65.

138. Anne-Marie Marchetti, "Pauvreté et trajectoire carcérale," in Faugeron, Chauvenet, and Combessie, *Approches de la prison*, 197; and Marchetti, *Pauvretés en prison*, 185–205.

139. Maud Guilloneau, Annie Kensey, and Philippe Mazuet, "Les resources des sortants de prisons," *Cahiers de démographie pénitentiaire* 5 (February 1998): 3.

140. "Les détenus sont des pauvres comme les autres" (Inmates Are Poor People like the Others), *Dedans–Dehors* 8 (July–August 1998): 3.

141. On the variegated forms of sexual violence in the carceral milieu, their incidence, meanings, and effects, read Daniel Welzer-Lang, Lilian Mathieu, and Michaël Faure, *Sexualités et violences en prison* (Lyon: Aléas Éditeur, 1996).

142. See Tony Bunyan, ed., *Statewatching the New Europe* (London: Statewatch, 1993); Jean-Claude Monet, *Polices et sociétés en Europe* (Paris: La Documentation française, 1993); Michael Anderson, ed., *Policing the European Union: Theory, Law, and Practice* (Oxford: Clarendon Press, 1995); and James Sheptycki, "Transnationalism, Crime Control, and the European State System," *International Criminal Justice Review* 7 (1997): 130–40.

143. Didier Bigo, *Polices en réseaux. L'expérience européenne* (Paris: Presses de Science Po, 1996), 12 and 327; and Didier Bigo, ed., *L'Europe des polices et de la*

sécurité intérieure (Brussels: Éditions Complexe, 1992). See also Anderson, *Policing the European Union*.

144. See Kuhn, "Populations carcérales," 63–71, and Snacken, Beyens, and Tubex, "Changing Prison Populations in Western Countries," 36–37. The German policy of decarceration is described by Johannes Feest, "Reducing the Prison Population: Lessons from the West German Experience," in Muncie and Sparks, *Imprisonment*, 131–45, and Thomas Weigand, "Germany Reduces Use of Prisons Sentences," in Michael Tonry and Kathleen Hatlestad, eds., *Sentencing Reform in Overcrowded Times: A Comparative Perspective* (New York: Oxford University Press, 1997), 177–81. On the political and cultural causes of the penitentiary drop in Finland, see the analysis of Nils Christie, "Éléments de géographie pénale," *Actes de la recherche en sciences sociales* 124 (September 1998): 68–74.

145. Marcel Mauss, "Les civilisations: éléments et formes," in *Œuvres*, vol. 2, *Représentations collectives et diversité des civilisations* (Paris: Éditions de Minuit, 1968 [1929]), 470. See Pierre Tournier's demonstration in the French case, "La population des prisons est-elle condamnée à croître?" and, from a broad international perspective, Christie, "Éléments de géographie pénale."

146. David Garland shows this in *Punishment and Welfare: A History of Penal Strategies* (Aldershot: Gower, 1985), for the paradigmatic case of Victorian England.

147. Philippe van Parijs, *Refonder la solidarité* (Paris: Éditions du Cerf, 1996); Loek Groot and Robert J. van der Veen, eds., *Basic Income on the Agenda: Policy Objectives and Political Chances* (Amsterdam: Amsterdam University Press, 2001); and the works of the BIEN (Basic Income European Network, online at www.etes. ucl.ac.be/BIEN) demonstrating that the institution of an unconditional "citizen's income" is at once feasible on a fiscal level, efficient on the economic plane, and desirable from a civic and moral standpoint. The only genuine obstacle to its institution is the absence of political vision and will. A germane case for the centrality of systems of market regulation and social protection in advanced societies is offered by Gøsta Esping-Andersen, *Social Foundations of Postindustrial Economies* (Oxford: Oxford University Press, 1999). Similar arguments for basic income guarantee are made in the United States by members of the BIG (Basic Income Guarantee) network (see the publications available online at http://www.usbig.net).

3. The Great Penal Leap Backward

1. President's Commission on Law Enforcement and Administration of Justice, *Task Force Report: Corrections* (Washington, D.C.: U.S. Government Printing Office, 1967).

2. National Advisory Commission on Criminal Justice Standards and Goals, *Task Force Report on Corrections* (Washington, D.C.: U.S. Government Printing Office, 1973), 597.

3. The two key articles developing the "homeostatic theory" of imprisonment are Alfred Blumstein and Jacqueline Cohen, "A Theory of the Stability of Punishment," *Journal of Criminal Law and Criminology* 64.2 (1973): 198–207, and Alfred Blumstein, Jacqueline Cohen, and Daniel Nagin, "The Dynamics of a Homeostatic Punishment Process," *Journal of Criminal Law and Criminology* 67.3 (1977): 317–34. The most thorough critique of theories of the incarceration rate is provided by Franklin Zimring and Gordon Hawkins, who inventory the specific blindness that caused diverse analysts of the prison, from sociologists and criminologists to historians,

economists, and statisticians charged with forecasting within correctional administrations, to stubbornly ignore or misstate the problem (*The Scale of Imprisonment* [Chicago: University of Chicago Press, 1991]).

4. David J. Rothman, *The Discovery of the Asylum: Social Order and Disorder in the New Republic* (Boston: Little, Brown, 1971), 295. See also Michael Ignatieff, *A Just Measure of Pain: The Penitentiary in the Industrial Revolution, 1750–1850* (New York: Pantheon Books, 1978).

5. Michel Foucault, *Discipline and Punish: The Birth of the Prison* (New York: Vintage, 1979 [1975]), 306, my translation.

6. Andrew T. Scull, *Decarceration: Community Treatment and the Deviant, a Radical View* (Englewood Cliffs, N.J.: Prentice-Hall, 1977); Stanley Cohen, "Community Control: A New Utopia," *New Society* 858 (March 15, 1979): 609–11; and Jessica Mitford, *Kind and Usual Punishment: The Prison Business* (New York: Random House, 1973), 291.

7. Robert Adams and Jo Campling, *Prison Riots in Britain and the United States* (London: Macmillan, 1992). There is an intriguing parallel here with the trajectory of U.S. slavery in the revolutionary era: with the gradual abolition of bondage in the North and its prohibition in the Northwest, the facilitation of manumission in the South, and the incipient termination of the foreign slave trade, opponents of the "peculiar institution" in the 1780s had "good grounds to be cautiously optimistic. Slavery appeared to be in full retreat, its end only a matter of time" (Peter Kolchin, *American Slavery: 1619–1877* [New York: Hill and Wang, 1993], 80). Yet it would go on to endure and indeed expand for nearly another century and its demise would require a civil war leaving 4 million dead, much of the South shattered, and the country deeply divided.

8. For a detailed account of this movement and its impact, see Eric Cummins, *The Rise and Fall of California's Radical Prison Movement* (Stanford, Calif.: Stanford University Press, 1994). For a linked series of case studies from an organizational perspective, see Bert Useem and Peter Kimball, *States of Siege: U.S. Prison Riots 1971–1986* (Oxford: Oxford University Press, 1991).

9. Richard Frase, "Jails," in Michael Tonry, ed., *The Handbook of Crime and Punishment* (New York: Oxford University Press, 1999), 476. By Frase's computation, lockups could hold more than 30,000 at any moment, a figure equal to twice the inmate population of the Netherlands that is erased from official correctional statistics.

10. Bureau of Justice Statistics, *Prison and Jail Inmates, 1995* (Washington, D.C.: Bureau of Justice Bulletin, August 1996).

11. Cf. William J. Chambliss, *Trading Textbooks for Prison Cells* (Alexandria, Va.: National Center on Institutions and Alternatives, 1991), on city and county expenditures; and William DiMascio, *Seeking Justice: Crime and Punishment in America* (New York: Edna McConnell Clark Foundation, 1995), on state budget planning.

12. Sidra Lea Gifford, *Justice Expenditures and Employment in the United States, 1999* (Washington, D.C.: Bureau of Justice Bulletin, February 2002).

13. The statistics on costs in this paragraph are drawn or computed from James Stephan, *State Prison Expenditures, 1996* (Washington, D.C.: Bureau of Justice Statistics, August 1999). Note that these figures exclude capital outlays (purchase of land, facility construction and renovation, major repairs, and debt service), as well as probation and parole services, juvenile corrections, and nonresidential community sanctions.

14. Corrections Corporation of America, *Annual Report 1996: Leaps and Bounds* (1997), 5. Corrections Corporations of America is the leader of this economic sector

with nearly half the country's private beds. Founded in 1983, the Nashville firm was then in charge of fifty-nine custodial establishments located in nineteen states and abroad (Puerto Rico, Australia, and England), with gross sales of $300 million growing by 40 percent per year in the 1990s.

15. Michael B. Katz, "Redefining the Welfare State (1996)," in *In the Shadow of the Poorhouse: A History of Welfare in America* (New York: Basic Books, 1996), 314.

16. By one estimate, to construct the prisons required to house these extra inmates alone would have required a veritable correctional Marshall Plan of $6.6 billion per year (Charles Thomas and Charles Logan, "The Development, Present Status, and Future Potential of Correctional Privatization in America," in Gary Bowman et al., eds., *Privatizing Correctional Institutions* [New Brunswick, N.J.: Transaction Press, 1993], 213–40).

17. Richard W. Harding, "Private Prisons," in Tonry, *The Handbook of Crime and Punishment*, 635.

18. Based on interviews conducted by the author over the four days of the 127th Congress of Corrections, a biannual meeting of corrections professionals held under the auspices of the American Correctional Association (a trade organization founded in 1870 with more than 24,000 members), in Orlando, Florida, in August 1997.

19. Randy Gragg, "A High Security, Low Risk Investment: Private Prisons Make Crime Pay," *Harper's Magazine* (August 1996): 50.

20. See Stephen G. Gibbons and Gregory L. Pierce, "Politics and Prison Development in a Rural Area," *Prison Journal* 75.3 (September 1995): 380–89, and the documentary movie by Tracy Hurling, *Yes, in My Backyard* (Galloping Girls Productions, 1999).

21. For an overview and critique of this thesis, read Peter Andreas, "The Rise of the American Crimefare State," *World Policy Journal* 14.3 (fall 1997): 37–45.

22. The criminological, sociological, legal, and policy literatures on criminal offending and victimization in the United States fill entire libraries. I limit myself here to pointing out those facts and figures that spotlight the consistent *disconnect* between trends in offenses and trends in incarceration. For a panorama of normal research on the topic, revealingly limited to "what the average person thinks of as predatory or street crime," consult James Q. Wilson and Joan Petersilia, eds., *Crime: Public Policies for Crime Control* (San Francisco: ICS Press, 1995).

23. The National Crime Victimization Survey (NCVS) is an annual questionnaire-based study conducted by the U.S. Department of Justice with a representative sample of 45,000 households using a rotating panel design that tracks the evolution of major categories of criminal infractions. It is considered the most reliable source of data on offending in the United States—more so than police statistics, which are known to conflate variations in police activity and procedures with changes in the incidence of criminal conduct.

24. U.S. Department of Justice, *National Crime Victimization Survey: Criminal Victimization, 1973–1995* (Washington, D.C.: U.S. Government Printing Office, 1997), and Alfred Blumstein and Joel Wallman, eds., *The Crime Drop in America* (Cambridge: Cambridge University Press, 2000).

25. Cited by Joel Best, *Random Violence: How We Talk about New Crimes and New Victims* (Berkeley: University of California Press, 1999), 3.

26. U.S. Department of Justice, *Sourcebook of Criminal Justice Statistics, 2000* (Washington, D.C.: U.S. Government Printing Office, 2001), 313 and 315; Federal Bureau of Investigation, *Uniform Crime Report 1995* (available online at www.fbi.gov/ucr/95cius.htmp), 17.

27. Loïc Wacquant, "The New Urban Color Line: The State and Fate of the Ghetto in Postfordist America," in Craig J. Calhoun, ed., *Social Theory and the Politics of Identity* (Cambridge: Basil Blackwell, 1994), 231–76; William Julius Wilson, *When Work Disappears: The World of the New Urban Poor* (New York: Knopf, 1996); and Elliott Currie, "Race, Violence, and Justice since Kerner," in Fred R. Harris and Lynn A. Curtis, eds., *Locked in the Poorhouse: Cities, Race, and Poverty in the United States* (Lanham, Md.: Rowman & Littlefield, 1998), 95–115.

28. Department of Justice, *Correctional Population of the United States, 1997* (Washington, D.C.: U.S. Government Printing Office, 2000), 11, table 1.22.

29. James Austin and John Irwin, *It's about Time: America's Imprisonment Binge* (Belmont, Calif.: Wadsworth, 1997), 23.

30. On the profile of Texas prison convicts, see Tony Fabello, *Sentencing Dynamics Study* (Austin, Tex.: Criminal Justice Policy Council, 1993); on the criminal profile of California and federal inmates, Stephen R. Donziger, ed., *The Real War on Crime: The Report of the National Criminal Justice Commission* (New York: Harper, 1996), 17–19.

31. Austin and Irwin, *It's about Time,* 32–57.

32. For a fuller demonstration than is possible here, read Loïc Wacquant, *Punishing the Poor: The Neoliberal Government of Social Insecurity* (Durham, N.C.: Duke University Press, 2009), chapters 1, 4, and 5.

33. The classic account of the collapse of the normalizing and therapeutic model that dominated corrections in America from the interwar years until the mid-1970s is Francis A. Allen, *The Decline of the Rehabilitative Ideal: Penal Policy and Social Purpose* (New Haven: Yale University Press, 1981).

34. This moral fairy tale receives an impeccably academic treatment in James Q. Wilson, *Thinking about Crime* (New York: Vintage, 1975).

35. There is a striking parallel here with the 1996 "reform" of welfare passed in Congress with the willful consent of President Clinton—a "reform" that amounted to abolishing the right of impoverished single-parent families and resident aliens to assistance and to making precarious labor a civic obligation at the bottom of the class structure. For, in this case too, it is the "liberal" reformers (those on the left of the American political spectrum) who made possible the passage of this retrograde law by adopting themes dear to conservatives (starting with the idea that the welfare state is fundamentally dysfunctional) and by endorsing coercive and paternalistic measures (such as mandatory work at the end of two years and lifetime caps on assistance), on the pretext that their harmful effects would be compensated for later by the adoption of other progressive measures (like the creation of public jobs, which one could easily foresee would not see the light of day), and on grounds that any reform is better than no reform because the existing system mistreats the dispossessed.

36. David Rothman, "American Criminal Justice Policies in the 1990s," in Thomas G. Blomberg and Stanley Cohen, eds., *Punishment and Social Control: Essays in Honor of Sheldon L. Messinger* (New York: Aldine de Gruyter, 1995), 29–44. A germane diagnosis had been offered a decade earlier by James Austin and Barry Krisberg, "The Unmet Promise of Alternatives to Incarceration," *Crime and Delinquency* 28.3 (July 1982): 374–409.

37. Lawrence Hazelrigg, ed., *Prison within Society* (Garden City, N.Y.: Doubleday, 1968), flap-cover text; the confession is by Donald Cressey, "The Nature and Effectiveness of Correctional Techniques," in ibid., 371.

38. Timothy J. Flanagan, James W. Marquart, and Kenneth G. Adams, eds., *Incar-*

cerating Criminals: Prisons and Jails in Social and Organizational Context (New York: Oxford University Press, 1998), x.

39. James Button, *Black Violence: Political Impact of the 1960s Riots* (Princeton, N.J.: Princeton University Press, 1978), 163–66.

40. Jill Quadagno, *The Color of Welfare: How Racism Undermined the War on Poverty* (New York: Oxford University Press, 1994).

41. David C. Anderson, *Crime and the Politics of Hysteria: How the Willie Horton Story Changed American Justice* (New York: Times Books, 1995). William Chambliss offers a succinct and precise analysis of the fabrication of this moral panic that makes especially clear how opinion polls (on "the main challenges facing the country") constituted as a national problem a question that the public was barely concerned about until politicians, the media, and pollsters thrust it upon them (William J. Chambliss, "Policing the Ghetto Underclass: The Politics of Law and Law Enforcement," *Social Problems* 41.2 [May 1994]: 177–94, esp. 187–92).

42. Robert S. Lichter and Linda S. Lichter, *1993—The Year in Review: TV's Leading News Topics, Reporters, and Political Jokes* (Washington, D.C.: Media Monitor, 1994), and idem, *1999—The Year in Review: TV's Leading News Topics, Reporters, and Political Jokes* (Washington, D.C.: Media Monitor, 2000). That the rise of crime to the top of the national list of public concerns in 1994 was the result of a "network TV news scare" is shown by Dennis T. Lowry, Tarn Ching, Josephine Nio, and Dennis W. Leitner, "Setting the Public Fear Agenda: A Longitudinal Analysis of Network TV Crime Reporting, Public Perceptions of Crime, and FBI Crime Statistics," *Journal of Communication* 53.1 (March 2003): 61–72.

43. Mark Fishman and Gray Cavender, eds., *Entertaining Crime: Television Reality Programs* (New York: Aldine, 1998).

44. Franklin Zimring, "Populism, Democratic Government, and the Decline of Expert Authority: Some Reflections on 'Three Strikes' in California," *Pacific Law Journal* 28 (1996): 243–56.

45. Loïc Wacquant, "Elias in the Dark Ghetto," *Amsterdam Sociologisch Tidjschrift* 24.3/4 (December 1997): 340–48.

46. Douglas Massey, "Getting Away with Murder: Segregation and Violent Crime in Urban America," *University of Pennsylvania Law Review* 143.5 (May 1995): 1203–32; also Jeffrey D. Morenoff and Robert J. Sampson, "Violent Crime and the Spatial Dynamics of Neighborhood Transition: Chicago, 1970–1990," *Social Forces* 76.1 (September 1997): 31–64.

47. Michael Tonry, "Crime and Punishment in America," in Tonry, *The Handbook of Crime and Punishment,* 17. The proportion of blacks among arrests for property crimes remained roughly constant during that period, oscillating between 29 percent and 33 percent.

48. Robert Crutfield, George S. Bridges, and Susan Pitchford, "Analytical and Aggregation Biases in Analyses of Imprisonment: Reconciling Discrepancies in Studies of Racial Disparity," *Journal of Research in Crime and Delinquency* 31.2 (May 1994): 166–82.

49. Michael Tonry, *Malign Neglect: Race, Crime and Punishment in America* (New York: Oxford University Press, 1995).

50. A synoptic expression of this scholarly myth is Ronald Mincy, "The Underclass: Concept, Controversy, and Evidence," in Sheldon Danziger et al., eds., *Confronting Poverty: Prescriptions for Change* (Cambridge: Harvard University Press, 1994), 109–46; for a methodical critique of its tenets and bases, see Loïc Wacquant,

"L'*underclass*' urbaine dans l'imaginaire social et scientifique américain," in Serge Paugam, ed., *L'Exclusion. L'état des savoirs* (Paris: La Découverte, 1996), 248–62.

51. Chambliss, "Policing the Ghetto Underclass," 194; Wesley G. Skogan, "Crime and the Racial Fears of White Americans," *Annals of the American Academy of Political and Social Science* 539 (May 1995): 59–71; and Martin Gilens, "Racial Attitudes and Opposition to Welfare," *Journal of Politics* 57.4 (November 1995): 994–1014.

52. Loïc Wacquant, "The New 'Peculiar Institution': On the Prison as Surrogate Ghetto," *Theoretical Criminology* 4.3 special issue, "New Social Studies of the Prison" (2000): 377–89.

53. Tonry, *Malign Neglect,* 104.

54. Jonathan Simon and Malcolm M. Feeley, "True Crime: The New Penology and Public Discourse on Crime," in Blomberg and Cohen, *Punishment and Social Control,* 147–80.

Afterword

1. I prefer the term *civic* to *public* sociology (which has recently come into fashion among American sociologists), since such sociology seeks to bridge the divide between instrumental and reflexive knowledge and to speak simultaneously to both academic and general audiences—albeit in different harmonics. The dichotomous opposition between "public" and "professional" sociology is a peculiarity of the U.S. intellectual field, expressive of the political isolation and social impotence of American academics, that does not travel well outside the Anglo-American sphere and does not adequately capture the positional predicament of university sociologists in America either. See Dan Clawson et al., eds., *Public Sociology: Fifteen Eminent Sociologists Debate Politics and the Profession in the Twenty-first Century* (Berkeley: University of California Press, 2007), and, for contrast, Gisèle Sapiro, ed., *L'Espace intellectuel en Europe* (Paris: La Découverte, 2009).

2. Starting with the logics of urban polarization from below in the United States and Europe, plumbed in Loïc Wacquant, *Urban Outcasts: A Comparative Sociology of Advanced Marginality* (Cambridge: Polity Press, 2008). I trace the analytic linkages between my forays into urban relegation and penalization in "The Body, the Ghetto, and the Penal State," *Qualitative Sociology* 32.1 (March 2009): 101–29.

3. The differential push toward labor-market deregulation in postindustrial nations is analyzed by Thomas P. Boje, ed., *Post-Industrial Labour Markets: Profiles of North America and Scandinavia* (London: Routledge, 1993); Gøsta Esping-Andersen and Marino Regini, eds., *Why Deregulate Labor Markets?* (Oxford: Oxford University Press, 2000); and Max Koch, *Roads to Post-Fordism: Labour Markets and Social Structures in Europe* (Aldershot: Ashgate, 2006). The spread and adaptation of U.S.-inspired "workfare" to other advanced societies is traced by Heather Trickey and Ivar Loedemel, eds., *An Offer You Can't Refuse: Workfare in International Perspective* (London: Policy Press, 2001); Jamie Peck, *Workfare States* (New York: Guilford Press, 2001); and Joel Handler, *Social Citizenship and Workfare in the United States and Western Europe: The Paradox of Inclusion* (Cambridge: Cambridge University Press, 2004).

4. The meeting led to the publication of a book widely read and used by justice activists in France, Gilles Sainati and Laurent Bonelli, eds., *La Machine à punir: Pratique et discours sécuritaires* (Paris: L'Esprit frappeur, 2001). Extensions and updates of the diagnosis of the penalization of poverty in France under the sway of American-style schemas proposed in *Les Prisons de la misère* include Gilles Sainati

and Ulrich Schalchli, *La Décadence sécuritaire* (Paris: La Fabrique, 2007); Laurent Bonelli, *La France a peur: Une histoire sociale de l'insécurité* (Paris: La Découverte, 2008); and Laurent Mucchielli, ed., *La Frénésie sécuritaire: Retour à l'ordre et nouveau contrôle social* (Paris: La Découverte, 2008).

5. Loïc Wacquant, "Towards a Dictatorship over the Poor? Notes on the Penalization of Poverty in Brazil," *Punishment & Society* 5.2 (April 2003): 197–205. For a fuller analysis of the distinctive modalities and implications of punitive containment as antipoverty policy in Latin American countries, see idem, "The Militarization of Urban Marginality: Lessons from the Brazilian Metropolis," *International Political Sociology* 1.2 (Winter 2008): 56–74 (first published in Portuguese, "A militarização da marginalidade urbana: lições da metrópole brasileira," *Discursos Sediciosos: Crime, direito e sociedade* [Rio de Janeiro] 15–16 (Fall 2007): 203–20).

6. Just one indication on Argentina: the main campaign leaflet of the center-left candidate Anibal Ibarra, "Buenos Aires, un compromiso de todos," put fighting crime at the top of his commitments to the voters: "El compromiso de Ibarra-Felgueras: Con la seguridad: vamos a terminar con el miedo y a combatir el delito con la ley en la mano." After I had appeared on national television to discuss *Cárceles de la miseria,* the candidates of the Peronist Party asked through my publisher if I would agree to appear with them at a press conference to support their tactical denunciation of Ibarra's commitment to *mano dura.*

7. Juan Gabriel Valdès, *Pinochet's Economists: The Chicago School in Chile* (Cambridge: Cambridge University Press, 1984).

8. All figures are from International Center for Prison Studies, *World Prison Brief* (London: King's College, 2007). See also Fernando Salla and Paula Rodriguez Ballesteros, *Democracy, Human Rights, and Prison Conditions in South America* (São Paulo: Núcleo de Estudos da Violência, USP, November 2008).

9. For a Colombian illustration, see Manuel Iturralde, "Emergency Penality and Authoritarian Liberalism: Recent Trends in Colombian Criminal Policy," *Theoretical Criminology* 12.3 (2008): 377–97.

10. A deft dissection of the long-standing intersection of U.S. foreign policy and criminal justice norms and goals is Ethan A. Nadelmann, *Cops across Borders: The Internationalization of U.S. Criminal Law Enforcement* (University Park: Pennsylvania State University Press, 1994).

11. South American allies of the Manhattan Institute include the Instituto Liberal, the Fundação Victor Civita, and the Fundação Getúlio Vargas in Brazil; the Instituto Libertad y Desarrollo and the Fundación Paz Ciudadana in Chile; and the Fundación Libertad in Argentina. Blind faith in the direct transportability of "zero tolerance," in spite of the vast social, political, and bureaucratic differences between the two continents, is expressed by William Bratton and William Andrews, "Driving out the Crime Wave: The Police Methods That Worked in New York City Can Work in Latin America," *Time,* July 23, 2001.

12. "The Americas Court a Group That Changed New York," *New York Times,* November 11, 2002.

13. Lucia Dammert and Mary Fran T. Malone, "Does It Take a Village? Policing Strategies and Fear of Crime in Latin America," *Latin American Politics and Society* 48.4 (2006): 27–51. For a Brazilian illustration, read Juliana Resende, *Operação Rio. Relato de uma guerra brasileira* (São Paulo: Página Aberta, 1995), and view Jose Padilha's award-winning documentary, *Tropa de Elite* (2007).

14. Eric Hershberg and Fred Rosen, *Latin America after Neoliberalism: Turning the Tide in the Twenty-first Century?* (New York: New Press, 2006), 432.

15. Jordi Pius Lorpard, "Robocop in Mexico City," *NACLA: Report on the Americas* 37.2 (September–October 2003). A brief account of the "thirty-six-hour whirlwind of mean streets and chic suites" in Mexico City by "the world's best-paid crime-fighting consultant" is Tim Weiner, "Mexico City Journal: Enter Consultant Giuliani, His Fee Preceding Him," *New York Times,* January 16, 2003.

16. Henrik Tham, "Law and Order as a Leftist Project? The Case of Sweden," *Punishment & Society* 3.3 (September 2001): 409–26; Laurent Mucchielli, "Le 'nouveau management de la sécurité' à l'épreuve: Délinquance et activité policière sous le ministère Sarkozy (2002–2007)," *Champ pénal* 5 (2008); Juanjo Medina-Ariza, "The Politics of Crime in Spain, 1978–2004," *Punishment & Society* 8.2 (April 2006): 183–201; and Diane E. Davis, "El factor Giuliani: Delincuencia, la 'cero tolerancia' en el trabajo policiaco y la transformación de la esfera pública en el centro de la ciudad de México," *Estudios Sociológicos* 25 (2007): 639–41.

17. Loïc Wacquant, "Ordering Insecurity: Social Polarization and the Punitive Upsurge," *Radical Philosophy Review* 11.1(Spring 2008): 9–27.

18. One indicator: a full decade of publication by the *Journal of Scandinavian Studies in Criminology and Crime Prevention* contains not a single reference to William Bratton or Rudolph Giuliani, and only eleven mentions of "zero tolerance," always to note the inapplicability of the concept to the Nordic setting.

19. Jock Young, *The Exclusive Society: Social Exclusion, Crime, and Difference in Late Modernity* (London: Sage, 1999) and *The Vertigo of Late Modernity* (London: Sage, 2007); David Garland, *The Culture of Control: Crime and Social Order in Contemporary Society* (Chicago: University of Chicago Press, 2001); John Pratt, *Punishment and Civilization: Penal Tolerance and Intolerance in Modern Society* (London: Sage, 2002); Hans Boutellier, *The Safety Utopia: Contemporary Discontent and Desire as to Crime and Punishment* (Dordrecht: Kluwer Academic Publishers, 2004); Pat O'Malley, ed., *Crime and the Risk Society* (Aldershot: Ashgate, 1998); and Jonathan Simon, *Governing through Crime: How the War on Crime Transformed American Democracy and Created a Culture of Fear* (New York: Oxford University Press, 2007).

20. Loïc Wacquant, "Crafting the Neoliberal State: Workfare, Prisonfare, and Social Insecurity," *Theoretical Criminology* 14.1 (Spring 2010).

21. Jamie Peck and Nikolas Theodore, "Variegated Capitalism," *Progress in Human Geography* 31.6 (2007): 731–72.

22. Just as the transatlantic spread of American penal categories and policies was booming, Tonry wrote that "the USA in particular is neither a successful importer nor an influential exporter" of crime-fighting measures, claiming that "countries in Western Europe actively emulate seemingly successful innovations from elsewhere in Europe but seem largely impervious to U.S. influence" (Michael Tonry, "Symbol, Substance, and Severity in Western Penal Policies," *Punishment & Society* 3.4 [October 2001]: 517–36, at 519). A broad panorama of recent social science studies of "the carceral state" in America is typically mute on the foreign ramifications of U.S. developments: Marie Gottschalk, "Hiding in Plain Sight: American Politics and the Carceral State," *Annual Review Political Science* 11 (2008): 235–60.

23. Desmond King and Mark Wickham-Jones, "From Clinton to Blair: The Democratic (Party) Origins of Welfare to Work," *Political Quarterly* 70.1 (December 1999): 62–74; Jamie Peck and Nikolas Theodore, "Exporting Workfare/Importing Welfare-to-Work: Exploring the Politics of Third Way Policy Transfer," *Political Geography* 20.4 (May 2001): 427–60; and Trevor Jones and Tim Newburn, "Learning

from Uncle Sam? Exploring U.S. Influences on British Crime Control Policy," *Governance: An International Journal of Policy* 15.1 (January 2002): 97–119.

24. Loïc Wacquant, "Racial Stigma in the Making of the Punitive State," in Glenn C. Loury et al., *Race, Incarceration, and American Values* (Cambridge, Mass.: MIT Press, 2008), 59–70, and Loïc Wacquant, *Deadly Symbiosis: Race and the Rise of the Penal State* (Cambridge: Polity Press, 2010).

25. It is not by chance that the United States has simultaneously exported its folk notions of, and policies toward, crime with "zero tolerance," poverty with the tale of the "underclass," and race defined by (hypo)descent: see Pierre Bourdieu and Loïc Wacquant, "On the Cunning of Imperialist Reason," *Theory, Culture, & Society* 16, no. 1 (February 1999 [1998]): 41–57.

26. See, in particular, Tim Newburn and Richard Sparks, eds., *Criminal Justice and Political Cultures: National and International Dimensions of Crime Control* (London: Willan, 2004); Trevor Jones and Tim Newburn, *Policy Transfer and Criminal Justice* (London: Open University Press, 2006); John Muncie and Barry Goldson, eds., *Comparative Youth Justice* (London: Sage, 2006); and Peter Andreas and Ethan Nadelmann, *Policing the Globe: Criminalization and Crime Control in International Relations* (New York: Oxford University Press, 2006).

27. An authoritative review of social research on the transnational spread of public policies is mum on crime and punishment and contains a single mention of think tanks (Frank Dobbin, Beth Simmons, and Geoffrey Garrett, "The Global Diffusion of Public Policies: Social Construction, Coercion, Competition, or Learning?" *Annual Review of Sociology* 33 (1997): 449–72.

28. A provocative account of American and international influences in recent trends toward, and reactions to, the "repenalization" of youth crime that turns up such a mix is John Muncie, "The 'Punitive Turn' in Juvenile Justice: Cultures of Control and Rights Compliance in Western Europe and the USA," *Youth Justice* 8.2 (2008): 107–21.

29. Loïc Wacquant, *Punishing the Poor: The Neoliberal Government of Social Insecurity* (Durham, N.C.: Duke University Press, 2009).

Index

Institute for Economic Affairs (IEA), 2, 27–28, 36–37, 43
intellectuals, 9–10, 26, 119, 135, 164, 174, 178n5, 204n1; heteronomous, 41, 46, 47, 172–73
Inter-American Policy Exchange (IAPE), 168–69
internationalization of policy ideas and formulas. *See* exportation of policy ideas and formulas
"invisible hand" of the market. *See* market: "invisible hand" of
Ireland, 130
"iron fist" of the state. *See* state: "iron fist" of
Irwin, John, 63
Islamism, 22
Italy, 21, 61, 88, 97, 99, 100, 117, 122, 135, 138, 163, 180n32, 194n96

jails, 4, 59, 62–63, 69–72, 80, 83, 86, 93, 96, 101–2, 126–27, 134, 136–37, 140, 149, 157, 170
Japan, 58, 163
Johnson, Lyndon B., 133
Jospin, Lionel, 3, 20, 39, 41, 50, 54, 115, 177n2, 183n69, 184n72, 195n113
Juppé, Alain, 112
juveniles. *See* youth

Kansas, 61
Kelling, George, 14, 15, 43–44, 46, 168–70
Kelly Services, 188n28
Kensey, Annie, 192n76
Keynesian social compact. *See* Fordist-Keynesian social compact
K-4 Committee, 128
Kirchheimer, Otto, 92
Knobler, Peter, 180n26
Konica, 72
Kosovo, 23, 154
Kouchner, Bernard, 111

labor. *See* wage labor
Lastman, Mel, 22
late modernity, 172–74
Latin America, 9, 167–70, 172, 181n33
law, 15, 53; conformity to, 116; en-

forcement, 16, 25–26, 33, 156; labor and social, 116; Law on Crime and Disorder (UK), 38; Law on Informatics and Liberties (France), 108; Law on Orientation and Planning on Security (France), 107; and order, 8, 17, 19, 38, 39, 42, 53, 59, 63, 78, 103, 108, 111, 148, 196n118; repressive, 155; "Three Strikes and You're Out," 60, 155. *See also* courts
Law Enforcement Administration Agency, 65
Lazerges, Christine, 41, 50
League for Human Rights, 108
libertarianism, 5, 14, 29, 151, 163
London, 2
López Obrador, Andrés Manuel, 170–71
Los Angeles County, 62
Louima, Abner, 24
lower class. *See* class: lower
Loyola, Ignacio, 170

Maastricht Treaty, 97, 128
Maine, 61
Major, John, 27, 29, 120
Mandelbrot, Benoît, 52
Manhattan Institute, 11–15, 18, 19, 28, 29, 43, 52, 168–70, 179n16
Manpower Incorporated, 188n28
Marest, Patrick, 102
marginality, 54, 83; in the labor market, 91–92; urban, 4, 161, 172, 176. *See also* poverty
market: bipartisan consensus on principle of, 142; "black," 103; crime driven by, 154; European integration, 129; ideology of, 1–3, 11, 14–15, 32, 39, 54, 88, 118–19, 122, 169; "invisible hand" of, 1, 131, 171; labor, 1, 27, 32, 39, 55, 79–81, 89, 91–93, 103, 105, 109, 122–26, 162, 167; rule of, 171, 175; unfettered extension of, 54, 62, 122, 158. *See also* libertarianism; neoliberalism
Martin, Hubert, 41
Massey, Douglas, 156
Mauss, Marcel, 130
McLeish, Henry, 20

214   *Index*

Mead, Lawrence, 2, 31–36, 182n56, 183n59
media, 5, 10, 11, 12, 18, 22, 37, 41–42, 51, 57, 64, 72, 98, 142, 144, 157, 162, 196n115, 206n6; exploitation of crime by, 150, 153–54, 196n114, 203n42; press, 28, 45, 48, 112, 164, 182n52; pro-business, 58
Medina, Carlos, 169
Mexico, 20, 169–71, 178n3, 206n15
Michigan, 68, 83, 141
Microsoft, 72
middle class. *See* class: middle
Minnesota, 137, 141, 151
Mississippi, 74, 137
Mitford, Jessica, 135
Mitterrand, François, 8, 90
modernity. *See* late modernity
Montebourg, Arnaud de, 53
Moore, Mark, 66
moralization. *See* crime: moralization of; incarceration: moralizing dimensions of
Moss, Mark Richard, 66
Murdoch, Rupert, 28, 29
Murray, Charles, 2, 11–14, 28, 29–31, 34–36, 43, 178n14, 179n15, 181n44, 182n52, 183n59, 183n62
myth: activist, 4, 72–73, 86; demonic, 84–87; scholarly, 45, 47–48, 203n50

National Association for the Advancement of Colored People (NAACP), 24
National Commission on the Future of DNA Evidence, 67
National Front, 48, 184n72, 193n82
National Urban League, 24
neoconservatism, 11, 29, 36, 38, 119, 142
neoliberalism: hegemony of, 162; as ideology, 10, 11, 27, 88, 118, 122, 131, 170, 174; monetarism, 167; neoliberal turn, 98, 109, 171, 186n1; nexus of punitive penality and, 175; as policy, 37, 47, 54, 55, 79, 88, 168, 175; punitive doctrine of, 45–46, 54, 167, 173, 175; unevenness of, 173. *See also* privatization
Netherlands, 56, 88, 94, 100, 103, 109–10, 117, 123, 194n96, 200n9

Nevada, 141
New York, 65, 67, 68, 71, 78, 114, 167, 180n29
New Zealand, 22, 55, 123
Nixon, Richard, 113, 133, 150, 153, 158, 196n118
normalization, 2, 54, 124, 135, 168, 202n33
North Carolina, 137
Norway, 99–100, 134

Occident Chrétien, 44
Oklahoma, 74

panhandling, 121, 197n131
panopticism, 134–35; and computerized data collection, 106–10, 128, 195n106; social, 105–10
parole, 64–65, 67, 90, 92, 102, 103, 125, 134, 138, 157, 200n13
Pataki, George, 71
Pena, Alfred, 169
penalization, 2–4, 9, 10, 32, 38–39, 48, 52, 58–131, 161, 170, 172; deautonomization of the penal field, 150–55; ideological attraction of, 87, 159; new punitive ethos, 39; penal dualization, 115; penal pauperization, 124; of the social, 195n104. *See also* homelessness: criminalization of; immigrants: criminalization of; incarceration; poverty: criminalization of; precariousness: criminalization of; youth: criminalization of
penitentiaries, 4, 20, 40, 59, 62–63, 65, 72, 74–75, 88, 97, 100, 120, 133, 135–37, 143, 149, 152, 155, 199n144
police, 11, 16, 19–27, 43–44, 65, 67, 103, 121, 123, 154; brutality, 23–26, 103, 111; community policing, 16, 18, 38; criminal database, 65–67, 117, 105–10, 181n35; as discriminatory, 77, 112; growth of, 17, 68; harassment by, 23–26, 42; legitimation of, 184n73; "New York model," 2, 15–19, 162, 164–67, 181n33; policing as technique of government, 110; "policy transfer," 174, 178n4; "proactive policing," 37; as regulating the poor, 112, 195n107;

stations, 102; statistics, 49; surveillance, 42; transformation of, 17–18, 39, 179n21; viewed as threat, 25–26; views of, 44. *See also* exportation of policy ideas and formulas
policy transfer. *See* exporation of policy ideas and formulas
political overdetermination, 85
politics of knowledge, 167
Portugal, 88, 99, 100, 103, 122, 163–64
post-Fordism, 4, 105, 162
post-Keynesianism, 3, 82, 85, 162
poverty, 3, 12, 19, 47, 53; criminalization of, 37, 50, 76, 79, 111–12, 120–22, 124, 126, 151, 158, 167, 182n55; and dependency, 32; disciplining the poor, 19, 33, 39, 158; as function of penalization, 125–26; "gap," 56; level, 122; "line," 56, 57, 63, 156; public contempt for, 79; rates of United States and Europe compared, 56; as resulting from welfare retrenchment, 55; in the Second World, 167, 178n3
Pratt, John, 206n19
precariousness: criminalization of, 121, 124; of employment, 3–4, 9, 32, 44, 51, 52, 54, 55, 63, 79–80, 87–103, 105, 107, 108, 112, 124, 130, 171
Premier Prisons, 121
"prison-industrial complex," 4, 84–87
prisons, 1–4, 20–21, 23, 36, 39–40, 59–104, 109, 111, 115–59, 161, 163, 165, 168, 170, 171–72, 175; overcrowding, 62, 100–103, 194n96; reform of, 119, 151; regional disparities in operating costs, 141; as tools for economic development, 75–76; wages of employees, 70
private sector, 11, 80; intertwined with public sector, 84. *See also* privatization
privatization: during Clinton years, 69; of criminal justice services, 38; doctrine of, 141–42; of incarceration, 40, 73–75, 80, 85, 117, 119–21, 141–44, 188n28; opposition to, 143; of policing, 45; Private Industry Enhancement (PIE) Program, 72; of public services, 118–19; of state enterprises, 54; of welfare, 83

probation, 64–65, 67, 157, 200n13
proletariat. *See* class: working
public housing, 53, 69, 175
public opinion, 48, 203n41
public order. *See* law: and order
public space, 15–16; recapturing, 19
punitive containment as technique of government, 1, 4–5, 19–27, 33, 39, 44, 54, 58–131, 167, 173

"quality of life," 2, 14, 16, 24, 26. *See also* zero tolerance

race. *See* ethnicity
racial profiling, 24–25
Raufer, Xavier, 44–45
Réa, Andréa, 194n93
Reagan, Ronald, 11–12, 45, 60, 68, 70, 77, 119, 142, 157, 185n80, 185n87; era of, 1
Reno, Janet, 67
repression, 48, 104; and policy, 44; state, 84, 117, 149, 179n21. *See also* law: repressive
responsibility: versus collective irresponsibility, 118; cost shifting, 72; for criminal acts, 45; individual, 19, 23, 32, 34–35, 117–18, 173–74; parental, 42, 117; "responsibilization," 122; trope of, 32
Right, New, 14, 15, 29
Rocard, Michel, 127
Roché, Sébastian, 43–44
Romania, 94
Roriz, Joaquim, 20
Rothman, David, 134, 151
Rusche, Georg, 92
Russia, 61

Safir, Howard, 25
Scandinavia, 56, 99, 100, 122, 206n18
Schengen Agreement, 97, 128–29
Schröder, Gerhard, 21, 39, 180n31, 186n1
Schwartz, Richard, 15
Scull, Andrew, 135
Securicor, 74, 121
Securitas International, 121
Serco, 121

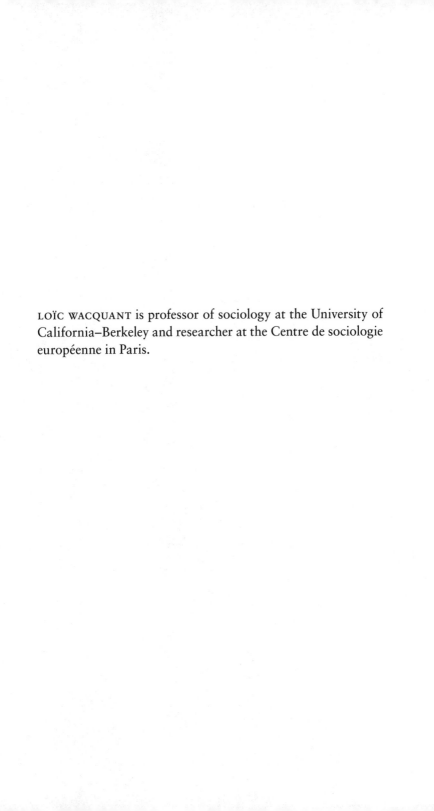

LOÏC WACQUANT is professor of sociology at the University of California–Berkeley and researcher at the Centre de sociologie européenne in Paris.